# LIVING NO LONGER FOR OURSELVES:

## *Liturgy and Justice in the Nineties*

Edited by
Kathleen Hughes, R.S.C.J.
Mark R. Francis, C.S.V.

*A Liturgical Press Book*

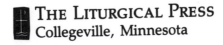
THE LITURGICAL PRESS
Collegeville, Minnesota

Cover design by Fred Petters.

1     2     3     4     5     6     7

**Library of Congress Cataloging-in-Publication Data**

Living no longer for ourselves : liturgy and justice in the nineties /
   Theodore Ross . . . [et al.] ; H. Kathleen Hughes, Mark R. Francis,
   editors.
       p.   cm.
   Includes bibliographical references.
   ISBN 0-8146-2035-3
   1. Catholic Church—Liturgy.  2. Christianity and justice—
Catholic Church.  I. Ross, Theodore.  II. Hughes, Helen Kathleen.
III. Francis, Mark R.
BX1970.L56  1991
264'.02—dc20
                                     91-12960
                                        CIP

*To*

Ralph A. Keifer

(1940–1987)

*who struggled all his life with these questions*

# Contents

# Acknowledgments

We wish to thank our colleagues at the Catholic Theological Union above all for the rich dialogue that we have sustained over these last few years. We are particularly grateful to those who have contributed essays for this volume. Several pieces have previously appeared in print and are here reprinted in revised form with permission: The Liturgical Press for John Pawlikowski, "Worship after the Holocaust" *(Worship* 58 [1984] 315–329); Michael Glazier for Kathleen Hughes, "The Voice of the Church at Prayer," *Biblical and Theological Reflections on the Challenge of Peace,* ed. John Pawlikowski and Donald Senior, Wilmington: Michael Glazier, 1984, 135–147; The Pastoral Press for Edward Foley, "Liturgy and *Economic Justice for All,"* published under the title "Liturgy and Social Justice," *Economic Justice: CTU's Pastoral Commentary on the Bishops' Letter on the Economy,* ed. John Pawlikowksi and Donald Senior, Washington: The Pastoral Press, 1988; and Harper-CollinsPublishers for "Liturgy and Justice: An Intrinsic Relationship," pp. 36–51, reprinted with revisions from "Liturgy, Justice and Peace" by Kathleen Hughes from *Education for Peace and Justice* edited by Padraic O'Hare. Copyright © 1983 by Padraic O'Hare. Reprinted by permission of HarperCollinsPublishers. Finally, we acknowledge with gratitude the editorial assistance of Frances Krumpelman, S.C.N.

M.R.F.

H.K.H.

# Introduction

Most of the essays included in this collection were first written as catalysts for a series of conversations at the Catholic Theological Union in Chicago. One day there had been some lighthearted bantering between the members of the Word and Worship department and the ethics faculty about the irrelevancy of each other's respective disciplines! Bantering led to more serious discussion—not only about the importance of these two disciplines in the life of the Church, but of their essential relationship and interdependence. We recognized that we needed to begin a sustained dialogue.

During the last few years we have met periodically among ourselves and with students to pursue the interrelationship between liturgy and just living. Our conversations have ranged broadly. We have approached our topic from the perspectives of history, anthropology, economics, biblical studies, and catechesis. Certain overarching concerns of Catholic Theological Union have colored our thought: feminism, mission, cross-cultural and global realities. We have told stories and have read prayers aloud. We have also drawn upon the insights of others; our conversations have coincided with a burgeoning collection of books and articles and with major addresses and conferences on the topic (sponsored, for example, by the North American Academy of Liturgy, the Federation of Diocesan Liturgical Commissions, and the Center for Pastoral Liturgy at the University of Notre Dame). We have repeatedly probed our own experience of worship and found it often estranged from life—and we have tried to articulate why we have found it so.

In these pages you will find some of our concerns and many of our open questions. We offer them with a sense of urgency about the fundamental task in which we have been engaged, for we ignore the estrangement of liturgy and life at the risk of making the message of Christ celebrated in worship and enacted in our lives irrelevant to the world.

Two background essays establish the context of the discussion in the American Church. Jesuit historian Ted Ross, a specialist in U.S.

Church history, gives the issue of liturgy and justice a human face. In a series of portraits, Ross sketches the lives of five men and women whose influence predates Vatican Council II: Virgil Michel, Reynold Hillenbrand, Dorothy Day, Peter Maurin, and Paul Halli-nan. These individuals embodied a synthesis between liturgy and just living. Each one is unique; each portrait suggests a different emphasis in their labors: writing, speaking, organizing, feeding and housing, shepherding. What binds them together and makes them apt representatives of the synthesis of justice and worship is that each recognized, in the words of another liturgical pioneer, William Busch, that "incorporation into Christ is of little value if it ceases to function the moment we step out onto the church porch."

A key characteristic of the liturgical movement in the United States prior to the Second Vatican Council was precisely this emphasis on the ethical demands of *being* the body of Christ. In light of this heritage, it is surprising that The Constitution on the Sacred Liturgy does not mention the issue of justice, although it is possible that "the joy and hope, the grief and anguish of the men [and women] of our time, especially those who are poor and afflicted in any way" *(Gaudium et spes,* no. 1), would have found its way into the liturgy document had this document been treated last rather than first at the council. In any case, Kathleen Hughes describes the postconciliar dichotomy that began to appear in the North American Church between social justice concerns and liturgical renewal. Subsequent debates about ritualism on the one hand and ritual manipulation on the other decried two extremes that mute the liturgy's inherent power to put us in contact with the Just One who alone redeems and transforms our lives. Hughes concludes with some reflections on the meaning of "active participation" and its claims on our daily lives.

John Pawlikowski makes concrete Hughes' "transforming power of worship" with the caveat that worship must recover the root metaphor, body of Christ; highlight the dignity of all creation and the community's power and responsibility as cocreators; and suggest the vulnerability of God, which invites *even* enemy love. In Pawlikowski's view it is the role of liturgy to discover and celebrate a compelling God, rather than a commanding God, in light of the Holocaust and similar atrocities. He further urges recovery of a

**Introduction**

symbol system that will enable an encounter with the living presence of our Creator God.

Ralph Keifer, professor of liturgy at Catholic Theological Union until his death in July of 1987, poses some provocative questions to a community too often concerned with "what we get out of" liturgy. Keifer's essay suggests that the genesis of this problem is not found in the contemporary community but in the relationship that developed in the Middle Ages between the Church and society; a relationship that devalued culture and its expression, particularly among the laity. Keifer proposes that the solution lies less in recovering the relationship between liturgy and culture than in discovering the relationship between liturgy and mission.

Mark Francis, who studied in Rome with Anscar Chupungco, a specialist in liturgical inculturation, advances a case for cultural pluralism as an issue of justice. Francis demonstrates that the liturgical renewal was influenced—and thus hampered—by an incomplete understanding of the relationship between liturgy and culture. While the "genius of the Roman Rite" has long guided liturgists, Francis proposes that the liturgical reform will be successful to the extent that it is also faithful to local experience and expression.

Kathleen Hughes then forcefully argues that liturgy too often functions as a neglected source and an underestimated means in the development of the community's self-understanding. Using the bishops' pastoral letter *The Challenge of Peace: God's Promise and Our Response* as a case study and drawing upon some of the new texts in The Sacramentary, Hughes examines the self-involving and performative nature of liturgy, which places obligations upon the community and commits worshipers to just ways of being in the world.

Ed Foley also employs the pastoral letter *Economic Justice for All* to bolster his argument that ritual is a corporate rehearsal of mission. In Foley's view liturgy is not an escape nor simply a way of holding God at bay, but thrusts us into the social arena where the reign of God is discovered and proclaimed.

Worship is at the center of the Christian experience, as Foley demonstrates, because it is the very heart of Jesus' life. It is the life and ministry of Jesus that serves as foundation for Barbara Reid's essay on a Church of equal disciples, for the women around Jesus were prominent as model disciples and ministers. Reid addresses feminism as a justice issue which she defines as a commitment to work for changes in structures and relationship patterns for the humanity, dignity, and equality of all persons. This is a vision that presents worshipers with tremendous challenges, calling us to reinterpret the language and symbols of liturgy and redistribute the roles in the liturgical assembly so that our worship might more faithfully reflect the innate equality of all in Jesus Christ.

Reinterpretation and the redistribution of roles imply changes in our worship patterns, but is it possible "to add, remove, or change anything" (can. 846.1) on one's personal initiative? What about canon law? John Huels, in his typically candid and lucid approach to canonical interpretation, takes up the question of changing language. He demonstrates that the spirit of the law not only does *not prohibit,* but actually *favors,* the use of inclusive language in liturgical celebrations.

Language is also the focus of Paul Wadell's essay, but language of another order. Wadell describes the moral life as the ongoing endeavor of learning and being disciplined in the language of God and as a training in right vision. In each instance, Eucharist serves as the primary context helping us to become eloquent speakers of the Word to our world. The Eucharist also opens the eyes of our hearts to a contemplative vision of reality. The language of God is difficult to learn because it challenges us and judges our sinfulness. It calls us to leave all forms of death behind and to live a paschal life open to continual conversion.

How does liturgy assist us in learning the grammar of God? Such learning is a concern of Gilbert Ostdiek whose essay focuses on liturgical catechesis. Catechesis for Ostdiek is one element of pastoral ministry that involves evangelization, catechesis, liturgy, and mission—all of which forms and instructs the Christian community in an awareness and habitual practice of justice. The strategy he proposes in order to make justice an explicit concern of liturgical catechesis—not limited to children, but including adult believers—includes attention to content, environment, and symbol as well as collaboration between liturgists and catechists. Ostdiek provides an "examination of conscience" which clarifies and concretizes his liturgical concerns.

There is an Ignatian dictum: "that we may end where we began." We come full circle in our examination of the relationship

**Introduction**

12

between liturgy and justice in a final essay, which gives our topic once again a human face, but this time one with which we are surely less familiar. Anthony Gittins urges us to consider liturgy and justice as a global concern. Writing out of his experience of the disenfranchized and forgotten both in this country and the developing world—and including their stories along the way—he describes the too-frequent dichotomy between liturgy and life. Worship detached from the concerns of flesh-and-blood people is only a step away from irreligion and impiety. Gittins poses the same question that preoccupied John Pawlikowski: How can we worship in face of the rampant injustice in our world? Gittins believes that we not only *can* worship, but we *must* worship, "for whenever we become conscious of our frightening tendencies to terrible evil, and whenever we realize just how broad has become the divide between the meaning attributed to our liturgies and the meaning we extract from and attribute to our lives, we must seek to build bridges and to reconstruct our world of meaning." *Living no longer for ourselves* and living justly in the nineties demands that we celebrate Eucharist, "not with formalism, but with appropriateness; not in strength, but in brokenness; not triumphantly, but repentantly; not in certainty but in self- questioning. Aware of human faithlessness, yet inspired by God's fidelity, we can loyally celebrate the memory of Jesus in order to restore our broken spirits and bring about what it signifies: unity, peace, love, reciprocity, universality."

We invite you, through these pages, to become part of our conversation, and to that end we have included, with each essay, questions for further reflection and possibly for discussion. We have also appended some suggestions for further reading.

Almost forty years ago, Hans Anscar Reinhold—liturgical pioneer who was often consumed by issues of justice and morality—wrote the following:

> Since we are members of that Mystical Body, which prolongs the incarnation, the state of the body social is a liturgical concern. We who claim to live by the sacraments must be found in the forefront of those who work for a new society built according to the justice and charity of Christ.

> Between shallow activism and naive optimism, this-worldly and natural on the one hand, and, on the other, an awareness of our

duty to lay down our lives for justice's and charity's sake in order to implement what we do in sacred signs, there is a world of difference. The same men and women who . . . strive for sanctity through a more intense living in the sacramental world of the liturgy and through their ascetic efforts, must be the ones who not only give alms—person to person or in drives—but who help unions, sit on employers' councils and housing committees, in interracial groups, in Catholic Action centers, who campaign for the medical services for the strata that cannot afford them, who oppose demagoguery and injustice to the freedoms needed by all people, and who make the cause of enslaved nations a matter of their own heart.

As Reinhold understood so well, *living no longer for ourselves* is first of all, and above all, a matter of the heart.

Mark R. Francis, C.S.V.
Kathleen Hughes, R.S.C.J.
The Feast of St. Ignatius of Loyola

**Introduction**

14

# Abbreviations

CSL     *Sacrosanctum concilium:* The Constitution on the Sacred Liturgy, Vatican Council II (1963)

DOL     *Documents on the Liturgy 1963–1979: Conciliar, Papal, and Curial Texts* (Collegeville: The Liturgical Press, 1982)

EACW     *Environment and Art in Catholic Worship,* Bishops' Committee on the Liturgy of the United States Catholic Conference (1978)

GIRM     *General Instruction on the Roman Missal,* 2nd edition, Sacred Congregation for Divine Worship, ICEL (1975)

ICEL     International Commission on English in the Liturgy

LG     *Lumen gentium:* Dogmatic Constitution on the Church, Vatican Council II (1964)

MCW     *Music in Catholic Worship.* Bishops' Committee on the Liturgy of the United States Catholic Conference (1972)

NAB     *New American Bible with Revised New Testament,* The Confraternity of Christian Doctrine (1986)

NCCB     National Conference of Catholic Bishops

NJB     *New Jerusalem Bible,* ed. H. Wansbrough, GC (1985)

NRSV     *New Revised Standard Version of the Bible with Apocrypha,* (New York: Oxford University Press, 1989)

USCC     United States Catholic Conference

Theodore Ross, S.J.

# The Personal Synthesis of Liturgy and Justice: Five Portraits

*The Best of Times! The Worst of Times!*

Charles Dickens' catchy little characterization of life in France during the Revolution is not unique to that country and that century. In actual fact any good historian can apply that description to most places in most centuries. It fits perfectly the American Catholic Church before the tension and turmoil of the Second Vatican Council.

The briefest bird's-eye glimpse would show that our churches were generally packed and paid for and more than half of all Catholic children were in Catholic schools and paying one-dollar-a-year book rent; young people were entering seminaries and religious houses faster than these could be built; the whole country was talking about a Trappist monk in Kentucky named Father Louis who had been Thomas Merton, a Greenwich Village playboy, and with him millions ascended his *Seven Storey Mountain;* the media were specially sensitive to Catholicism and all things Catholic, and the only sensationalism was the news of film starlet June Haver becoming a nun, or, as we said in those days, "entering the convent"; the Catholics who made the news were people like the attractive and modestly attired "pinups" Loretta Young and Ann Blythe, who brought the Boy Scout out of the millions of young, adoring males; there was a symbol system among Catholics that bonded them and gave them a common identity; Catholic children grimaced and finished their spinach to get Aunt Constance out of purgatory; everybody ate fish on Friday; our priests wore birettas and had the power to give dispensations; all students in Catholic high schools were taught such subtle distinctions as "invincible ignorance" and *ex opere operato* and the pitfalls of religious indifferentism; so close was the bonding and so common the Catholic experience that if one Catholic were scratched, they all bled!

Undeniably, it was a ghetto, historian Garry Wills reminds us, "but not a bad ghetto to grow up in." And the loss of this innocence, this stability, has caused tidal waves of nostalgia to continue to sweep over much of the Church in the United States. Yet nostalgia has a built-in deception: It compares the worst of the present with the best of the past. There *was* another side to the coin.

Historians looking back place identification tags on epochs and movements. The Church between the Council of Trent and the Second Vatican Council is conveniently labeled "the Ultramontane Church"—the Church "beyond the mountains." The "mountains" are the Alps. "Beyond the mountains" is Rome. This Church has for its driving force an obsessive reaction against Protestantism and everything connected to the Reformation movement.[1]

To be specific, the *bête noir* for sixteenth-century Protestantism was the papacy. No agreement would be possible between Catholics and Protestants unless Rome agreed to eliminate the Petrine office. Rome in this matter, as in all the Reformers' demands, would not even consider the slightest compromise. The result was the Catholic option of defending papal authority with a vengeance. In his introduction to *Lectures on the Prophetic Office* (1877), even the usually balanced Cardinal Newman described this top-heavy Church as a tyranny! Bishops were the losers and so were the universities and theologians. This was a very different situation from earlier centuries, notably the thirteenth and fourteenth, described by the same Newman as an age in which the intellect had a "licentious revel."

The papal question was not the only one to experience the Roman backlash. Rome opposed every Protestant demand. Sacred Scripture serves as another example. The battle cry of the Reformers was *sola Scriptura*. Scripture was the only authority they would recognize. Papal proclamations, medieval theologians, sage comments by the saints and founders of religious Orders—these carried absolutely no weight. The result of all of this was that Protestantism soon found itself without five of the seven sacraments, without papacy, purgatory, and pilgrimages, without prayers to the Mother of God and the saints, and on and on. Rome reacted to the use of this biblical criterion of authenticity with a strong suspicion

---

1. For further development of the mentality of the ultramontane Church, *see* Robert J. McNally, S.J., *The Unreformed Church* (New York: Sheed and Ward, 1965) and Hans Küng, *The Council, Reform and Reunion* (New York: Sheed and Ward, 1961).

**Theodore Ross, S.J.**

toward Sacred Scripture. This can be—and has been—exaggerated. Evangelical propaganda consistently claimed, then and now, that Catholics were forbidden to read the Bible. Catholics were *never* forbidden to read the Scriptures. Actually, they were mildly encouraged to read them. But Scripture was "under a Roman cloud" until the eve of the Second Vatican Council.

In no area did this polemical mentality take a bigger toll than in the matter of the Eucharist. The Roman Catholic community would have made many changes in its Mass long before Vatican II had it not been for the fact that the Protestants had clamored for these same changes four centuries earlier in the great trauma of the Reformation. Examples? A vernacular liturgy, a cup shared with the laity, a less clerical emphasis. All of these practices had been part of an earlier, healthier Catholic tradition. But these changes were delayed many centuries in the Latin Rite because of the hostile attitude to the 30 percent or so who broke off from Rome in the sixteenth century. To think of a vernacular liturgy was to join "them." One could speculate on the possibility today of optional celibacy were it not for the fact that one of the earliest innovations of the Protestants was a married clergy.

The above practices, however, were merely incidental to the really big wedge between Christians in the sixteenth century—the very nature of the Eucharist itself. Catholics insisted that the Mass was the real, albeit unbloody, sacrifice of Christ and that from this sacrifice Christ was truly and really present in the Eucharistic species. Protestants saw this as more unbiblical Roman "hocus-pocus." Due to a battalion of influences, not the least of which was nominalism and its influence on their interpretation of the Letter to the Hebrews, Protestants denied the sacrificial nature of the Eucharist. But they themselves had a veritable babel of opinions regarding the real presence. Luther held that Christ was consubstantially present along with the bread and wine; Calvin said the presence was spiritual; Zwingli maintained it was "only" symbolic.

The Catholic reaction to Protestant Eucharistic practice resulted in an exclusive sense of Christ's presence with emphasis on all the points that Protestants would not accept. Ultramontane catechesis stressed Christ's presence in the Eucharistic species to such an extent that many Catholics thought that Father said Mass in the morning to get a consecrated host for Benediction in the afternoon.

**The Personal Synthesis of Liturgy and Justice**

Christ was also present in the person of the priest, another "no-no" from a Protestant perspective, which saw this as a form of privilege and elitism. Finally, Christ was present in the liturgical action, the very Mass itself. The places where Protestants found Christ were not accentuated: in the word and in the worshiping community, even though these, too, are in an earlier, authentic Catholic tradition.

The effect of such a Eucharistic theology was the privatization of the liturgy. The social sense was always there, but it got lost in awe and transcendence. Holy Communion was a time of silent meditation. We saw only our union with Christ and did not develop the union that brought us together in our common food. Our relationship with Christ was vertical, "me and Jesus," not horizontal, "us in Jesus." With such emphasis on sacrifice, meal themes went undeveloped. *That* was for Protestants. In this privatized spirituality, concern for the poor and the demands of social justice had very little intrinsic, popular connection with the Holy Mass.

Understandably, the Catholic conscience would be restless in such an arrangement. Prophets rose to challenge it. Earlier in this century, the French poet Charles Péguy confronted his Church with the sting: "We must be saved together. What would God say if some of us came to him without the others?" The Old World spread its challenge to the New.

The remainder of this essay will concentrate on five American Catholic prophets who were grounded and inspired by the Mass in their quest for social justice: Virgil Michel, Reynold Hillenbrand, Dorothy Day, Peter Maurin, and Paul Hallinan. Few American Catholics heard their message, and fewer still listened. After all, these new voices were calling for dramatic change; and any kind of change, observed sixteenth-century Anglican theologian Richard Hooker, is "inconveniencing." Besides being prophets, these liturgical social activists *were* pioneers. And what happens to pioneers in most American movies? They generally end up with a *derrière* full of arrows. It would take an ecumenical council to recapture the Church's tradition that the body of Christ *means* the body of Christ.

Theodore Ross, S.J.

### A Radical Movement: Virgil Michel, O.S.B.

"We were feeding the hungry, clothing the naked and so on, but these needs of our brothers [and sisters] in Christ were overwhelming us! The day was indeed dark when this fiery priest, a bearer of light, warmth, and truth walked through the Blue Door. His name was Virgil Michel."[2]

Who was this priest with such saintly credentials who gave courage and vision to Catherine de Hueck Doherty, herself a Catholic social activist? And what was his vision?

If there was such a thing as a high priest for the movement to integrate liturgy with social activism, it was the humble, saintly, brilliant Benedictine, Virgil Michel, from St. John's Abbey in Collegeville, Minnesota. And if there were such a thing as a human dynamo, Father Michel qualifies for that as well. The most superficial glance at his *curriculum vitae* explains his problems with headaches, insomnia, depression, and an early death at the age of forty-eight. He was the founder of The Liturgical Press as well as the most prestigious Catholic liturgical periodical in the United States, *Orate Fratres,* changed in 1951 to *Worship.* Along with all this, he taught philosophy at St. John's University, wrote books and articles, and even held the position of dean. In addition, he became involved in the ministries of the Catholic Social Movement, especially those benefiting his beloved Chippewa Indians. After founding the Institute of Social Studies, he became its director in 1935. And in his "spare time" Father Michel pioneered programs for adult education. If this very zealous, talented priest had a breakdown, he deserved it.

With all these interests and diversions, it was the liturgy of the Church, however, that was Michel's obsession and first love. It is interesting to note that liturgical spirituality was not a treasure that originated in the United States. Almost all the pioneers of the American liturgical movement "struck gold" while studying in Europe, and Virgil Michel was no exception to this pattern. Louvain and St. Anselm's in Rome kindled his liturgical spark. Although he was converted to a strong liturgical orientation while in Europe, this is not to imply that social activism automatically came with it.

2. Catherine de Hueck Doherty, *Not Without Parables* (Notre Dame, Ind.: Ave Maria Press, 1977) 104, 106–107.

## The Personal Synthesis of Liturgy and Justice

His integration of liturgy and social responsibility actually came in two distinct phases.[3]

In the first phase (1926–1930) Michel concentrated on giving Catholics a sense of identity through the Mass and the sacraments of initiation. A common theme in his early work in *Orate Fratres* was his insistence that the Mass is not the action of the priest but a collective act of worship in which priest and people unite with Christ in offering sacrifice to God. All of the baptized are one with Christ. As such, they participate in the priesthood of Christ and they are made "co-offerers" of the Mass with the priest. Michel saw a need for each Catholic to renew his or her "baptismal consciousness," to put off the old self and put on Christ. Confirmation, he stressed, celebrates one's coming of age in Christ. The remedy for the apathy regarding confirmation's effectiveness, he believed, was twofold: (1) active appreciation and wholehearted answering of the promptings of the Holy Spirit, and (2) preparation for and celebration of confirmation as a parish event. All of this is ho-hum, at least in language, for the postconciliar Church. But in the first third of the twentieth century this insight was a blockbuster.

In the Foreword of the first issue of *Orate Fratres,* published in 1926, Dom Virgil mentioned for the first time the term that would become a key to all his later thought: "the mystic body of Christ." He challenged the Church to make the theology of the mystical body—strong from Pauline times until its decline after Aquinas— once again alive. The Church, he said, is a supernatural organism alive in Christ, and that makes each Christian a natural sacrament of Christ in the world as a member of Christ's body.

Two years later Michel pointed out the weakness of the Ultramontane Church: an overemphasis on its external juridicial structure, which fostered the passivity of the faithful. He contended that this same emphasis filled the vacuum caused by the loss of liturgical sense at the time of the Protestant Reformation.[4]

---

3. The same division is suggested by R. W. Franklin and Robert L. Spaeth, *Virgil Michel: American Catholic* (Collegeville: The Liturgical Press, 1988) 63–89.

4. *See* Virgil Michel, O.S.B., "The Liturgy and Catholic Women," *Orate Fratres* 3 (1929) 274.

**Theodore Ross, S.J.**

Such a theological base was just a hop, skip, and jump away from the second phase of Michel's liturgical thought: the liturgy as the basis for social regeneration. This position dominated his ministry from 1934 until his death in 1938.

Michel's first phase, which could be characterized as "liturgy, the source of Catholic unity," was born from his Benedictine vocation and his study in Europe. As a result of his ministry, Michel's second phase concentrated on a more activist stance against social injustice. This stance was inspired directly by the celebration of the liturgy. Michel had had a severe nervous breakdown and his superiors thought it best to get him away from heady academe to the more down-to-earth ministry of work with the Chippewa Indians. The injustice to, and suffering among, this beautiful people called forth from him a very empathetic response. His ministry was further fueled by the woes of the depression, an era so frought with social cancer of one kind or another that even the nation's chief executive began to question the traditional American way.

Pope Pius XI, in *Quadragesimo anno* (1931), emphasized the reconstruction of the social order. Michel, the zealous and committed priest, generously responded. He beat his drum for a cultural revival and urged a wholly new approach to every cultural expression, including art, literature, social theory, and education. Many during the depression were calling for the same thing, but Michel did it with this difference: *No cultural revival is Christian unless it is animated by and flows from the liturgical spirit.*[5]

Michel was not a wild-eyed dreamer, much less a revolutionary. Liturgy for him was a model and guide; it was *not* a full-scale plan. The organic unity of humanity in Christ cannot be reduced to a political or economic system. But it can act as a test for any system and as a model for generating principles for a system. Dom Michel judged four movements of his day to be in line with Christian ideals founded on liturgical spirituality: (1) the personalist movement, especially that found in the writings of Emmanuel Mournier, who had been a major influence on Peter Maurin and the Catholic Workers; (2) the corporative order, the best example of which was

5. Virgil Michel, O.S.B., "Nine Years After," *Orate Fratres* 10 (1935) 5. *See* the essay by Mark Francis in this volume for a further development of the relationship of culture and worship.

**The Personal Synthesis of Liturgy and Justice**

the industry council plan; (3) the cooperative movement as typified by Fr. James Tompkins and the Antigonish movement; and (4) the distributist-agrarian movement outlined in the *Manifesto on Rural Life,* published by the National Catholic Rural Life Conference. In each instance, the norm for his judgment was the Mass. As he insisted time and again, since it is the action of Christ that is realized in the Mass, the scope of it must be as extensive as the divine love of Christ. In an article in *Orate Fratres* he wrote: "In this holy fellowship we find a harmonious combination of the two complementary factors of humankind, that is, organic fellowship coupled with full respect for human personality and individual responsibility."[6]

Catherine de Hueck Doherty was only one person who found vision and strength from Father Michel's writing and lectures. Many others would be challenged by him. A luminary in the Midwest got for his own program a theological base from the brilliant theory of the Collegeville Benedictine. That person was the distinguished and respected Chicago legend, Msgr. Reynold Hillenbrand.

### That Toddlin' Town: Reynold Hillenbrand

If one wanted to find the creativity, the excitement of American Catholicism, Chicago—before the heavy hand of John Cardinal Cody—was "where it was happening." The Windy City anticipated the renewal of Vatican II a full thirty years before Pope John's *aggiornamento,* while Angelo Roncalli was exiled in Bulgaria and Turkey. Pioneer work in marriage and family life, the laity claiming more space in their Church, exciting catechetics, social awareness flowing from solid liturgical spirituality—a mere superficial index for a very impressive volume. And no one tells the story—no one knows the story so well—as Fr. Andrew Greeley. If few can match his touchiness and thin skin, fewer still are the equal to his background and knowledge of the details and personalities behind American Catholic movements.

A case in point is Greeley's "oldie but goodie," *The Catholic Experience,*[7] the book that convinces its reader of Chicago's place in

6. Virgil Michel, O.S.B., "The Liturgy: The Basis for Social Regeneration," *Orate Fratres* 9 (1935) 541.

7. Andrew M. Greeley, *The Catholic Experience: An Interpretation of the History of American Catholicism* (Garden City, N.Y.: Image Books, 1969).

**Theodore Ross, S.J.**

24

breaking the Ultramontane stranglehold. The Chicago story is about one personality and the story is about many personalities. Reynold Hillenbrand was the star, but in another city he would never even have made it to the stage. Chicago was a womb of leadership and activity. If Marxism was the craze for secular academe, the social teachings of the Church roused many Catholics. Auxiliary Bishop Bernard Sheil gave encouragement and protection to experimentation, even that which seemed "way out." The young in the Church "turned on" with CISCA (Chicago Inter-Student Catholic Action), the brainchild of Cecilia Himebaugh and Martin Carrabine, most unlikely charismatic leaders. But their movement produced Ed Marciniak, James O'Gara, Jack Egan, and John Cogley. Outside of the city on the affluent North Shore, Jesuit father Ed Dowling began a renewal of family life that burgeoned into the Cana Movement.

Carrabine and Dowling, with the aid of their brothers John LaFarge, S.J., in the East and Dan Lord, S.J., in Missouri, gave the impression that the Chicago Jesuits were the accelerator of the renewal bandwagon. It is a very wrong impression. When the tale is told, they will be seen to be its brake! But this is to get ahead of our story.

Reynold Hillenbrand[8] was truly "a man for all seasons"—the darling of George Cardinal Mundelein and the brain of the whole liberal operation, in a word, the guru—if such existed in the Church of the thirties and forties. He was in a position to deliver in all these areas, since he held the prestigious and influential office of rector for the archdiocesan seminary of St. Mary of the Lake, more commonly called Mundelein. It is to the cardinal's credit that he recognized authentic brilliance. Father Hillenbrand got this office at the ripe old age of thirty-one. Very early in his tenure as rector, Hillenbrand showed his hand. The influence of his travel and study in Europe, the great vision of the Catholic Workers, the brilliant theological theory of Virgil Michel, all came together in one of his early challenges to the seminarians to "see beyond their comfortable parishes and beyond their own comfortable lives, to

8. For an excellent overall picture of Hillenbrand *see* Robert Tuzik, "Reynold Hillenbrand: Teacher, Activitist, Pioneer," *Liturgy 90* 21:1 (1990) 6–9 and 21:3 (1990) 5–7.

### The Personal Synthesis of Liturgy and Justice

see the suffering in the world, to have a heart for the unemployed, not to shy away from misery, but to feel the injustice of inadequate wages . . . to have some of the vision that [Dorothy] Day and [Peter] Maurin and priests have who are coping with social problems."[9]

Hillenbrand was the product of one of Chicago's numerous ethnic parishes, St. Michael's on the Near North Side, which was the center for the German Catholic community. An insight from Father Greeley is very helpful here: The Germans had a tradition for active liturgical spirituality but no real concern for social activism; the Irish had a strong tradition for social activism but no real tradition of rich liturgical depth. Hillenbrand brought them together. The result was intoxicating! With a foot in both camps, Hillenbrand proved the confidence Cardinal Mundelein had in him. He became national chaplain for the Christian Family Movement, the Young Christian Students, and the Young Christian Workers. He *knew* the laity and what they could do.

Hillenbrand was a consultant for the Vatican II commission that gave the Church the decree on the laity. He was active in the Vernacular Society—a movement that was ultra taboo in the Ultramontane Church—and founding member of the Chicago Archdiocesan Liturgical Commission. But it was in the classroom that Hillenbrand made his biggest and most lasting impact. He taught liturgy to hundreds of future priests, and his interpretation of liturgical principles creatively assimilated his whole social orientation. Vignettes of Peter Maurin, Dorothy Day, Virgil Michel, Maisie Ward, and Frank Sheed made the liturgical picture he sketched a very interesting one. He was as historical as Joseph Cardijn, the Belgian priest who founded the Young Christian Workers in 1912. And he was as current as the trauma of the depression and the papal message that came out of it. *Quadragesimo anno* presented a solution to the economic ills of the thirties with the faith vision of the organic unity of Christ's mystical body. It was a challenge Hillenbrand accepted.

But the problem was the same for him as for Dorothy Day: They took the message of the popes more seriously than the popes did. Hillenbrand *certainly* took the message more seriously than did the

9. Tuzik, "Reynold Hillenbrand," *Liturgy 90* 21:1 (1990) 7.

**Theodore Ross, S.J.**

Jesuits teaching at Mundelein! Father Greeley has no great love for the Society of Jesus, but his evaluation is accurate when he claims that the Jesuit faculty at Mundelein was Hillenbrand's undoing. They considered the rector a social radical. And his orientation to real problems and social evils was a distraction from their abstract and often useless systematic theology! The Jesuits had the assistance of some very influential pastors throughout the city who wanted their young assistants to stay in the sanctuary and keep off the picket lines. Soon Hillenbrand found himself out of the seminary with a plum of a parish, but not before his impact was made. Fifty years later, some Hillenbrand-educated priests, sensitive to the pain and the wounds of a hurting people, continue to find in the Mass the motivation they need to challenge the greed and heartlessness of American affluence. These few are his legacy.

### A Radical Devotion: Dorothy Day and Peter Maurin

"I told him I feel like crying sometimes, or I flush with anger: to be in Church isn't to be calmed down, as some people say they get when they are at Mass. I'm worked up. I'm excited by being close to Jesus, but the closer I get, the more I worry about what he wants of us, what he would have us do before we die [Dorothy Day to her confessor]."[10]

Dorothy Day had a special, almost unique, role in the movement of integrating liturgy and social justice. The bigger guns, Virgil Michel and Reynold Hillenbrand among them, confronted the individualism that pervaded Catholic liturgical spirituality. They did this by developing theories, by research and eloquent writings, and by forming groups and organizations that planned and programmed renewal and reform. Their agenda was Church shaking: vernacular liturgies, less clericalism, greater participation, and more power to the laity. Inquisitions in the past would have burnt people for less.

Dorothy Day—model for the very best of authentic feminism: strength, competence, and compassion—was different. She followed her heart. Day could not go to Communion and be insensitive to the reality that someone was hungry; she could not enjoy the warmth of Eucharistic consolation and know that she had a

10. Robert Coles, *A Radical Devotion,* Radcliffe Biography Series (Reading, Mass.: Addison-Wesley, 1987) 77.

**The Personal Synthesis of Liturgy and Justice**

blanket while her brother or sister did not; she could not "go to the altar of God" and be aware that someone was sleeping over a grate on the sidewalk. All of this had little to do with theory or theology—what Newman would have referred to as a "notional assent." Her generosity and selflessness were not grounded on a reflective analysis of the paschal mystery. Nor was she necessarily motivated by the ethical dimension of Paul's instruction to the Church at Corinth. But she *was* persuaded by the Sermon on the Mount; she listened and she heard Jesus' words: "I was hungry . . . I was naked . . . " in Matthew's Gospel. The Mass was the place that centered and concentrated all of this for her because it was there that she became one with Christ and one with Christ's brothers and sisters. The bottom line was love, "a harsh and dreadful love"—personal commitment! Newman would call it "real assent."

This is not to say that her response was merely affective and personal. It was grounded in the theological. But the rational and intellectual came *after* the response of the heart, the prod of merciful grace. From her early childhood, Day had compassion for suffering humanity.

She reacted wildly and irresponsibly to status-quo society—"cut-throat capitalism"—that gave so much money to so few and so much misery to so many. It was before the Great Depression. If the old adage bears any truth—tell me who your friends are and I'll tell you what you are—then Dorothy Day was certainly a prominent member of the lunatic fringe. A list of her friends and confidants reads like a catalogue of the worst troublemakers in Greenwich Village. She did more than flirt with communism, and she did more than flirt with everybody else. No giddy flapper, she, with rouge on her knees and interests in flagpole sitters and goldfish eaters. Her situation was much more serious than that. She ended one pregnancy with an abortion; she lived with a man a full two generations before a permissive society would flaunt all permissions. Almost as if to make reparation for killing her unborn baby, she determined to have another baby—and she did, even though being an unwed mother in that time in history meant social leprosy.

But just as much as Dorothy Day flaunted society, she was totally dedicated to helping it. Her religion was not the transcendent

**Theodore Ross, S.J.**

but the humanistic. Her models were not the saints but Sigmund Freud, John Dewey, and the whole progressive litany. The cause of women's suffrage found her in jail; actually, to be honest, in solitary confinement for six full days. *That* will happen when one kicks a jailer and bites his hand! One cause after another intrigued her, and she sought desperately for something for which her life could be meaningful. Her goals were definite, but her existence was aimless. She even tried marriage, but that, like everything else, failed.

Her biography for the first thirty years reads like the "Hound of Heaven." Day was searching for God and God was searching for her. It was only a matter of time before they met—collided might be a more accurate term. Yet even in the darkest night or the most depressing failure, Day recognized that all was grace.

Roman Catholics, unlike Calvinistic Protestants, are reluctant, if not loathe, to admit the common phenomenon of irresistible grace. They will concede such a grace to the Mother of God. St. Paul *seems* to have had it. Some Jesuits, in fits of wishful thinking, might attribute such a gift to Ignatius of Loyola on the occasion of his battle injury at Pamplona and subsequent conversion. Did Dorothy Day receive such a grace? At times she seems to have said no to God, but God said only yes to her! She was no better or worse than dozens of her cronies and contemporaries, but they gave no indication of any change. They had little to claim except emptiness and frustration. Dorothy Day became a saint.

When she decided to become a Catholic, the whole conversion experience had none of the usual media hype of Catholic stereotype. She was not plagued with guilt or a pathological fear of hell, nor was she obsessed with her carnal lifestyle. Quite simply—and not easily rationalized—when her baby was born, she wanted little Tamar baptized even though it would be the decision that would lose Tamar's father and her lover. Then Day did what she knew she had to do: She, too, asked for baptism a few months later. In her personal notes she confided, "It was the glories of creation, the tender beauty of flowers and shells, the song of birds, the smile of my baby, these things brought such exultation, such joy to my heart that I could not but cry out in praise of God."[11] Up-

11. William Miller, "Dorothy Day, 1987–1980: 'All Was Grace,' " *America* 143 (December 13, 1980) 383.

**The Personal Synthesis of Liturgy and Justice**

beat, certainly! But the irony is that her desperate struggle to find God did not end there.

Baptism did not solve the problem of what seemed to be the deepest craving of her spirit. She had received from the Church, but the Church had a lot to receive from *her*. Not knowing much Catholic theology—she hardly knew any Catholics—Day had an intuition of the problems of the Ultramontane Church. She sensed that somehow her Catholicism had been turned aside from history, had been distorted in its meaning and even made into a sweet syrup to season bourgeois values.[12]

Day joined the Hunger March on Washington in December 1932. While in the nation's capital, she went to the National Shrine of the Immaculate Conception to pray for light and for a sense of vocation in her new faith. The answer to her prayer was not what she would have predicted. It came in the person of a French peasant, shabbily dressed and so eccentric that the most traveled and experienced cosmopolitan on passing him would turn for a second look.[13]

A veritable Niagara of words, Peter Maurin got in everybody's hair. As eccentric as he seemed, Dorothy Day saw what others had missed, for Maurin had experience and the wisdom that came from experience. A former member of the Brothers of the Christian Schools, he had also been active in Marc Sangnier's *Le Sillon* Movement in France and Vincent McNabb's Distributist League for land socialism in England. In addition he "knocked about" Canada and the United States experiencing desperate poverty and deep prayer. His knowledge, experience, and vision, coupled with Day's zeal and practicality, gave America the Catholic Worker Movement.

The Catholic Worker Movement (CWM) was a lay ministry whose foundation was liturgy and spirituality, and these challenged its members and the whole Church to create community, to affirm peace and denounce war, to restore true human dignity and creativity to the whole idea of work, to challenge a culture that ex-

12. This section is indebted to the fine, concise picture of the Catholic Worker Movement given in David O'Brien, *American Catholics and Social Reform* (New York: Oxford University Press, 1968) 182–211.

13. A recommended and reliable picture of Peter Maurin is found in Marc H. Ellis, *Peter Maurin: Prophet in the Twentieth Century* (New York: Paulist, 1981).

**Theodore Ross, S.J.**

ploited the helpless, to criticize big business and technology that were destroying personality and individuality and imagination.

The CWM was born in the height of the depression, when dozens of movements, philosophies, and isms surfaced. And all of them thought they held the antidote to what was poisoning America: skyrocketing unemployment, empty stomachs, constant uncertainty, fear and more fear. Solutions ranged from violent revolution to waiting out the status quo. What in this medley was distinctive about the CWM? What made it special? Quite simply, the answer is Peter Maurin and Dorothy Day. Pushing the question further: What made *them* special? The response to that is their balance, their perfectly blended integration of Christian ideals and social realities.

Maurin was convinced that the problem of the depression was rooted in the separation of the Church from political, economic, and social life. The Goliath of American industry and technology complicated human existence and rendered humans totally insensitive to the needs of each other. Government was not the answer. Actually it was much of the problem! Social workers were worthless in Maurin's analysis. Their data missed the point that was key to the solution: The oppressed were made in God's image and were brothers and sisters of Christ. All humanity was one and possessed unique dignity despite varying social conditions and situations. This faith vision of human worth and dignity was the heart of the Catholic Worker Movement.

Even the starry-eyed, ever-searching Peter Maurin had to have a plan. His program embraced three dimensions, all of which, taken together, offered fulfillment to human experience:

*Cult.* Quite simply this is prayer and worship. The Mass, of course, was central and pivotal, the soul of the whole vision. In the liturgy, Christ's action makes all one with him and with each other. Often when Dorothy Day "made her pitch" for more members in the CWM, she spoke on the Mass. Later, toward the end of her life, she was disappointed and somewhat depressed because the young workers did not see the liturgy as essential to the movement. For Maurin and Day, Eucharist and social action were two sides of the same coin.

*Culture.* This, for Maurin, was learning. His passionate interest in Church history helped him to distill the best of Catholic tradition.

**The Personal Synthesis of Liturgy and Justice**

The result was a synthesis of medieval ideals with the Christian personalism of the twentieth century. In this he was especially influenced by Nicolas Berdyaev.

*Cultivation.* All were expected to work. Here the movement was open to accusations of monasticism and medievalism because the work was basically agricultural. Maurin wanted to establish farming communes where the young could work the land, live together in Christian community, and initiate a whole new social order. Vincent McNabb's Distributionist League in England had the same ideals. The problem was to find a place for technology and modern science. The CWM was accused of being archaic and of rejecting the modern world before attemping to redeem it. Dorothy Day often challenged these conclusions, but, it seemed, never successfully. The CWM plan was never intended to ignore urban problems. Food grown on the farms was to be used to feed the poor and homeless in Hospitality Houses established in all of America's major cities. But the fact of the matter is that the dream of moving "back to the land" never became a reality.

All of this was to happen through discussions and dialogue— what Maurin referred to as "clarification of thought." The process involved some of the nation's finest intellectuals. These would learn from the poor and those serving the poor and would, in turn, lead them into a more enlightened vision.

The Church greatly benefited from the Catholic Worker Movement. Maurin and Day challenged Christians whose lives risked nothing and lost nothing of self for others, or even worse, assumed no responsibility for the powerless and used their "faith" to serve their own good. Those challenged were people who received the sacraments and whose lives supposedly revolved around the Mass.

Nevertheless, the Catholic Worker Movement in many ways was a child born out of time. Thirty years and one ecumenical council later, the Catholic Church somewhat caught up with it. Liturgy became the nourishment for the Church's commitment to make a "new heaven and a new earth"; laypeople began to regain their power not by concessions from Church authorities but by right of their baptism.

This was the goal and aim of the liturgical movement in the United States: the restoration of the laity. This was the "hidden

**Theodore Ross, S.J.**

32

agenda'' behind the movement for the vernacular and many other practices that were mandated by Vatican II. The CWM was from the beginning nonclerical in its organization and its decisions, even when it sometimes meant hitting the hierarchy head on. Peace, pacifism, and protests became common fare in the sixties. The Catholic Workers had held these as linchpins for their whole program even during the jingoistic days of World War II when such talk was most unpopular. But Maurin and Day saw the human family as members of a single body. This was the whole thrust of the Eucharist.

No symbolism captures the life and work of Dorothy Day and Peter Maurin so vividly as Day's funeral: St. Patrick's Cathedral, a cardinal prince of the Church, bishops, priests, city and government dignitaries, famous personalities, just plain people who loved and admired her! After the funeral liturgy, as her body was taken from the cathedral, a confused, ragged, homeless man—"bum" in a less sensitive age—pushed dignitaries aside in order to see what was happening. They all moved to let the man come closer.

Dorothy Day and Peter Maurin surely would have made room for him. Strengthened by the Mass, they bound the wounds of a hurting world.


### A Bishop Carries the Ball!

Monsignor Hillenbrand could never have done what he did for as long as he did it without some type of cooperation from the ruling echelon in the Church. Cardinal Mundelein and Bishop Sheil, as we have seen, were very much in his corner. And brass, not in the hierarchy but just as shiny, protected him, notably Msgr. Joseph Morrison, the strong and influential rector of Holy Name Cathedral, and Msgr. Edward Burke, chancellor of the archdiocese. One can only fantasize what impact Hans Anscar Reinhold would have made in Seattle and the whole American Church if *he* had had the support that Hillenbrand had. But *that's* another book. Most of the hierarchy are very much threatened by a model of Church that comes from the Catholic Workers or Virgil Michel or Father Reinhold or Reynold Hillenbrand. *Most,* but not *all!* This story ends with a very inadequate postscript of a tribute to one of the hierarchy who *was* the exception.

**The Personal Synthesis of Liturgy and Justice**

Paul J. Hallinan, bishop of Charleston, South Carolina, and later first archbishop of Atlanta, broke the episcopal mold. Archbishop Hallinan was a cosmopolitan from Cleveland, a true intellectual who, as bishop, earned a Ph.D. in history from Case Western Reserve University. He was also a shrewd judge and patron of quality who thirty years ago recognized the leadership potential of a young southern priest by the name of Joseph Bernardin. Archbishop Hallinan reacted to the Ultramontane Church, but he did so with balance and with ministerial compassion. In 1967, during the era of turmoil following Vatican II, he told the tiny Catholic flock in Georgia: "Those who nostalgically look back at a Church whose note was immobility, whose language was obscure, whose altars were ornaments are not on the right path. Those who carelessly seek the new, without regard to the sacred tradition that was so dear to the many they call their patron, Pope John XXIII, will not find a refreshed, revitalized faith."[14]

In that desperate decade, the sixties, after the euphoria of the council, pessimism gripped the Catholic community, but it never touched Hallinan. He retained to the end his Chestertonian sense of optimism and holy expectancy, the same mood he had in the beginning of the decade when he told an audience at Notre Dame on the eve of the council: "Only those who are devoid of Christian hope can look at the world today and throw up their hands. Only a philosophy that is drained of all meaning can find expression today in a shudder, or worse, a tired yawn."[15] God knows he would need the buoyancy. The lone American on the liturgical commission at Vatican II, Hallinan fought every delay tactic and dodge that would compromise the renewal of the Church's life of worship. Liturgy was his first love but by no means his only love. He was something of the American enfant terrible at the council. He was reacting to the evils of sexism long before most of the curia were even aware of two sexes. And, man of the gospel, "he hungered for justice." His cautious but dogged pursuit of racial integration in the very heart of Dixie gained him as many enemies as admirers.

14. Thomas J. Shelley, *Paul J. Hallinan: First Archbishop of Atlanta*, Foreword by John Tracy Ellis (Wilmington: Michael Glazier, Inc., 1989) 2.
15. Ibid.

**Theodore Ross, S.J.**

34

As a young priest Paul Hallinan had a firsthand experience of the pain and misery of war. The new, more sophisticated weapons for killing and wounding brought out his most humanitarian compassion and his strongest, most vocal opposition. Every reform, every move of renewal from Vatican II had been first lived and engrained in the heart, soul, and life of Archbishop Hallinan. But the motive for his "new heaven and new earth" was his conviction of the treasure of the human person purchased with the blood of Christ. The Mass and liturgy are where the redemption happens. The Eucharist was the start of social awareness; the Eucharist was its culmination and completion.

*Conclusion*

All the great characters in this essay found what they were looking for in the Mass. They died, all of them, exhausted from their labor of love for their brothers and sisters. They experienced pain and opposition and sickness and indifference. But "burnout" was not a word they used or an idea they would understand. In each instance, the liturgy was the full harvest that fed their enthusiasm. As a result, the problem and challenge of integrating faith and justice was not something they would understand. "To live is Christ," they would say with Paul. To separate worship from social commitment was a problem somebody else might have. It was not theirs.

**For Further Reflection**

1. How would you characterize Virgil Michel's understanding of mystical body theology?

2. What accounts for the key role of the Church of Chicago in issues of justice?

3. How did the approach of Dorothy Day and Peter Maurin differ from that of Virgil Michel or Reynold Hillenbrand?

4. Which portrait best describes how you would like to forge the synthesis of liturgy and justice in your own life?

**The Personal Synthesis of Liturgy and Justice**

H. Kathleen Hughes, R.S.C.J.

# Liturgy and Justice: An Intrinsic Relationship

*Introduction*

The renewal of the Church's liturgical life must be counted among the distinct achievements of the Second Vatican Council. It has been a renewal that in varying degrees has affected all the Christian Churches as each has pondered and probed the integral relationship between word and sacrament, the nature of the assembled Church, the many modes of the presence of Christ in the worshiping community, and the symbolic language of ritual action. Printing presses shifted into high gear, scarcely able to keep up with the new service books of the various communions that were issued in the late 1960s and throughout the 1970s. Worship offices and liturgy committees sprang up. Liturgical studies programs trained a cadre of professional theologians and liturgical practitioners who, in turn, offered study days and workshops and ground out reams of treatises dealing with the history and theology of worship and practical guides to its concrete expressions. Whatever one may think of its results, the fact is undeniable that the worship life of the Church has been radically and irrevocably altered in the aftermath of Vatican II.

The renewal of the Church's life of prayer corresponded, in time, to increased concern for issues of justice and peace in the world. During these recent decades of liturgical renewal, the Churches simultaneously became more involved in the needs of the human community. The parish liturgy committee found its analogue in committees for peace and justice. Study days and workshops raised the consciousness of thousands who, in turn, participated in peace marches and demonstrations, joined the Catholic Committee on Urban Ministry (CCUM) or Bread for the World, supported the Equal Rights Amendment or Ban the Bomb, wrote members of Congress or letters to the editor—in diverse ways probing and picketing and prophesying the Christian response to the injustices in our world. Whatever one's position on individual issues, the fact is equally undeniable that the Christian social conscience has been pricked.

**H. Kathleen Hughes, R.S.C.J.**

Two realities shaping the post-Vatican II Church. Two ground-swells of renewal. Consciousness has been raised simultaneously on two levels, yet only recently have liturgists and social activists attempted to recover the essential relationship between liturgy and just living, which was so integral to the liturgical movement in the United States prior to Vatican II.[1]

Our contemporary concern for articulating the relationship of liturgy and justice—as if they were two separate entities—would have been inconceivable to the pioneers of the liturgical movement in the United States. Our liturgical ancestors recognized that the way we live our lives is a litmus test of the authenticity of our worship, that we must worship the same God on Sunday and during the week, that the equality we know at the table of Christ's Body must be celebrated at all our other tables, that daily more deeply we must come to embrace the demands of every spoken "Amen."

So, for Virgil Michel, to take just one example, the racial question, and justice with regard to the distribution of the land, and the crusade to establish a Christian social order, and the movement for the reunion of the churches—all of these were the most logical and consistent concerns of one who entered into the sacrifice of Christ.[2]

Why two separate movements evolved in the wake of the council is a great puzzle.[3] *That* a chasm developed between them is un-

1. For a development of the liturgical movement in the United States prior to Vatican II, *see* my essay "The History and Hopes of the Liturgical Movement: A Tribute on the Twenty-Fifth Anniversary of the Constitution on the Sacred Liturgy" in *Proceedings of the Annual Meeting of the North American Academy of Liturgy* (Valparaiso, Ind.: North American Academy of Liturgy, 1989) 5–26; *see also* my book *How Firm a Foundation: Voices of the Early Liturgical Movement* (Chicago: Liturgy Training Publications, 1990).

2. The essay by Theodore Ross in this volume includes a portrait of Virgil Michel. For a recent treatment of Michel *see also* R. W. Franklin and Robert L. Spaeth, *Virgil Michel: American Catholic* (Collegeville: The Liturgical Press, 1988).

3. The word "movement" is used here in its more popular connotation. Strictly—and technically—speaking, the liturgical movement ended when it became institutionalized at Vatican II.

In a series of interviews I conducted in the course of other research, I asked a variety of people why liturgy and justice seemed to have grown apart in the sixties. I was offered as many reasons as there were persons I interviewed.

deniable. One had only to be present during a summer session at the University of Notre Dame in the late 1970s to discover how antithetical was the perceived relationship between liturgy and social justice. The participants in the liturgical studies program celebrated sung morning and evening prayer and a full Sunday Eucharist in Sacred Heart Church with vestments and incense, dignity, and formality. They understood themselves as participants in the recovery of the Church's tradition of worship who were, at the same time, contributing to its adaptation through model celebrations. Meanwhile, the participants in the CCUM summer session met in lounges, celebrating alternative, experimental worship services created around justice themes.

This latter group observed the former as "playing church with bells and smells," unconcerned with or even oblivious to real human issues, tinkering with trifles while cities burned and hearts eroded. The former observed the latter as "mucking around with tradition," creating liturgies *ex nihilo,* and manipulating participants by using worship as a weapon of social transformation. The lines were clearly drawn.

This vignette, while something of a caricature, nevertheless provides some truth and insight into the complexity of the relationship between worship and justice, between liturgy and life experience. For, on the one hand, the temptation to religious ritualism remains a constant threat to genuine liturgical renewal. It *is* possible to delude oneself, to worship different gods on Sunday and during the week, to count oneself part of the body of Christ yet remain unmoved by the needs of Christ's members. On the other hand, to superimpose themes on the celebration of liturgy is to distort the experience of worship in a different way. We gather for worship to celebrate not an idea but a Person, not what we can, should, or will do but what God has done and continues to do for us in Jesus, dead and risen. Anything less is neo-Pelagian.

In the remainder of this essay we will look more closely at these two distortions of authentic liturgy, which seem to hamper a true rapprochement between liturgy and justice in our day. In a third section it will be proposed that the relationship between liturgy and justice is intrinsic to both realities and that the way to bridge the gap between them may lie in taking seriously the meaning of participation in the paschal mystery which liturgy makes present, a

H. Kathleen Hughes, R.S.C.J.

participation that would issue in conscious Christian commitment to the vision of justice inherent in the celebration.

## The Gap Between Liturgy and Just Living

The temptation to religious ritualism is not a new problem, stirred up by the liturgical renewal of our day. It was a temptation to which our forebears in the faith succumbed, as witness the stinging rebuke that the prophet Amos places on the lips of the Holy One:

> I hate, I despise your festivals,
>     and I take no delight in your solemn assemblies.
> Even though you offer me your burnt offerings and grain offerings,
>     I will not accept them;
> and the offerings of well-being of your fatted animals
>     I will not look upon.
> Take away from me the noise of your songs;
>     I will not listen to the melody of your harps.
> But let justice roll down like waters,
>     And righteousness like an everflowing stream.
>
> Amos 5:21-24[4]

A similar diatribe is found in First Isaiah. In this passage the prophet castigates the people of Israel, who, despite copious prayer and sacrifice, are not living their lives according to the covenant:

> Hear the word of the Lord,
>     you rulers of Sodom!
> Listen to the teaching of our God,
>     you people of Gomorrah!
> What to me is the multitude of your sacrifices?
>     says the Lord;
> I have had enough of burnt offerings of rams
>     and the fat of fed beasts;
> I do not delight in the blood of bulls,
>     or of lambs, or of goats.
> When you come to appear before me,
>     who asked this from your hand?
>     Trample my courts no more;
> bringing offerings is futile;
>     incense is an abomination to me.

4. Scripture citations are taken from the NRSV.

New moon and sabbath and calling of convocation—
    I cannot endure solemn assemblies with iniquity.
Your new moons and your appointed festivals
    my soul hates;
they have become a burden to me.
    I am weary of bearing them.
When you stretch out your hands
    I will hide my eyes from you;
even though you make many prayers,
    I will not listen;
    and your hands are full of blood.
Wash yourselves; make yourselves clean;
    remove the evil of your doings from before my eyes;
cease to do evil,
    learn to do good;
seek justice,
    rescue the oppressed,
defend the orphan,
    plead for the widow.

                                                    Isaiah 1:10-17

And finally, in the Book of Micah, the prophet considers the perennial human dilemma: What kind of worship, what sacrifice of praise should be offered to God? What liturgy does God desire of us?

With what shall I come before the Lord,
    and bow myself before God on high?
Shall I come before God with burnt offerings,
    with calves a year old?
Will the Lord be pleased with thousands of rams,
    with ten thousands of rivers of oil?
Shall I give my firstborn for my transgression,
    the fruit of my body for the sin of my soul?

                                                    Micah 6:6-7

God responds to the prophet, but not with a solution for the worship committee! They are offered instead a way of life: to do justice, and to love kindness, and to walk humbly with God (Mic 6:8).

    What Micah, Isaiah, and Amos provide is a very salutary warning. They are not condemning ritual worship out of hand. They are condemning religious formalism. They oppose a cult performed with mechanical exactness but no inner devotion. They decry external rites unrelated to interior morality. The prophets remind us that there is an *intrinsic* relationship between cult and conduct—that worship is an expression of, and not a substitute for, social responsibility.

Care for libation of oil and fattened cattle, for albs and incense and programs and pauses, is commendable. But more is surely required, says the God of the prophets. Worship is rooted in justice, that is, worship is a concrete expression of right relationships or it is worse than worthless. It is an abomination!

*Justice* cares for the establishment of right relationships. Justice implies the recognition within us and among us of our growth as unique human persons with gifts and grace, with potential and desires, with anxieties and hopes and fears. Justice includes unity and solidarity, the linking up of our destinies as brothers and sisters who rise and fall together without domination or constraint, without exploitation or manipulation, without discrimination or violence.

Blessed are those who hunger and thirst when human rights are violated in various ways, when discrimination is encountered in its numerous forms, when situations are burdened with injustice in whatever guise. Justice instills in those who embrace it a hunger and thirst for the indispensible transformation of the structures of social life so that each person may find himself or herself in Christ and may mature, through Christ, in the one body of the human community.

While justice cares for the establishment of relationships, *liturgy* is their celebration. We gather to give praise and thanksgiving, to recall the mighty acts of God in human history, to make the memorial of Jesus' victorious death, to pray for the needs of our world, and to celebrate the kingdom of justice and love which is already and which is yet to be. Liturgy is our activity, our service as human persons in all our fragility and weakness, our hunger and thirst for justice still unsated, yet struggling to give expression to the life we are shaping in Christ. Liturgy is not a stepping outside of daily life into some mystical realm but a lifting up of our dailiness, recognizing that we are God-touched yet incomplete. It is a gathering of persons who need to let go, to give ourselves over, to surrender to the God of mystery, and to receive grace and strength

**Liturgy and Justice**

to live no longer for ourselves. And in the very process of confessing the one true God and Jesus Christ whom God has sent, the confessing community's self-awareness is purified and deepened, its commitment to justice reaffirmed.

Sometimes this commitment to just living is made explicit in the language of our prayer:

> God our Father,
> your Word, Jesus Christ, spoke peace to a sinful world
> and brought [hu]mankind the gift of reconciliation
> by the suffering and death he endured.
> Teach us, the people who bear his name,
> to follow the example he gave us:
> may our faith, hope and charity
> turn hatred to love, conflict to peace, death to eternal life.
> We ask this through Christ our Lord.
>
> > *The Sacramentary*
> > Fourth Sunday of Lent
> > Alternative Opening Prayer

> Keep, O Lord, your household the Church in your steadfast faith and love, that through your grace we may proclaim your truth with boldness, and minister your justice with compassion; for the sake of our Savior Jesus Christ, who lives and reigns with you and the Holy Spirit, one God, now and for ever.
>
> > *The Book of Common Prayer*
> > The Season After Pentecost
> > Proper 6

> Eternal Lord, your kingdom has broken into our troubled world through the life, death, and resurrection of your Son. Help us to hear your Word and obey it, so that we become instruments of your redeeming love; through your Son, Jesus Christ our Lord, who lives and reigns with you and the Holy Spirit, one God, now and forever.
>
> > *Lutheran Book of Worship*
> > Third Sunday of Lent
> > Prayer of the Day

"Followers," "ministers," "instruments"—keeping the memorial of Jesus' death and rising places obligations on the people who bear Christ's name. Confessing faith in God has social implications. It is interesting to note in some recent liturgical compositions that the focus of prayer has shifted from asking God to take care of those

**H. Kathleen Hughes, R.S.C.J.**

in need—thus perhaps relieving the community of its social obligations—to asking God to give the community the appropriate gifts of strength and courage to make us agents of change.[5]

As the liturgical renewal has progressed, various criteria have been propsed to measure the quality of the celebration, for example, careful planning, artistic integrity, theological accuracy, appeal to the senses, repetition and variety in careful balance—a whole series of objective criteria that form a kind of liturgical examination of conscience, a way of judging the progress of the reform. But there are larger questions:[6] Does this progress, of which we may be the promoters, make human life on earth more human? In the context of this progress are we becoming truly better, more mature spiritually, more aware of the dignity of our humanity, more responsible, more open to others, especially the neediest and the weakest, and readier to give and to aid all? Is there a growth of social love, of respect for the rights of others, for every person, or, on the contrary, is there an increase of various degrees of selfishness, the propensity to dominate, the propensity to exploit? Can we speak of progress in the liturgical renewal at all unless the liturgy has had a profoundly humanizing effect in our lives as well as in our celebrations?

That being said, it must also be stated that the claims the liturgy might make upon our lives sometimes cannot be heard because of the way in which they are delivered to us. The words and the gestures will only mediate the presence of the transforming Christ if they are spoken in a language that can be heard and appropriated by the entire community: "Liturgy requires the faith community to set aside all those distinctions and divisions and classifications (stemming from color, sex and class). By doing this

---

5. In the prayers here cited the community expresses its understanding of its obligation to just action, asking God for those graces necessary to strengthen it in its resolve. For other examples, see the prayer "In Time of Famine" in *The Sacramentary* (Collegeville: The Liturgical Press, 1974); the prayer for "The Oppressed" in *The Lutheran Book of Worship,* prepared by the Churches participating in the Inter-Lutheran Commission on Worship (Minneapolis: Augsburg, 1979); the prayer for "Social Justice" in *The Book of Common Prayer* (New York: The Church Hymnal Corporation, and Seabury, 1977).

6. The questions that follow have been inspired by the first encyclical of John Paul II, *Redemptor hominis,* March 4, 1979.

the liturgy celebrates the reign of God, and as such maintains the tension between what is (the status quo of our daily lives) and what must be (God's will for human salvation—liberation and solidarity)."[7] The many languages of liturgical prayer, including the words, the space, the choice of ministers, and the multiplicity of ritual actions, cannot transform the human heart if they are not heard; they cannot be heard if spoken in a way that excludes anyone in the community from full participation.[8]

The prophets' warning must sound again in our ears, urging us to examine not simply the quality of our celebrations—including their inclusive dimensions—but the quality of our Christian lives as well. Throughout human history ritualism has been a temptation. Our age is not exempt from its lures.

### The Manipulation of the Liturgy

Worship can be distorted in another, far more subtle way and this second problem is of recent origin: It is the superimposition of a theme on the celebration of liturgy.[9] Themes are a threat to genuine liturgical renewal and, in the context of the present discussion, a threat to genuine social justice as well, for they tend to promote a truly superficial idea of Christian justice and of its celebration.

There *is* an appropriate way to understand theme celebrations, of course. One might think of the mystery of God or the person

7. Bishops' Committee on the Liturgy, *EACW* (Washington: NCCB, 1978) 32.

8. It is impossible in the present article to treat either the question of the inclusion of women in the ministries of the liturgy or the question of language that discriminates because it is racist, sexist, clericalist, or anti-Semitic. These issues are, however, pressing justice questions in light of my thesis, namely, that the liturgy is a summons to *everyone* in the assembly to transformation into Christ, a summons that must not be muted by any word or action that tends to exclude. Other essays in this volume address some of these questions. *See,* particularly, the essays by Gilbert Ostdiek, Barbara Reid, and John Huels.

9. Theme celebrations are not limited to any one sector of the Church. The United States Catholic hierarchy broadly promotes the use of themes by specifying National Catechetical Sunday, National Mission Sunday, National Vocation Sunday, etc. Furthermore, a Jewish colleague confided to me that his Reform congregation was also busy at the xerox machine with celebrations such as "Manger, Mistletoe, and Menorah."

**H. Kathleen Hughes, R.S.C.J.**

44

and work of God come among us in Jesus Christ as compared to a prism with many facets, only a few of which are visible to the eye at any one time. Every Eucharistic liturgy celebrates the paschal mystery—the event of Jesus, dead and risen. It is the Scripture passages of the day that highlight one or other facet of this many-faceted mystery. It is the word of God that gives the theme or lends the nuance to a celebration; it is the Scripture that differentiates celebrations one from another.

But such is often not the way in which themes are used. The more detrimental thematizing looks something like this: A group gathers to plan a worship event. A theme is proposed, say for example, one of society's ills together with the appropriate Christian response. The group chooses Scripture passages that "speak to the issue," songs and prayers that support it. And, lest the theme is not already crystal clear, the sermon is designed to drive the point home. It is all very tidy. The choice of justice themes, it is anticipated, will fire up the community to do works of justice. But the problem is, that's not how the liturgy "works," nor how women and men become just.

We do not gather in the presence of the Holy One in order to discuss what we intend to do but to surrender to God's designs for us, a surrender that cannot be predetermined or controlled because it is not up to the initiative of the community. Liturgy is God's initiative, not ours! Liturgy is our response to the God who gathers a people together, who counts us worthy to stand in the divine presence, as we are reminded in Eucharistic Prayer II, and to offer our service—not because of anything we have done or intend to do but because of the victim whose death has reconciled us to God, in whose Spirit we become one. The celebration of ideas will not make us just; Jesus Christ will make us just, and so we pray to God: *May Christ make us* an everlasting gift to you.

Liturgy is not logical explanation, nor can its end be reduced to a political or ethical "goal"—a series of "shoulds" or "oughts." Theme liturgy, whether it be "right to life" or "peace" or "disarmament" or whatever, makes of the liturgy an exposition of ideas. But surely there are other more appropriate forums for such discussion. We do not celebrate the liturgy in order to think about ideas, however worthy, but to place ourselves in contact with the person and work of Jesus Christ and to submit to Christ's redemptive action in our lives. Liturgy is less a matter of the head than of the heart, an experience less of formation than of transformation, *if* we let God have God's way with us.

The liturgy has a unique potential for inviting transformation in the Christian community. The liturgy gives expression to the community's faith experience, or to borrow a phrase from Victor Turner, the liturgy transmits the community's "deep knowledge" from one generation to another.[10] In this function, it is true, liturgy is formational. At the same time, liturgical prayer deepens and enlarges the community's experience of faith, depicting what the community is summoned to become in the power of the Spirit, inviting wholehearted response. It is this second function of the liturgy that is potentially transformational.

Rosemary Haughton captured the essence of human transformation some years ago. She spoke of transformation as a total personal revolution that begins in an act of repentance, the rejection, along with actual sins, of the whole apparatus of natural virtue as irrelevant and misleading. Repentance proceeds eventually to the desired dissolution of all that ordinary people ordinarily value in themselves or others. The result of this dissolution, this death of the natural human being, is birth of the whole human being. It involves an integration and perfection of all that is most authentically human—and it takes place in Christ and nowhere else. It is what Christians call the resurrection, or eternal life.[11]

The insights of Victor Turner and Rosemary Haughton will help to clarify how the community may be transformed through its ritual prayer. For Victor Turner, nearly all rituals of any length and complexity have the function of placing men and women temporarily outside of everyday structural positions and demands— what Turner calls "status incumbencies"—and into a liminal betwixt-and-between state. In specifically religious rituals, the liminal interval may be an experience of stripping and leveling before the transcendent:

> In liminal sacredness many of the relationships, values, norms, etc.,
> which prevail in the domain of pragmatic structure are reversed, ex-

10. Victor Turner, "Passages, Margins and Poverty: Religious Symbols of Communitas," *Worship* 46 (1972) 399.

11. Rosemary Haughton, *The Transformation of Man* (Paramus, N.J.: Deus Books, 1967) 7–8.

**H. Kathleen Hughes, R.S.C.J.**

punged, suspended, reinterpreted, or replaced by a wholly other set. . . . [Those] who are heavily involved in the jural-political overt and conscious structure are *not* free to meditate and speculate on the combinations and oppositions of thought; they are themselves too crucially involved in the combinations and oppositions of social and political structure and stratification. They are in the heat of the battle, in the "arena," competing for office, participating in feuds, factions and coalitions. This involvement entails such affects as anxiety, aggression, envy, fear, exultation, etc., an emotional flooding which does not encourage either rational or wise reflection. But in ritual liminality they are placed, so to speak, outside the total system and its conflicts; transiently, they become [people] apart—and it is surprising how often the term "sacred" may be translated as "set apart" or "on one side" in various societies. If getting a living and struggling to get it, in spite of social structure, be called "bread," then man [or woman] does not live "by bread alone."[12]

"Liminality" for Turner describes the state of freedom and creativity realized by people set apart for awhile from what Turner calls inhibiting "status-incumbencies" in order to contemplate "the mysteries that confront all [human persons], the difficulties that peculiarly beset their own society, their personal problems and the way in which their own wisest predecessors have sought to order, explain, explain away, cloak or mask these mysteries and difficulties."[13]

Haughton might agree that ritual liminality provides an opportunity for contemplation, but she would emphasize that the point of such contemplation would be decision for action. In her schema, ritual provides the medium for the experience of withdrawal from—and indifference to—inhibiting social structure in order to afford a frame for encounter with the sacred—encountered only in the breakdown of structures. Such liminality she describes as "wilderness," "ambiguity," "in-betweenness." The point of ritual withdrawal and the point of encounter with the sacred in the breakdown of ritual structures is the possibility of transformation. Ritual "is directly and solely concerned with the occurrence of transformation,"[14] its limits, only the willingness of human re-

12. Turner, "Passages, Margins and Poverty," 393, 402.
13. Ibid., 402.
14. Haughton, 248.

sponse to the invitations to a real, personal surrender. Participation in liturgy demands decision. God's covenant with humankind requires the response of the obedience of faith. The event of liturgical prayer invites conversion and transformation, and the words and the gestures of the liturgy contribute to the invitational process.

Haughton proposes that it is in embracing *ambiguity* that transformation happens. This basic ambiguity upon which Christianity is based is Christ himself, who belongs securely to no category whatsoever:

> He cannot be thought of as a divine being, in human form, nor as a man seized by divine inspiration, but is a disconcerting complex that nobody has even managed to define satisfactorily, because the whole point is that you can't. He wasn't a priest yet offered sacrifice, he was ruler yet ended up on a gallows. Master and servant, carpenter and king, a dead man who was known and recognized as living. A total failure and a total success. These are ideas to which we are well accustomed, so they don't easily feel contradictory. But if one reflects on any one of these points it can be seen that while each member of each pair is clearly a true description, the truth of each one is a totally different mental and emotional "area" from the other. If both are put into one sphere of thought they are really contradictory, really nonsense. For each has to be kept in its own proper sphere in order to be true, and the mental shift from one to another, if one really makes this move and doesn't merely slide over the top of both, involves a kind of psychological distortion.[15]

The ambiguity of Christ shatters all categories. It makes *all* Christian language an experience of ambiguity, a challenge to its hearers, a summons to transformation in Christ.

The liturgy provides numerous invitations to transformation. The language of ritual prayer, reflecting as it does God's saving encounter with humankind in and through Christ, deliberately shatters our ordinary categories, using ordinary words and gestures in extraordinary ways, often presenting logic-defying irreconcilables in juxtaposition. At one and the same time the community is sinner and saved, powerless and graced by God, active subject of the praise of God and needy receiver of empowering grace.

15. Ibid., 277–278.

**H. Kathleen Hughes, R.S.C.J.**

The liturgy invites the praying community, bound to God by covenant love, to let go of all other ties that bind; to become powerless that God might fill it with power; to be utterly confident not because of its own worth but because God is faithful; to be leveled and to be lifted up by the God whom it encounters in its prayer. The liturgy of the Christian community is simultaneously an expression of its experience of faith and a summons to conversion and transformation in Christ.

The summons will not come because of carefully crafted but ultimately extrinsic themes that are imposed on the celebration. The summons to transformation is *intrinsic* to genuine worship. Only as we open ourselves to the event of Jesus' death and rising and as we allow ourselves to be purified in the abundant and life-giving divine presence shall we grow in holiness and justice. We shall, in fact, overcome. But let there be no illusion. We shall overcome only by God's transforming grace.[16]

*Make of Your Lives a Living Worship*

In the celebration of the liturgy, Jesus' death for the life of the world becomes available to us. Jesus, the Just One, the perfect response to the will of the one he called Abba, the source of God's continued gift to us, becomes present in the celebration and in the persons celebrating—in the words and gestures, the sacrifice and the meal. The liturgy summons us to *become* the sign of Christ's presence to and with one another. Such is our participation in the worship of the Church.

There is perhaps no statement from the Second Vatican Council's Constitution on the Sacred Liturgy more often quoted and more frequently misunderstood than that which refers to participation: "The Church earnestly desires that all the faithful be led to that full, conscious, and active participation in liturgical celebrations called for by the very nature of the liturgy. Such participation by the Christian people as 'a chosen race, a royal priesthood, a holy nation, God's own people' (1 Pet 2:9; see 2:4-5) is their right and duty by reason of their baptism" (CSL 14; DOL 14).

16. Other authors develop the transformative dimension of worship. *See* the recent work by William R. Crockett, *Eucharist: Symbol of Transformation* (New York: Pueblo, 1989) 227–263.

Full, conscious and active participation—our right and duty by reason of baptism. How easy it is to water down that statement! How easy it is to be full throated in our singing, to follow along in our "participation aid," to make all the appropriate responses, to give a warm and friendly greeting of peace, to receive the Eucharist—and to walk away, untouched at the core of our being. How easy it is to participate with a certain mechanical exactness, like Pavlov's dogs, scarcely aware of what we are doing, glad that the sermon is brief on hot summer days, wondering what we should serve for dinner next Wednesday when company comes, making mental notes to catch so-and-so in the parking lot . . . all the while muttering our "Amens" and our "And also with yous." How easy it is to come away unscathed by the reality of what we are doing when we gather to make this memorial of Christ's death and resurrection!

But what would it be like if we took the liturgy seriously, or rather, let the liturgy take us seriously—take us, for example, into that world of justice and love as expressed in the words of one of the Roman Eucharistic Prayers:

> To the poor [Jesus] proclaimed the good news of salvation,
> to prisoners, freedom,
> and to those in sorrow, joy.
> In fulfillment of your will
> he gave himself up to death;
> but by rising from the dead,
> he destroyed death and restored life.
> And that we might live no longer for ourselves but for him,
> he sent the Holy Spirit from you, Father,
> as his first gift to those who believe,
> to complete his work on earth
> and to bring us to the fullness of grace.[17]

Participation in the liturgy means participation in the life, death and rising of Jesus, *truly* dying and rising with him, *truly* laying down our lives. Participation means working mightily for the establishment of the reign of God by letting the spirit of God work in us to complete Christ's work on earth. Participation means living Christ's life: pouring ourselves out for the poor and the imprisoned

17. Eucharistic Prayer IV, *The Sacramentary.*

**H. Kathleen Hughes, R.S.C.J.**

50

and the suffering, wherever we encounter these realities in our every day. Participation means living "no longer for ourselves but for God." Otherwise, how can we say amen to such a prayer?

Participation in the liturgy means hearing the word of God as it is proclaimed in our midst, week after week after week, and letting that word take root in our lives. Participation means saying "the prayer which Jesus taught us" and recognizing ourselves as sons and daughters, brothers and sisters, consciously embracing the relationship thus implied when we name God "Abba." Participation means taking up the cup of salvation, remembering it is the cup of suffering as well, and not drinking unworthily. Participation means *meaning it* when we say of the Body of Christ: Amen. So be it. Yes, it is. Yes, I will be, with God's grace.[18]

Liturgy and justice have an intrinsic relationship to one another precisely because liturgy places us before the Just One to whom we say "Amen." We need not change the liturgy in order to highlight themes of justice. We need simply to celebrate the liturgy with genuine participation and allow the Just One gradually to work a transformation in us.

With every Amen we join ourselves to the paschal mystery and pledge ourselves to that vision of justice and love that is inherent in the celebration. Amen is an act of faith and an act of commitment. Full, conscious, and active participation in the celebration of the liturgy demands that we will, *in deed,* live what we proclaim.

### For Further Reflection

1. What do the prophets teach about ritualism? Do you think ritualism is still a temptation in the twentieth century?

2. How do you understand "theme" when used of liturgy and the process of liturgy planning?

3. Is it possible for the celebration of liturgy actually to perpetuate injustice?

4. What does "active participation in liturgy" mean, and what is its role in the process of human transformation?

18. See the recent monograph by Frederick R. McManus, *Liturgical Participation: An Ongoing Assessment,* American Essays in Liturgy, series ed. Edward Foley (Collegeville: The Liturgical Press, 1988).

John T. Pawlikowski, O.S.M.

# Worship After the Holocaust: An Ethician's Reflections

## Introduction

In a major reflective essay published several years ago in the *National Catholic Reporter,* Msgr. John Egan called for the renewed linkage of liturgy and justice in the Church. It is a connection that sadly was missed by the Second Vatican Council despite its genuine accomplishments in each individual area. Neither The Constitution on the Sacred Liturgy nor the Pastoral Constitution on the Church in the Modern World *(Gaudium et spes)* spoke to the connection. As a result, Egan concludes, the council "by its silence lends sad confirmation to what was a fact of life at that time: the failure of Christian people and Christian leaders to acknowledge the essential connection between liturgy and society, much less liturgy and social justice."[1]

Because I am strongly supportive of Egan's contention I genuinely welcome the opportunity to dialogue with liturgists.[2] From the perspective of an ethicist I feel no hesitation in saying unequivocally that such a partnership is necessary if we are to rebuild a strong commitment to justice in the Christian community and in the society at large. This partnership becomes even more crucial as we reflect on the world in which we live, one that has experienced the trauma of the Nazi Holocaust and approximately similar genocides such as in Cambodia. Additionally, we have witnessed the unleashing of atomic power, and we stand on the threshold of even greater human destruction through nuclear warfare, as the American bishops have so prophetically warned us.

## The Meaning of the Holocaust

From a study of these modern realities, the Nazi Holocaust in particular, I have become convinced that we cannot stop the de-

---

1. "Getting Liturgy and Justice to Merge" (September 30, 1983) 9.
2. This essay was originally prepared for presentation at the annual North American Academy of Liturgy convention in 1984.

terioration of and we cannot rebuild the moral ethos of humankind unless we can once again come to experience a living and challenging God through liturgical expression truly reflective of our era. In saying this I am endorsing the comments made to the 1983 meeting of the North American Academy of Liturgy by David Power: "The greatest temptation threatening liturgical reform is that of a retreat into the past, or a retreat into abstract universalism. It is one to which Churches succumb when they find themselves doomed to silence by the inability even to face, let alone make any sense of, current reality. Can we in truth celebrate Eucharist after the Nazi Holocaust and in face of an imminent nuclear holocaust, and in a world half-populated by refugees, in the same way as we did before the occurrence of such horrors?"[3]

I have been persuaded by such scholars as the Israeli historian Uriel Tal that the Holocaust represents something more than the final, most gruesome sequel in the long and tragic history of Christian anti-Semitism. This is in no way meant to minimize the central role played by the classical anti-Semitic tradition in public cooperation with the Nazi Final Solution. There is little question that Christian anti-Semitism provided an indispensable seedbed for Nazism.

But the Holocaust also represented an attempt to create a "new person," a superbeing, in a social atmosphere in which growing technological capacity combined with bureaucratic efficiency and the erosion of traditional religious restraints upon human behavior to open the doors to virtually unlimited and morally unchallenged use of power to reshape human society and even the human person. Though the Nazis used the Christian Churches in some instances in their primal attack on the Jews, their philosophy deep down was profoundly anti-Christian. And their calculated genocidal plan for "renewing" humankind included the elimination of gay people, Gypsies, and the mentally and physically handicapped, in addition to the subjugation of the Slavs, especially the Polish nation. The creation of mobile killing units and execution centers modeled on modern industrial plants that processed their victims with conveyor-belt efficiency, with a high premium placed on the elimination of waste and the creation of by-products from the human remains as well as the establishment of branches of leading

3. "Response: Liturgy, Memory and the Absence of God," *Worship* 57 (1983) 328.

German firms such as I. G. Farben and Krupp in the vicinity of the gas chambers and crematoria to make some profit from every last ounce of life in the inmates—this is human perversity almost beyond belief.

The challenge to human integrity as well as to any notion of a loving, caring God assumes even greater proportions when we recognize that this "social development" was the work of some of the best and brightest people in a society many consider among the most advanced yet generated by the human spirit. Leo Kuper speaks well to this especially sinister aspect of the Holocaust in his volume *Genocide:* "Then there was the extreme bureaucratic organization of the genocide. This was one of its most dehumanized aspects. We know all too well the passionate outbursts by murderous mobs under incitement of their leaders. These fall well within the expected range of human behavior. But to use bureaucratic planning and procedures and regulation for a massive operation of systematic murder throughout a whole continent speaks of an almost inconceivably profound dehumanization."[4]

Auschwitz truly opened up a new era in human possibility. The perpetrators of the Holocaust seized upon the destructive side of this possibility. In so doing they challenged many traditional Christian theological notions that had previously grounded the conduct of human affairs. They passed beyond many previous barriers in their use of human power and ingenuity. They clearly showed that religious concepts such as divine punishment, hell, the wrath of God, divine Providence—to name but a few—that had dominated human consciousness since biblical times were indeed waning in their influence. By implication, any form of prayer and liturgy rooted in these beliefs was likewise profoundly affected. Auschwitz, it is my contention, was but the most extreme example to date of a growing awareness that is touching people everywhere. The experience is not all negative, as I shall shortly explain. But if it is to parent a constructive advancement in human consciousness, it will need the guidance of God's spirit. Such guidance, however, will not reach humankind with sufficient force if, to repeat David

---

4. *Genocide: Its Political Use in the Twentieth Century* (New Haven, Conn.: Yale University Press, 1982) 120.

John T. Pawlikowski, O.S.M.

Power's warning, the Church in worship falls back on the mere repetition of old formulas.

The fundamental reality that has emerged from my research into the Holocaust is the new sense of human freedom present among the Nazi theoreticians.[5] The Nazis had correctly assessed modern human experience in at least one crucial respect. They rightly understood that profound changes were at work in human consciousness. Under the impact of the new science and technology, the human community was starting to undergo a transformation that can aptly be described as "Prometheus Unbound," and that on a mass scale. The doctor-killer in Rolf Hochhuth's *The Deputy* says it well: 'We are the Dominicans of the technological age.''[6]

An awareness was beginning to dawn of a degree of human autonomy and power far greater than most of Christian theology had allowed for in the past. The possibility now existed to reshape human society, perhaps humanity itself, to an extent never previously imaginable. This new possibility created a new responsibility—to liberate humankind from the "polluters" of authentic humanity, the dregs of society, as these were arbitrarily determined by the Master Race. People now began to use death to solve the problem of human existence. As Uriel Tal has maintained, the Final Solution was meant to answer a universal crisis of the human person. It aimed at a total transformation of human values at the heart of which was the loosing of the "shackles" of the historic God-idea with its attendant notions of moral responsibility, redemption, sin, and revelation. To quote Tal directly: "God became man, but not in the theological New Testament sense of the incarnation of the word . . . or in accordance with Paul's understanding of the incarnation of God in Christ. . . . In the new conception, God becomes man in a political sense as a member of the Aryan race whose highest representative on earth is the Fuehrer.

5. My writings on the Holocaust include *The Challenge of the Holocaust for Christian Theology*, rev. ed. (New York: Anti-Defamation League, 1982); "The Holocaust: Its Implications for the Church and Society Problematic," *Christianity and Judaism: The Deepening Dialogue*, ed. Richard W. Rousseau (Montrose, Penn.: Ridge Row, 1983); and "Christian Perspective and Moral Implications," *The Holocaust: Ideology, Bureaucracy, and Genocide*, ed. Henry Friedlander and Sybil Milton (Millwood, N.Y.: Kraus, 1980).

6. New York: Grove, 1964, p. 248.

**Worship After the Holocaust**

Communication with the Fuehrer became communion. This transformation took place through public mass meetings which were staged and celebrated as sacred cults as well as by means of education, indoctrination and inculcation of discipline."[7]

The Christian theologian Michael Ryan and the late Jewish historian J. L. Talmon basically concur with Tal's analysis of the implications of Auschwitz. Ryan speaks of the Hitlerian "salvation history" as "a resignation to the conditions of finitude combined with the total assertion of power within these conditions." Hitler's worldview, Ryan writes, "amounted to the deliberate decision on the part of mass man to live within the limits of finitude without either the moral restraints or the hopes of traditional religion."[8]

Talmon describes the Nazi heresy as the denial of any "final station of redemption in history," which gave birth to a cult of power and vitality as ends in themselves. Having abandoned any belief in "eternal verities," the Nazis "were ensnared by a perverted, murderous idealism which gave them absolute belief in their own superiority." The awesome question, Talmon asks, is whether the Holocaust served "as an eternal warning, or merely the first station on the road to the extermination of all races and the suicide of humanity?"[9]

*A New Sense of Freedom*

In light of the Holocaust and related examples of the brutalization of human power, it is incumbent upon contemporary Christianity to discover ways to affirm the new sense of freedom that is continuing to dawn within humankind while channeling it into constructive outlets. Post-Holocaust Christian faith expression, including its liturgical dimension, must fully recognize and welcome this development of a new sense of human liberation and elevation as a positive, crucial, and central part of the process of human sal-

7. "Forms of Pseudo-Religion in the German *Kulturbereich* Prior to the Holocaust," *Immanuel* 3 (Winter 1973–1974) 69–70.

8. "Hitler's Challenge to the Churches: A Theological-Political Analysis of Mein Kampf," *The German Church Struggle and the Holocaust,* ed. Franklin H. Littell and Hubert G. Locke (Detroit: Wayne State University, 1973) 160–161.

9. Cf. J. L. Talmon, "European History—Seedbed of the Holocaust," *Midstream* 19:5 (May 1973) 22–24.

**John T. Pawlikowski, O.S.M.**

vation. But in view of the Nazi experience, Christianity cannot blindly or naively applaud this new sense of human freedom. Its challenge is whether it can now provide an understanding and experience of the God-human person relationship that can guide this newly discovered power and freedom creatively and constructively. Somehow faith encounter and faith expression today must be such that they can prevent the newly discovered creative powers of humanity from being transformed into the destructive force we have seen expressed in all its ugliness in the Holocaust. It must begin to address the contemporary human condition that the philosopher Hans Jonas has described as one in which "we shiver in the nakedness of a nihilism in which near omnipotence is paired with near emptiness, greatest capacity with knowing least what for."[10]

### The Recovery of Transcendence

For this to happen in a meaningful way we shall have to recover a fresh sense of transcendence. And I am convinced the realm of the symbolic remains our only viable hope in this regard. Men and women will once more need to experience contact with a personal power beyond themselves, a power that heals the destructive tendencies still lurking within humanity. The newly liberated person, to be able to work consistently toward the creation of a just and humane society, must begin to sense that there exists a judgment upon human endeavors that goes beyond mere human judgment. The old sense of judgment rooted in a notion of divine punishment will no longer work. The modern experience of the human community is that the worst atrocities can be perpetrated with apparent impunity. The only norm that can finally curb such atrocities is one rooted in an experience of love and unity beyond the narrow dimensions of this earth, joined to the concomitant realization that actions such as those that shaped the Holocaust ultimately block the attainment of such love and unity. The Holocaust has destroyed the simplistic "commanding God." But it has likewise revealed our desperate need to restore a relationship with a "compelling God," compelling because we have experienced through symbolic encounter with this God a healing, strengthen-

10. *Philosophical Essays* (Boston: Beacon Press, 1974) 124.

ing, an affirming that buries any need to assert our humanity through the destructive, even deathly, use of human power. This sense of a compelling Parent God who has gifted humanity, who shares in our vulnerability through the cross, is the foundation for any adequate moral ethos in the contemporary world.

## The Integration of Liturgy and Ethics

With this statement you may perhaps begin to see why I deeply welcomed the opportunity as an ethicist to address liturgists. We in the discipline of ethics cannot hope to make the impact we deem absolutely necessary in today's world without your assistance. Unless we can begin to create liturgical experiences that will lead to a genuine experience of a compelling God together with a consciousness of such realities as sin, freedom, dependence, solidarity, vulnerability, and oppression, we have little chance to influence human decision making. And the absence of such influence will leave the human condition increasingly in a situation in which there exist fewer and fewer constraints on the use of human power, which technology is enhancing day by day.

In other words, moral sensitivity remains an indispensable prelude to moral reasoning. We ethicists can provide the necessary clarifications of human response mandated by such sensitivity. Such clarifications are absolutely essential if religious experience is not to degenerate into religious fanaticism. But, as an ethicist, I cannot create the sensitivity itself. Mere appeals to reason, authority, and/or natural law will prove ineffective by themselves. Such sensitivity will reemerge only through a new awareness of God's intimate link with humankind through symbolic experience. Nothing short of this will suffice.

Let me say at this point that I view the Holocaust as the culmination of a long-term process in which a sense of God's personal relationship with people has been gradually lessening. Gerardus van der Leeuw pointed to one aspect of this reality in his comments about the breakdown between dance and religion in modern culture. Dance has not lost its appeal in our world, but it has largely shed its sacral character. This has resulted in the closure of one of the primary channels for the experience of God's relationship to people. "Primitive man," says van der Leeuw, "views the dance as a most serious affair, with religious significance. It sets into motion

**John T. Pawlikowski, O.S.M.**

powers which are holy to man; it touches on all levels of life and raises it to a higher level. All other meanings are included in the religious."[11] Van der Leeuw feels that the religious dimensions of dance will reemerge as we again become conscious of the unity of body and soul.

As Western society has moved through the centuries, it has gradually, though somewhat subtly, closed off more and more avenues to the personal encounter with God. Secularism may be far more advanced in theory in certain Marxist societies; but in practice we in the West may not be far behind. The loss of a sense of dance as link with the divine is just one small example of this trend. The substitutes have simply not worked. Reliance on the mind could not ultimately save Greek society from destruction any more than power could save the Roman Empire. The discovery of reason by the Greeks, though it led to many genuine contributions to humanity, represented in the last analysis an exaggerated rebellion against Homeric religion. Greek philosophy made a contribution to Western thought only as long as that thought remained somehow tied to religious roots.

The gradual breakdown in the West of this union during the Enlightenment and its aftermath found reason trying to assume a role as source and foundation for moral values. The disjunction occurred much earlier on the Continent than it did in North America, where a popular piety never gave the rationalism of Jefferson, Franklin, and the other architects of the republic the free hand it enjoyed in Europe. Reason's child, technology, which has more and more tried to disassociate itself from its parent, moved us further in the direction of one-dimensionality. In ways the Holocaust is the climax of this process. A leading commentator on Auschwitz, Irving Greenberg, is perfectly right in my judgment when he argues that the Holocaust challenges the Enlightenment tradition at least as much as the Christian tradition and undercuts the validity of any ethic based solely on the possibilities of human reason:

> How naive the nineteenth-century polemic with religion appears to be in retrospect; how simple Feuerbach, Nietzsche, and many others. The entire structure of autonomous logic and sovereign human rea-

---

11. *Sacred and Profane Beauty: The Holy in Art* (New York: Holt, Rinehart, and Winston, 1973) 35.

son now takes on a sinister character. It is like Hawthorne's pilgrims in "The Celestial Railroad," who speak so sweetly and convincingly of heavenly bliss, while all the time the barely stifled flames of hell rage in their breasts. For Germany was one of the most "advanced" Western countries—at the heart of the academic, scientific, and technological enterprise. All the talk in the world about "atavism" cannot obscure the way in which such behavior is the outgrowth of democratic and modern values, as well as pagan gods.[12]

One person who saw the transformation was Immanuel Kant. He tried to establish a new basis for ethics beyond that of the biblical divine-human encounter. Kant was tremendously insightful in his grasp of how modern developments were undercutting the traditional bases for ethics. But his solution—a model based on reason and universal consistency—has proven inadequate as a response. While the philosopher Dorothy Emmet is correct in arguing that the Kantian model is not so simplistically based on universal consistency as some commentators would have it,[13] it nonetheless assigns a primacy to reason that renders the Kantian system by itself unusable as the touchstone for modern societal morality. It participates too much in the cleavage between body and spirit. Until this cleavage is overcome, no solid moral footing will be found for contemporary humanity. Unfortunately, the Kantian model still dominates far too much in significant segments of Christian ethical thought.

Recently, some ethicists have begun to challenge the dominance of the rational model. Daniel Maguire is one example. He has pointed to affectivity, to the heart, as the birthplace of moral sensitivity: "Ethics moves on to confirmatory reason and theory, to demonstrations of the coherence and fruitfulness and truthfulness of one's positions; but it is in feeling that its roots are found and nourished. The foundational moral experience is an affective reaction to value. It is not a metaphysical or a religious experience primordially. It is not a conclusion to a syllogism, though it may subsequently be supported by syllogisms and reasoning. The value

12. "Cloud of Smoke, Pillar of Fire: Judaism, Christianity and Modernity After the Holocaust," *Auschwitz: Beginning of a New Era?* ed. Eva Fleischner (New York: Ktav, 1977) 17.
13. *Rules, Roles and Relations* (New York: St. Martin's, 1966) 70.

**John T. Pawlikowski, O.S.M.**

of persons cannot be taught, subjected to proof, reasoned to, or computerized. It can only be affectively appreciated.''[14]

Maguire is on the right track in his analysis, but he does not go far enough. The fundamental moral experience, as I see it, is not merely an affective reaction to value, though it is that to be sure. Ultimately it depends, it is precipitated by, a personal encounter with the living presence of the Creator God. And the contexts of such encounters are the prayer experience and, first and foremost in my judgment, the symbolic experience of the liturgy. I give primacy to the liturgy because of its communal setting, its greater link to the tradition, and its potential for more explicit direction of the encounter's vitality toward genuine moral ends.

### Life Is Multidimensional

By this time I trust my basic thesis is clear. I see an urgent need to counter the growing one-dimensionality in Western society in the midst of a growing awareness of human power and freedom through the development of new moral sensitivity. This moral sensitivity must be engendered by symbolic encounter with the Creator God who speaks to us in a newly compelling way. Strange as it may seem, the Holocaust provides us with some help in this regard. For if Auschwitz reveals one permanent quality of human life, it is the enduring presence of, the enduring need for, symbolic communication. What my mentor in social ethics, Reinhold Niebuhr, called the vitalistic side of humanity has not been permanently obliterated. But it has increasingly in the West been relegated almost exclusively to the realm of play and recreation.

### Social Themes and the Liturgy

Its link to moral formation has become more and more tenuous. It is the power inherent in this vitalistic side of the human person that liturgy has the greatest potential for channeling into constructive moral commitment. Here lies the fundamental link between ethics and liturgy, a link whose reestablishment becomes imperative in light of the Holocaust. In this sense I agree up to a point with my CTU colleague Kathleen Hughes, who argues against see-

14. *The Moral Choice* (Garden City, N.Y.: Doubleday, 1978).

ing this link primarily through the creation of "cause" liturgies: "Liturgy is not logical explanation, nor can its end be reduced to a political or ethical 'goal'—a series of 'shoulds' or 'oughts.' Theme liturgy, whether it be 'right to life' or 'hope' or 'disarmament' or whatever, makes of the liturgy an exposition of ideas. . . . We do not celebrate the liturgy in order to think about ideas, however worthy, but to place ourselves in contact with the person and work of Jesus Christ and to submit to Christ's action in our lives."[15]

I am not as opposed to more specialized "cause" liturgies on an occasional basis so long as the basic thrust of the liturgy set out by Professor Hughes is not distorted. Also, I believe we need to go somewhat beyond her in trying to create within the liturgy certain basic attitudes intimately connected with the experience of a caring God and a transforming Christ. In terms of her examples, I see a significant difference in "hope," which I think far more central to the liturgy than the other more specific themes she mentions in the above quotation.

In addition to hope, I would suggest the following as very important themes if the liturgy is to have a transforming effect on the worshiping community relative to the grounding of its moral commitment. Time constraints will permit only a brief treatment of each. It may be that a dialogue needs to begin between ethicists and liturgists on how these can best be expressed in our celebrations. The context for such a dialogue might indeed be John Egan's call, a call I strongly second, for the generation of a pastoral letter on the link between liturgy and social justice.

The first of these themes would be the sense of community. John Egan stresses this in his essay referred to earlier, going back to Virgil Michel's root metaphor of the body of Christ: "We do not stand alone before God, but as a community of people vitally and organically bound to one another in Christ. In the social apostolate, the doctrine of the mystical body affirmed the fundamental truth that the human person is created as a social being, a being whose existence and growth is defined and developed in interaction with other human beings."[16]

15. *See* "Liturgy and Justice: An Intrinsic Relationship," in this volume.
16. Egan, "Getting Liturgy and Justice to Merge," 9.

**John T. Pawlikowski, O.S.M.**

62

A development of a sense of human cocreational responsibility for the earth is likewise vital. The post-Auschwitz divine-human relationship will need to be one in which there is a clear recognition of God's utter and inescapable dependence upon the human community in the process of creational salvation. The God whom we used to invoke in the liturgy to intervene and correct the ills of the world by himself died in the ashes of the Holocaust. God will not intervene to stop such perversions of authentic human freedom. Auschwitz has taught us that God will not, perhaps even cannot, effect the full redemption of that part of his being that he has graciously shared with humankind unless human beings assume their appointed role of cocreators. The American bishops' energy statement, with whose development I was closely connected, puts it this way:

> Since we derive all our energy from nature, the relationship of humanity and environment has the broadest implications for energy policy. In the religious community, this relationship is often described as "responsible stewardship"; we are stewards to whose care the Master has entrusted his creation. The technological strides we have made since World War II require a sharpening of that concept. The human race has the capacity to alter nature, even to destroy it, and the scope of our responsibility grows with the scope of our power. We are no longer called upon simply to tend the garden God has given us. It is now in our hands to determine whether our descendants will inherit an earth capable of sustaining them."[17]

I must acknowledge that some of my colleagues have challenged such a cocreationship orientation. Stanley Hauerwas has argued against my position, insisting that in light of the Holocaust we need to assert human limitation rather than human power, to regain a proper sense of humility.[18] I have to say that on the whole he has not persuaded me. In fact, failing to take seriously the depth of our new responsibility may well lead to further catastrophes. But we do share some communality in our analysis. For me the assertion of cocreatorship must be done in the context of a newly height-

17. USCC Committee on Social Development and World Peace, *Reflections on the Energy Crisis* (Washington: USCC Publications, 1981) 4–5.
18. *See* "Jews and Christians among the Nations," *Cross Currents* 31 (Spring 1981) 34.

**Worship After the Holocaust**

ened sense of humility, a clear recognition that any measure of cocreatorship we enjoy is not self-generative but a gift of God and a forthright recognition of the other side of this power—the destructive tendencies that surfaced so prominently in the Nazi era. The fear and paternalism that has frequently characterized the God-human person relationship in the past is fast eroding. But the new relationship being born cannot fully be made whole unless the human community develops a profound humility, evoked by the presence of the ultimate Creator of all human power. Without this sense of humility, the potential for goodness and love inherent in the new consciousness will become a reality that is one long nightmare of hate and destruction.

A proper incorporation of humility into twentieth-century consciousness is imperative for survival. Here is where Hauerwas and I profoundly agree. But so is the sense of cocreatorship. Here is where we profoundly disagree. Some Scripture scholars strongly object to the term "cocreator" as unbiblical. I am not absolutely wedded to the term, and I acknowledge that my use of it exceeds biblical boundaries. But somehow we must bring to the fore in liturgical celebration the new power and, subsequently, the responsibility for creation that is now a reality. Older terms like stewardship are simply too weak in my judgment.

Linked to the cocreatorship emphasis is an equal stress on the dignity of nature itself. One does not have to join the extreme environmentalists to recognize the deterioration in the human community-natural world relationship. Reversal of such deterioration is crucial for the continued sustainability of all life forms, including the human. We have done precious little in Christian liturgy to celebrate nature in its own right. Here is where we can profit from our increased contacts with Jewish liturgy. And what little we have done in the past along these lines has virtually disappeared in recent times. The inherent dignity of creation is another crucial sense that the liturgy must help to develop as part of contemporary moral awareness.

Another side of this same awareness is a genuine belief in the goodness of the earth. Some Holocaust interpreters such as Richard Rubenstein look to the philosophy of Nietzsche as providing roots, albeit indirect, for Nazi philosophy. The Catholic Holocaust commentator Frederich Heer shares this perspective with Rubenstein,

**John T. Pawlikowski, O.S.M.**

64

interpreting Nazi philosophy as in part a reaction to the anti-world sentiment buried deep in the Christian consciousness. Heer quotes fellow commentator Karl Erlingagen who has asked: "Could not Nietzsche's cry, 'Remain faithful to the earth,' be interpreted as the cry of protest of a misunderstood and mistreated world, and be echoed in its truest sense by the Christian? . . . The contempt for the world of which we speak goes far beyond contempt for the material and the basely sensual: it extends to the purest realms of the spirit."[19]

Somehow the liturgy needs to make us aware of the fundamental compatibility of earthliness and spirituality if the quest for authentic earthly existence is to avoid the destructive paths taken by Nazi philosophy.

Let me mention only two additional themes that need exposure in the liturgy in the process of moral development. The first is what Jurgen Moltmann in his volume *The Crucified God,*[20] the first comprehensive Christology based on the Holocaust experience, has termed the "vulnerability of God." Only a modification of God's omnipotence, through participation in human suffering and dependence on the human, will finally curb the combination of pride and power that has proven so destructive in the course of human history. And from the human side there is need to raise up Jesus' central emphasis on reconciliation to the point that my colleague Donald Senior has called "enemy love."[21] This must be done within a context of clear acknowledgement of Jesus' confrontational side as well.

### Significance of Symbols

Before concluding let me address one other dimension of the liturgy-ethics link in light of the Holocaust. Increasingly I have been intrigued with the role of symbolism in forging social cohesion and providing society with public values. As we examine the Holocaust, we begin to detect how purely rational ideals were to-

19. *See God's First Love* (New York: Weybright and Talley, 1970) 401.
20. New York: Harper & Row, 1974.
21. *See* "Enemy Love: The Challenge of Peace," *The Bible Today* 21 (1983) 163–169.

tally ineffective in combating the upsurge of Nazism. Here lies the fundamental flaw in classic liberalism. To their "credit," if I may put it that way, the Nazis recognized that symbols are extremely important in determining the public values of a society. They were quite aware that symbols bind people in ways that ideas alone cannot. They understood that acts of celebration strengthen resolve in ways that mere discussion cannot. So public liturgy became vital for the implementation of the Nazi scheme for society.

As we examine the public life of this republic today, the question haunts me. Are we not faced with a situation that in some ways parallels that of Germany at the time of the Nazi ascendancy? Some years ago Rollo May offered reflections on the meaning of symbols that may have application to the public state of America's soul, that may help illuminate a proper response to this question. He writes: "I would suggest that the difference between a 'sign' and a genuine 'symbol' lies at this point: when a word retains its original power to grasp us, it is still a symbol, but when this is lost it deteriorates into being only a sign, and by the same token when a myth loses its power to demand some stand from us, it has become only a tale."[22]

The question before us is whether the symbols of transcendence that have undergirded American public morality are now collapsing, becoming signs and tales with no power to grasp us. The success of the Nazis in presenting new symbols to an alienated and frustrated society may contain a vital lesson for those of us identified with liberal Christianity and liberal Judaism. People need symbols. If in opposition to the Moral Majority and other kindred groups, we simply join with those who oppose all public religious symbols, then we may in effect be paving the way for the triumph of religious symbolism motivated by religious fanaticism.

A central challenge before the mainline Churches today is the creation of new symbols of transcendence for American society and the clarification of the proper limits of such symbols in terms of their specific religious content. It is a challenge that we have not yet adequately addressed. If the challenge is to be met, however, it is my conviction that liturgists will have to consider assuming a sig-

22. "The Significance of Symbols," *Symbols in Religion and Literature,* ed. Rollo May (New York: Braziller, 1966) 17.

**John T. Pawlikowski, O.S.M.**

nificantly new role. They will need to step beyond denominational boundaries to look at what current symbols in society might be reinvigorated and what new ones might be developed. There is no other group on the current American scene with the creative potential to deal with this reality. Our universities frequently study ancient myth and ritual and analyze social symbols from a sociological perspective. But virtually nowhere, including our most prestigious theological faculties, is there attention in any great measure to the creation and maintenance of symbolic bondings in contemporary America that acknowledge our dependence on a Creator God while clearly asserting our newly realized cocreational responsibilities. It would be my plea that liturgists might begin to explore more deeply, in an interreligious context to be sure, this aspect of their calling.

In the frontispiece to his *Holocaust Kingdom,* Alexander Donat quotes from Revelation 6:8: "And I looked, and beheld a pale horse: and his name that sat on him was Death, and Hell followed with him. And power was given unto them over the fourth part of the earth, to kill with sword, and with hunger, and with death, and with the beasts of the earth."

Unless we can recreate a new dynamic sense of a God-human person relationship through symbolic experience and thus shape a new moral sensibility within humankind, we have little chance of preventing the horse from riding through our lands again as it did during the Holocaust. Our cooperative mission as ethicists and liturgists is truly death defying.

### For Further Reflection

1. Has modern technological society made us "one-dimensional" in our experience? Has this affected worship in the Church today?
2. Do we need a sense of a loving, merciful, but still judging God to maintain moral standards in society?
3. What role do symbols play in maintaining a moral tone in society?

Ralph A. Keifer

# Liturgy and Ethics:
# Some Unresolved Dilemmas

### The Eucharistic Action and Social Justice

In one sense, the relationship between liturgy and ethics in general and social justice in particular is obvious, and this is true of the heart and center of the liturgy, the Eucharistic action itself. It is the business of the Eucharist to constitute a foretaste of the heavenly kingdom, as it is an enactment of the covenant between God and humankind. Its fundamental gestures and dynamism are unitive and reconciliatory. Moreover, the intentionality of the Eucharistic action is that of a public act in the widest and deepest sense of the term—an enactment of what it means that the world is good and graced yet standing under judgment because the work of creation and redemption is unfinished. It is at the same time blessing and reproach, thanksgiving and lament, divine promise and human pledge. As an interpretation of the event of God in the *world* (not just in the Church—what else can the consecration of common bread and wine mean?), the Eucharist patently has everything to do with ethics in general and social justice in particular. To borrow a few lines from Rosemary Haughton, "if we take seriously the baffling but undoubted interrelatedness of the spiritual and the material, of culture and environment, mind and body, individual and community, then belief in the resurrection of Jesus is an assertion not only about what happens to this one man but about the nature of reality. It is saying first, that the ultimate bliss, the goal of all human decision, is not a liberation from material and bodily existence, but a transformation with it and in it."[1] If liturgical and sacramental action have to do with celebrating this estimate of the human situation—and who would deny they do—then clearly liturgy, ethics, and social justice have everything to do with one another.

---

1. *The Catholic Thing* (Springfield, Ill.: Templegate, 1979) 232.

**Ralph A. Keifer**

## Our Compelling Liturgical Symbols

Without in any way disagreeing with the major issues that John Pawlikowski raised in the previous essay in this volume, and in particular agreeing that the need of our times is to evoke for society an image of a compelling rather than a commanding God, I have some uncertainties about his appeal to liturgists to find or utilize new symbols of a compelling God for our time. Agreeing with everything else he has said, I find myself pondering that we *have* those symbols—water, oil, bread, wine, bodies, caresses, a flowing wealth of metaphor and parable clustered into a marvelously rich and variegated mythology of a power in but not of this world, real now yet coming to us out of the future, in every way on the side of wholeness and freedom, and in every way affirming the utterly precious uniqueness of every human being and the call of the race into unity, harmony, and cooperation in the mutual care of one another, spun out into tapestries of prayer and proclamation and woven into a gorgeous three dimensional kaleidoscopic organism of ritual speech and action. This is not something for liturgists to dig out of the dust of antiquity, wrest from society by anthropological expedition, or invent by some peculiar ingenuity of their craft. It is the common heritage and possession of the community of the faithful.

Yet to note all this is to highlight a fundamental problem already developed by Kathleen Hughes: Liturgy on one side and ethics-social justice on the other are frequently, indeed commonly perceived as entirely separate spheres of concern. If the fundamental intentionality of liturgical action has everything to do with ethics-social justice, why the disjuncture? I suggest that this is the basic question that demands exploration, and ultimately demands an effort between and across all the major disciplines of theological concern, far beyond the bounds of what is presently, or has been recently, constituted as liturgical studies or sacramental theology. Liturgical action (not just Eucharistic activity) is, I suggest, the Church's ritual enactment of the relationship between God and the world. Since that is a socially structured world, and it is the Church's doing of the enactment, liturgical and sacramental questions thus involve not only questions of ethics and social justice but also questions of ecclesiology, the relation of the Church to the world, mission, and others.

**Liturgy and Ethics**

Closer attention needs to be paid to the ambivalent nature of symbols: that what they "mean" for people is radically conditioned by the social and historical context within which they are used. To take the simplest of examples, the swastika means very different things to Jews and to Hopi. To describe the liturgy as "speaking for" social justice without reflection on how much this may be qualified by varying sets of experience of both Church and world is to ignore its nature as symbolic activity. Symbols do not actually "speak for themselves": in many ways, their ability to "speak" is derived from what a people is willing or able to attribute to them, and most especially, the context within which they are used. The Polish upheaval in the 1980s over crucifixes on public buildings and the very different conclusions of the United States Supreme Court about a municipality's erecting a nativity scene reflects this ambivalent nature of symbols. In Poland, the crucifix focused the continuing confrontation between society and government, Church and state; whatever the inadequacies of the Supreme Court's notion of "passive" symbolism, the nativity scene has, in the American context, far less charged power. There is a peculiar obliqueness to symbols such that they are unintelligible without reference to the community that uses them. Mary Douglas notes, for instance, that the Jewish horror of eating pork arose not out of any particular disgust for pigs and their supposedly filthy habits but because of the function of the pig in a particular perception of the ordering of the universe and out of resistance to the point of death when that perception was threatened.[2]

Given this rootedness of symbols in social, historical, and cultural context, I agree with the Jewish liturgist Lawrence Hoffman, who insists that the fundamental liturgical icon is the assembling community itself. From that perspective, the issue of the relationship between liturgy and ethics-social justice is less the particular symbols the community uses than how the community that uses those symbols actually behaves as a community living in the world. If the assembling community is one that in actual fact and public perception does justice and loves mercy, its liturgical symbols will speak for those things. It may be the particular province of liturgists to suggest which among the Church's panoply of symbols

2. *Purity and Danger* (London: Routledge & Kegan Paul, 1979) 57.

**Ralph A. Keifer**

best and most adequately speak for those things, but it is an intolerable and inadequate narrowing of the issue to reduce it *simply* to the one of the discernment of appropriate symbols. Much liturgists' discourse about liturgy floats in detachment from this question of the assembling community, yet I would suggest that this is a primary one, perhaps *the* primary one. To put the matter another way, the Church's *liturgia* does not float free in some special world but is intimately and inextricably bound up with its *kerygma, koinonia,* and *diaconia,* and its quality is in every way affected by the quality of those functions.

## The Privatization of Worship

The quality of liturgical celebration and its social impact is also in every way conditioned by the extent to which it is perceptible as a truly public act: an event that enacts a worldview, that perceptibly functions as embracing the whole of life, and that indeed is perceptible as a statement about the nature of human and cosmic reality, affirming the interconnectedness of the gathered assembly and its interconnectedness with the world. In one sense, the liturgical movement was well aware of the problem of the privatization of worship. Especially when it is perceived less as the public service of responsible citizens one to another and for the sake of the world than as service in the sense of a service provided by an agency for the benefit of its clients, and usually for benefits of a rather individualistic and private nature. The movement was especially critical of the cluster of private devotions that had overlaid the official liturgy and of the religious individualism that this encouraged.

The liturgical movement may have grasped the right issue and proposed the wrong solution—or at least proposed a solution that does not go to the heart of the matter. In many ways, particularly in this country, the liturgical reform that came as a result of the liturgical movement succeeded in uprooting many conventions of devotion inherited from the past. A variety of devotional patterns have been superseded by a Eucharistic cafeteria of "high," "low," and "folk." This does not necessarily render liturgical action—as perceived by the ordinary worshiper—as any more constituting a fully public act than the liturgy of yesteryear. It is possible to see the apparently rapid and revolutionary changes in North American

Catholic liturgical life as a simple Americanization of traditional pieties that answered more to private need than they spoke to public concern. Whatever their form, the old devotions had the important function of giving the ordinary believer access to a benign God, a space of comfort, assurance, and affirmation where one could put the toil and woe of everyday life. The present variegation of "high," "low," and "folk" allows that sacred space to unfold, either in terms of a certain numinous sense of connection with the past and tradition (high), a mantric backdrop of monotony so conducive to meditation or the respite of reverie (low), or within an atmosphere of modernity and affability so congenial to North Americans (folk). The disappearance of a hieratic language, the repositioning of the priest, and the granting of space for such things as vernacular hymns (usually of a very sentimental sort) created a situation in which the liturgical forms themselves could now function as pegs on which to hang popular private piety. It may be noted in this regard that the great litanies of the liturgy (penitential rites, general intercessions, Lamb of God) are normally interpreted in such a way that they take on the quality and content of prayers and examinations of conscience formerly found in devotional manuals, assuming an individualistic and privatistic character not at all foreseen by the agents of liturgical reform.

This is not to suggest that there is anything "wrong" with devotion as such, as if it were in some way inimical to the Christian gospel. Indeed, liturgical studies have probably underestimated the import of a variety of patterns of devotion as public worship. The devotions that developed in the eleventh and twelfth century, for example, had everything to do with an emergent new Christian humanism and the reshaping of the Church's relationship with the world. Certainly the problem of devotional prayer is not its supposed subjectivism or emotionalism—can there be real prayer without feeling subjects? Rather, the problem is that the gamut of needs given expression in many devotional patterns can be readily attended to without advertence to wider public issues, people can pray through them as isolated individuals without any significant reference to their interconnection with a wider world. The present tone and shape of many a contemporary Eucharistic Sunday celebration is such that it is readily perceptible simply as a "service"—not the service of citizens responsible to one another

**Ralph A. Keifer**

72

and to the world but as a service to clients who get out of the liturgical act what they can for their private and domestic benefit.

This privatization of worship is in certain significant ways fed by a heritage of interpretation that concentrated far more on sacramental activity as special avenue of access to the sacred than as disclosing the event of God in the world. Through most of our history, particularly in the Christian West, the perception of the sacraments as "means of grace" has, for all practical purposes, including the mode of their enactment, eclipsed their function as signs: revelatory actions that disclose the action of God already present in the world and to the whole of life. Both liturgical development and reflection on that life have tended in the Catholic tradition to the identification of liturgical activity as what can only be described as sacred cult, a special sphere of activity that gives special access to the realm of the sacred. This was all the more dramatized by a progressive heightening of the sense of difference between the primary agents of the cult (the clergy) and the ordinary worshiper, in both liturgical act and in reflection on it. Within the cultural context of medieval Christendom, liturgy could retain its public character. Whatever its failings, and whatever the variegation of formulation it produced in terms of questions of the relationship of the Church to the world, a number of characteristics of Christendom were evident. A certain hegemony of the Church over culture and society was assured, whatever the various trades made between Church and state and Church and culture at various times during that epoch. At least as the people of the time saw it, that hegemony of the Church over culture and society was assured as a given effort to permeate the world with the values of the Christian gospel. Hence, whatever the failings of individuals and the limits of its own interpretation of what it was doing, the Church's self-enactment in liturgical celebration inexorably pointed to the shaping of the world according to those values—a point made all the clearer by negation, the imposition of interdict when some particular community had radically failed to uphold them. If the liturgy took on the trappings and language of sacralized cult, it may also be noted that all significant institutions and their enactments were so clothed. Civil power was in the hands of anointed kings, and treaties were signed in the name of the Trinity.

**Liturgy and Ethics**

That cultural and societal hegemony of the Church has been breaking up since the Great Western Schism, but it is only since Vatican II that Roman Catholicism has officially and as a whole acquiesced in a situation where it no longer enjoys such hegemony. During that time between the end of the Middle Ages and the twentieth century, the Catholic Church neither essentially modified its interpretation of its basic patterns of worship nor essentially modified its interpretation of its liturgical life. On both of these counts, until very recently, it chose to defend and protect the medieval heritage rather than criticize it in light of the new situation. The result was perforce a certain privatization of liturgy, because the society role of the Church was itself hedged on all fronts. To the extent that the Church lost its power or credibility as a public agent, so too its liturgy inevitably lost that public dimension. The liturgical movement criticized the liturgy as being swamped by private devotions, but I suggest that criticism may have been somewhat beside the point, missing the heart of the matter. In a variety of ways, religion in the modern world has become a department of public life rather than its binding tie. Inevitably, then, acts of worship become some *part* of life, not bespeaking the whole.

In a cultural context where the Church's societal role is as ambiguous as it has become in the modern world, concentration on sacraments as "means of grace" and their cultic interpretation inevitably tends to a certain privatization of the sacramental event: The individual worshiper is cast in the role of a consumer-client rather than as an active agent with other co-worshipers. The ethical life becomes somewhat tangential to the actual act of worship, functioning either as a preparation ("worthy reception") or consequence ("responding to the grace of the sacraments") but not as constitutive of the liturgical event itself. Granted, both the agents of liturgical reform and contemporary sacramental theology have resisted this kind of interpretation of what sacramental action is about. But these are recent efforts at reinterpretation, in many ways incongruent with actual pastoral practice and liturgical experience.

Avery Dulles noted the problem with the image of the Church as sacrament: "It suggests a conspicuousness which the Church as a whole does not possess, since most Catholics, or other Christians,

**Ralph A. Keifer**

74

do not go about in uniform. And finally, there is some ambiguity about what the Church as sign or sacrament represents. Is this Church as we commonly experience it, a convincing sign of unity, love, and peace for which we hope in the final kingdom? The Church in its pilgrim state is still far from adequately representing the heavenly Jerusalem, even in a provisional manner."[3]

## The Church and Contemporary Culture

Dulles underscores the problem with perceiving a liturgical event as an event of disclosure of God's grace at work in the world. People tend to experience the Church as institution, not sacrament. This does not necessarily carry all the pejoratives frequently associated with the term "institution." I simply mean that the Church is commonly perceived less as a community of fully enfranchised citizens than as a kind of agency providing for certain needs and aspirations that other agencies do not. Ordinary worshipers perceive themselves as audience, receivers, clients, only tangentially connected with the other worshipers present. A variety of movements and currents of thought are tending to the breakdown of that perception of acts of worship. But at the same time, social and geographical mobility, the breakdown of ethnic bonds through intermarriage and assimilation into the cultural melting pot of the United States, the disappearance of genuine neighborhoods, all tend to the dissolution of a sense of common bonds among co-worshipers. The normal experience of Catholic worship is not that of an assembly where all are responsible to each and each to all but of a largely amorphous crowd of individuals coming somewhat tangentially together to receive the benefits of the services of a religious institution.

It should be noted that in a variety of ways the average congregation is what can only be described as "ethically amorphous." Whatever may be the limits of Robert Bellah's thesis on American civil religion[4] one thing is certain—in all sorts of spheres of contemporary life, the Church is no longer the arbiter of right and wrong, and it functions as one source among many for the values

3. *A Church to Believe In* (New York: Crossroads, 1982) 5.
4. Robert Bellah, "Civil Religion in America," *American Civil Religion,* ed. Russell Richey and Donald Jones (New York: Harper & Row, 1974) 21–44.

that people embrace. The preoccupation of the papal magisterium with matters of sexual ethics may have much to do with the fact that until recently, the Church was more readily accepted as the ultimate arbiter of issues of ethics culturally understood as private, and the membership of the Church is increasingly unwilling to accept even that tutelage.

What we get as a result is a model of the Church that I can only describe as "cookie jar"—people select from the Church what they find of value and disregard what they do not. That description is an attempt at accuracy, not flippancy—people commonly value liturgical activity for what they "get out" of it.

I suggest, then, that the issue of the disjuncture between liturgy and ethics-social justice is at root an issue of the relationship of the Church to contemporary culture, particularly as the role of the Church is perceived and lived out within contemporary culture. The evocative power of symbols is in every way conditioned by the life and the perception of the community that uses them. As the Catholic community of faith is currently shaped, it exists as one agency among many public agencies, catering to the needs and aspirations of a vast clientele which more or less partially identifies itself with that agency but which in contemporary democratic and pluralistic society finds no need for full and total identification. The cosmic and reconciliatory symbolism of which the liturgy is so redolent is thus significantly muted. The praying community approaches those symbols as the possession of a group with which it is not fully identified, "the Church," both Church as institution and Church as "cookie jar," and thus cannot make those symbols fully their own. Our most powerful evocative symbols, which could speak most eloquently to the fundamental issues of ethics and social justice, recede to the status of a kind of denominational pageantry.

### Toward a Solution

So much for the problem. What about the solution? It is frequently asserted that our liturgical problem is a problem of "community"—that the amorphous and anonymous nature of the liturgical assembly has everything to do with the failure of people to grasp the social dimensions of liturgical activity. There is truth to this assertion; but stated in such a vague manner, it is not very

**Ralph A. Keifer**

76

helpful. The communities of the *volk,* of the oppressed minority, or of the sect are either inaccessible or undesirable options within the mainstream of contemporary pluralistic culture in democratic societies. Much discussion of the problem of "community," however, reflects a nostalgia for those sorts of models. I would suggest that we need to begin with what we have—the cookie jar—and ask what are its possibilities and potentialities; and this is not only for pragmatic reasons. The detachment of churchgoers from the Church-as-institution cannot be interpreted as so simple a matter as an individualistic and narcissistic detachment from the demands of the gospel, but rather can also be seen as a theologically defensible living-out of a perspective that the Church has no corner on grace or goodness or truth, while admitting there is "something there" in the Church that makes it worthwhile to continue one's association with it. The fierce tensions that people are willing to bear between their own ways of living out the gospel and what the official Church often tells them is *the* way to live it out suggest not narcissism and individualism but a willingness to live with an inevitable tension between individual and community. This in its own way is a quiet heroism of fidelity to the community and to tradition. The Pastoral Constitution on the Church in the Modern World's concept of the "signs of the times" is a frank acknowledgment of the movement of grace within contemporary culture and, implicitly, an acknowledgment that such movement may occur in the teeth of official and conventional Church opposition. One could scarcely urge, for instance, that the movement for the liberation of women owes much to the official and conventional Church of the past century, yet it is singled out by the constitution as the "signs of the times." Hence, if we have managed to create a Church-as-cookie-jar in this country, whatever its liabilities it is defensible as a response to an intuitive perception that for all the limitations on either side, grace is to be found both in the Church and in contemporary society.

### Evoking a God Who Is Compelling Rather than Commanding

I agree with John Pawlikowski that the fundamental issue is one of our ability to evoke liturgically a sense of the compelling rather than the commanding God. For Catholicism, the image of God has everything to do with the image of the Church. What has clearly happened on the U.S. scene is that people are unwilling to accept a commanding Church, but even behind its facade of commands they find something compelling. The problem is that in the present impasse, the context of liturgical celebration is such that the image of a compelling God is readily diluted into one of a merely acquiescent God, providing assurance without challenge, comfort without criticism, substituting nostalgia for a sense of tradition, approval for encouragement. The revivalistic ethos of the way the Catholic Church in this country has taken up the right-to-life issue would seem to be symptomatic of a deep-seated uneasiness that perhaps we no longer stand for anything or any commitment, and that we had better find some last-ditch issue around which we can all rally. Likewise, the steady flow of sentimental syrup in some contemporary Church hymnody (commonly, the creative edge of liturgical praxis) bespeaks a rather flaccid religion of assurance, comfort, nostalgia, and approval—a religion of escape rather than engagement. The image of a compelling rather than a commanding God implies rather than excludes a sense that we stand under God's judgment; indeed more deeply and intimately so, because the refusal of a compelling God becomes a judgment we bring on ourselves. Within the present context of the Church-as-cookie-jar, the real problem of its ambiguity is that there is no effective way of celebrating God's grace in the world, nor of naming sin. Hence the current disarray of our whole penitential apparatus.

### Adaptation of the Liturgy to Mission

There are, I believe, ways out of that impasse, though it would take more courage than the American Church as a body ecclesiastical has hitherto been able to muster. We have yet to engage the issue of the implications of the adaptation of the liturgy to culture. The liturgical movement, as I have suggested, knew the problem: the privatization of religion. Its solution was in some ways useful—some significant adaptations of liturgical form, significantly paring down the medieval panoply of hieratic cult and effectively creating ritual patterns that abolished the distinction between official cult and private devotion. For reasons I have suggested here, that does not go far enough, and indeed scarcely begins to engage the issue. Aidan Kavanagh has asserted flatly that the issue of the

**Ralph A. Keifer**

78

adaptation of the liturgy to culture is a non-question: the culture adapts to liturgy, not the other way round.[5] It may be more to the point to suggest that liturgy adapts to *mission,* and that this proceeds not from any sort of predetermined principles but from where the Church finds itself in a given cultural epoch and milieu. Liturgical studies have developed in more-or-less splendid isolation from contemporary biblical studies and have been markedly inattentive to the discontinuities in liturgical development, particularly the discontinuity between the liturgical ethos of the Church before the crises of the late second and early third century and the development that emerges fully into the light of history after the fourth century. Even where there is continuity of form, for example, in the use of the Eucharistic Prayer, there are marked discontinuities of content, context, and interpretation.

Liturgy not only adapts to mission; it also adapts to eschatology and ecclesiology since, undoubtedly, both rise out of the experience of mission. Thus, for example, the prevailing line of interpretation of what the Eucharistic act is about in the second century is that it is a sacrifice because it is the action of God's holy ones (so *The Didache,* Justin Martyr, St. Irenaeus). After the third century, the Church did not enjoy such supreme confidence about the sanctity of its membership, but developed a supreme confidence in the sanctity of its institutions and embarked on its whole development of a theology of sacrament as the *opus operatum* at the hands of the priest. This is, of course, only fully developed in medieval theology, but the major lines of that perception are already well in hand among such architects of Christendom as Cyril of Jerusalem, John Chrysostom, Ambrose and Augustine, Theodore of Mopsuestia. Obviously, this had everything to do with the relationship between the Church, culture, and society and with the Church's present possibilities of carrying out its mission. In the first period, it was a persecuted sect; in the second, it was a major shaper of society and culture.

5. *Elements of Rite: A Handbook of Liturgical Style* (New York: Pueblo, 1982) 103–104. How Kavanagh explains the evolution of the essentially synagogal liturgical pattern of the early Church into the hieratic cult of the Middle Ages on those grounds is something of a mystery to me.

**Liturgy and Ethics**

## Collaboration Outside the Household of Faith

The critical question, then, is What are the present opportunities for mission? What is the cutting edge? It should go without saying that in a culturally diverse world, the opportunities will be different in different cultural contexts. I will therefore struggle with some suggestions only in the U.S. context. What, then, can Church-as-cookie-jar do? In a pluralistic and democratic society where the official Church lacks coercive and legislative power, it seems to me to be fairly obvious that the primary agents of the Christian mission are the convinced and convincing laity. Much if not most of the doing of that mission will be carried out in collaboration with others, not necessarily, certainly not exclusively, of the same household of faith and sometimes of none. Mission will be within the context of collaboration outside the household of faith. The implication of this is that the cutting edge of all mission in our culture is the conscientious individual decisions beyond the control of the Church, either as institution or as community. The disjuncture between liturgy and ethics-social justice is created precisely because we have not found a way to prize and celebrate this conscientious and highly individual sort of decision making. In a word, what our liturgy lacks is the significant marking of adult conversion, an ecclesial inaccessibility of testimony as to where this occurs. Not all of this need, ought, or can be liturgical in the strict sense, but if the Church as institution could bring itself to prize such events, it would be experienced as "standing for them." In a local context, for instance, if the Archdiocese of Chicago were to embrace—not co-opt—the Call to Action as an event of its own life, the liturgical enactments of this local Church would become perceptible as "standing for something" which they presently do not. There is a fundamental, official mistrust of the work of the Spirit among the laity, which is manifest in the assumption that an effort at consensus would lead to "wrong" conclusions. If our liturgy remains so unfortunately cultic and distant from the lives of ordinary believers, it has everything to do with its being perceptible only as an enactment of the Church-as-institution, because the Church-as-institution makes the testimony of the ordinary struggling conscientious believer inaccessible as witness to the life of the gospel.

The kind of process now being developed under the rubric of RCIA needs to be broadened and adapted so that there is a real

**Ralph A. Keifer**

celebration of turning points in the lives of the already baptized, and it needs to be worked out so that there is an audible and accessible testimony of those whose adult conversion has not represented simply a conforming to a commanding Church but a responding to a compelling gospel. John Pawlikowski underscores the need for the development of a liturgy that is more life affirming, and I agree. The major problem is that the official Church, in whose hands the liturgy is, tends to be less than affirming about where its membership lives and affirms life. It is usually only through special groups that many people can find a zone of affirmation for their own moral struggles as these actually shape the world in which they live. It seems to me, for instance, that it is wildly paradoxical that a Church whose major constituency is married should not have special moments to affirm the value of married life.

Moreover, I think serious consideration needs to be given to festival and commemoration, with due regard for our present cultural context, which is ecumenical. The commemoration of the Holocaust and Martin Luther King Day spring to mind; but if we are to take them seriously in this culture, we need to ask how we can enter into them as both fully ecumenical and fully liturgical events. In the present cultural context, and under the presupposition that the Church is not the exclusive mediator of God's grace in the world, some serious questions need to be raised about the imperatives for common sacramental participation, especially when it is a question of uniting with others in common human concerns.

### Liturgy and Eschatology

Finally, though not necessarily last, it strikes me that sacramental theology's critique of the medieval tradition has been excessively timid, not least of all because it has worked in some (not total) isolation from the revision of ecclesiology and eschatology that has been going on apace since World War II. A post-Holocaust sacramental theology needs to come to terms with a theology of "real absence." Liturgical action is a kind of conflation of time: past, present, and future. With its strong institutional bias, interpretation of sacramental action has long concentrated on time past and a historicized eschatology that radically oversacralizes liturgical action. We need to look much more seriously and more deeply at the possibility of interpreting the liturgical act less as a statement of "what is" than as of what is hoped for, as promise rather than fulfillment, as value rather than precept. The archaic forms of the liturgy such as the remaining trappings of imperial cult bespeak the link with a past tradition, for continuity. What is needed is the sense of the present, the prizing of adult conversion rather than ruling it out of ecclesiastical court, and a sense that we are not saying exactly who we are but what we see the world as called to be.

### Praying with the World

Vatican II made an epochal ecclesiological transition, not so much in what it had to say about Church structures, which is problematically inconsistent where it is not rigidly traditional, but in its affirmation of human history itself as the scenario of God's grace—especially manifest in the Pastoral Constitution on the Church in the Modern World's conception of the "signs of the times." The whole tendency of the Catholic tradition has been in the direction of understanding the Church as the exclusive mediator of that grace. The whole apparatus of theological distinctions between nature and supernature, Church and world, spiritual and temporal—which have everything to do with the disjuncture between liturgy and life—rests upon that understanding of the Church as mediator of grace. I think it can be safely said that what our liturgical tradition has hitherto considered us as praying about is, in the first place, what it means to be members of the Church, and if it was a question of relating to the world, simply of praying *for* the world. There is a liturgical task here of rediscovering our liturgical symbols as saying, in the first and last place, what it means to be a *human being,* and not of praying simply *for* the world but also *with* it.

## For Further Reflection

1. In your experience, do our liturgical symbols (water, oil, bread, wine, bodies, caresses) communicate an experience of a God who is compelling rather than commanding? Why or why not?

2. How has the Church's changed role in society promoted a privatized perception of the place of religion in human life? Should the Church seek to influence public policy in a pluralistic society such as our own?

**Ralph A. Keifer**

82

3. What would our liturgy look like if it were adapted to mission, understood as the work of the whole Church, including the laity? What would be the ecumenical implications of such adaptation?

Mark R. Francis, C.S.V.

# Liturgical Inculturation in the United States and the Call to Justice

*Introduction*

The relationship between liturgy and social justice was a hallmark of the modern liturgical movement, especially in the United States. Prominent figures in this movement such as Virgil Michel were convinced of the liturgy's power to convert and transform the "neopagan" culture of the United States into a society imbued with Christian values as it had done at the beginning of the Middle Ages in Europe. Writing in 1935, Michel declared his conviction that "the Liturgy itself is the highest cultural achievement of Christianity. It is also more than that. It is the one true basis of Christian culture and civilization."[1] The goal of the liturgical movement was not only to help Christians as individuals draw from this font but to renew the liturgy in such a way that it might also be "the fruitful source of a wider social growth in Christ, of the penetration of all human contacts and activities with the spirit of Christ."[2]

It was enthusiastic and eloquent proponents of the liturgical movement such as Michel, both in this country and in Europe, who paved the way for the reform of Roman Catholic worship, which found its expression in the first document promulgated by Vatican II, The Constitution on the Sacred Liturgy *(Sacrosanctum concilium)*. Although it has been more than twenty-five years since this document set in motion the liturgical reform, no one would seriously contend that Michel's ambitious goals for the liturgical movement have been fully realized. This is especially true of his contention that the liturgy should become the basis for the transformation of what he regarded as the "neopagan" civilization of the United States.

Various reasons have been advanced explaining why the liturgy has failed to be a source for the Christian renewal of U.S. society. This essay will focus on one particular reason for the often

1. Virgil Michel, "Nine Years After," *Orate Fratres* 10 (1935–1936) 5.
2. Ibid., 6.

problematic relationship between liturgy and justice. I would suggest that despite the breadth of vision of the liturgical pioneers at the beginning of the century, the seeds of the present disparity between liturgy and the call to justice were inadvertently sown by the liturgical movement itself, due to its understanding of the relationship between culture and the worship of the Church. This understanding in turn influenced the liturgical reform, as outlined in The Constitution on the Sacred Liturgy, and manifests itself in attitudes toward liturgical inculturation expressed in rectories, liturgy planning groups, and episcopal residences throughout the country.

In order to appreciate the relationship of culture to the liturgy, we must begin with a discussion of the terms "culture" and "inculturation."

### What Is Culture?

The meaning attached to the term "culture" in European languages has radically changed over the course of this century. Formerly, the word exclusively conveyed the idea of an elite "high culture," which found expression in the great works of art, literature, and music, especially those produced by Western civilization. Familiarity with Shakespeare's plays, Beethoven's symphonies, or the paintings of Leonardo da Vinci was the mark of a "cultured" person. Those who lacked this familiarity, either because they had not had the educational opportunities or because they belonged to a non-Western society, were considered "uncultured" or "barbarians." This use of the term was decidedly ethnocentric, consciously and unconsciously equating "culture" with European civilization and "barbarism" with all that was not European.

This equation of "culture" with Western European cultural forms also extended to religion as well. Hilaire Belloc's famous phrase, "The Faith is Europe and Europe is the Faith,"[3] aptly describes a prevailing Western attitude that long identified European culture, especially that of the Middle Ages, with the essence of Christianity. While Michel's conception of culture was more inclusive than that of Belloc, he was still influenced by a romantic ethnocentricism of another variety. Although he maintained that culture "embraces all the activities and abilities of [humanity], all the aspirations and in-

3. Hilaire Belloc, *Europe and the Faith* (New York: Paulist, 1920) 261.

spirations of [human] nature, the entire field of human existence,"[4] Michel regarded one particular cultural period as *the* point of reference for the efforts of the liturgical movement. That era was the late patristic period (the fourth to sixth centuries), which served as a model for Michel and others in the movement of how the liturgy could thoroughly permeate society with the spirit of Christ. It was this period that produced the Roman liturgy, "the highest cultural achievement of Christianity."[5]

With the rise of the social sciences such as anthropology and sociology at the end of the last century, the classicist conception of European civilization as being somehow universally superior and normative has given way to a very different understanding of culture. In the perspective of the human sciences, culture is envisioned as the way a particular group of people in a particular place and time orders its life and gives meaning to existence. Moreover, these cultural attitudes and presuppositions about life are inherited. They are handed down from one generation to the next in the traditions of society and communicated, perpetuated, and developed in symbolic forms such as language, music, and ritual.[6] Thus, speaking from the perspective of the human sciences, there is no "superior" or "normative" culture by which other societies are to be judged "civilized" or "barbarian."

The implications of this new understanding of culture for the Church and its worship profoundly influenced the Second Vatican Council. The documents of this council reflect the awareness that the Church is truly a global, multicultural reality that can no longer be considered simply a European institution. The last document of the council, the Pastoral Constitution on the Church in the Modern World *(Gaudium et spes)*, devoted an entire chapter to the rela-

4. "Liturgy and Catholic Life," 193 (unpublished manuscript), quoted in Paul B. Marx, *Virgil Michel and the Liturgical Movement* (Collegeville: The Liturgical Press, 1957) 257.

5. Ibid.

6. *See* the various definitions of culture presented by anthropologists such as Alfred L. Kroeber and Clyde Kluckhohn, "Culture: A Critical Review of Concepts and Definitions," in *Papers of the Peabody Museum of American Archaeology and Ethnology* 47, no. 1 (Cambridge, Mass.: Harvard University Press, 1952); and Clifford Geertz, *The Interpretation of Cultures* (New York: Basic Books, 1975) 3–30, 89.

**Mark R. Francis, C.S.V.**

tionship of faith to human culture and solemnly declared that "the Church, sent to all peoples of every time and place, is not bound exclusively and indissolubly to any race or nation, nor to any particular way of life or any customary pattern of living, ancient or recent."[7]

The council's gradual appropriation of this new understanding of human culture is also reflected by episcopal, curial, and papal teachings issued after Vatican II that speak of the Church's dynamic relationship to human cultures. Paul VI's acknowledgment that there has often existed a division between the gospel and culture highlighted both the new conception of culture and the need somehow to heal that division. In the apostolic exhortation Evangelization in the Modern World *(Evangelii nuntiandi),* he states that "the separation between the gospel and culture is undoubtedly a sad fact of our age as it has been of others."[8] In reference to the need to overcome that separation, he states that "evangelization loses much of its effectiveness if it does not take into consideration the actual people to whom it is addressed, if it does not use their language, their signs and symbols, if it does not answer the questions they ask, and if it does not have an impact on their concrete life."[9]

### Inculturation and Liturgy

"Inculturation" is one of the neologisms now current in a variety of theological disciplines. Along with such terms as "adaptation," "incarnation," "contextualization," and "indigenization," the way it is used largely depends on the author and the subject being treated. In a general way, however, inculturation can be described as the process by which Christianity is made "at home" in a particular culture. This process entails a respectful dialogue between those who proclaim the faith and the culture where it is proclaimed, transforming the way in which the Christian faith is presented through the use of the signs, symbols, and thought patterns of the host culture and in turn transforming the host culture through the good news of Christ.

7. *Gaudium et spes,* 58.
8. *Evangelii nuntiandi,* 20.
9. Ibid., 63.

**Liturgical Inculturation**

The need for an inculturated Christianity has been most keenly felt by those Christians who live in the so-called young Churches of Africa and Asia. In the past, to become a Christian in these cultures often meant abandoning one's identity as an African or Chinese. Indeed, in many of these countries, to call someone a "Christian" was equivalent to calling them a "European."

However, it would be a mistake to limit the concern for inculturation of Christianity to "mission lands." The civilization of Europe and the United States, long identified with the Christian religion, is increasingly becoming a "mission" territory itself. One only need look at recent statistics describing church attendance in Western Europe to appreciate the decline of Christianity's influence. The reasons for this decline are complex. The Enlightenment of the eighteenth century as well as the social, political, and economic transformations of the last hundred fifty years have radically changed the culture of the West. Because of a reluctance to cope with these changes, the Church's ability to speak the message of Christ in a meaningful way has been seriously compromised. Thus, inculturation of the Christian message, even in that part of the world regarded as most "Christian," is also becoming a pressing concern.

The need for inculturation of the faith, whether in "mission lands" or in cultures that are nominally Christian, is most graphically illustrated in the liturgy. The way in which the local Church worships speaks eloquently of its image of God, self, and world and of the interrelation between its members. The language of prayer, movement, gesture, song, and the organization of worship space all express a way of being Church and represent what the assembly holds important in its life of faith. Not surprisingly, many of the examples of inculturation given in missiological studies use the liturgy as a focus for the changes that need to take place in the local Church in order for Christianity to be truly "at home" in its cultural setting. In The Constitution on the Sacred Liturgy, Vatican II opened the door to such changes. But it is in this, the first document of the council, that we see a certain ambivalence toward culture, an ambivalence occasioned by the conscious and unconscious presupposition of the cultural superiority or normativity of the Roman Rite.

**Mark R. Francis, C.S.V.**

Behind the ceremonial modifications and rubrical simplifications mandated by the council, one can discern a renewed understanding of what the Church believes it does when it gathers for worship. This is especially obvious in the new introductions to these rites; the Eucharist as well as the other sacramental celebrations are now seen as the action of the entire assembly of Christians rather than solely the work of clerical specialists. To a large extent, this renewed emphasis on the assembly as the primary liturgical agent was made possible by the historical and theological groundwork done by scholars working during the first half of the twentieth century. Liturgists working in concert with other scholars in such disciplines as history, philology, and the textual criticism of liturgical documents were able to point to a time in the Church's life when its worship was understood as a truly communal enterprise. The worship of the late patristic period, which was characterized by communal participation, provided them with both a model and a traditional theological warrant for restructuring the rites of the Church along more participatory lines.

The liturgical scholars' focus on this period was both strategic and theological. Because of the Modernist crisis at the turn of the century, scholars were discouraged from theologizing outside of the official Scholasticism of the day, which tended to regard the Middle Ages, the "age of faith," as *the* golden age of Christianity.[10] Liturgists, afraid of being branded as Modernists, could identify the late patristic period as Christianity's "good old days" without fear of censure, since this period of the Church's life was just as orthodox and just as traditional as the Middle Ages. The worship of this era had the further advantage of substantiating their claims and hopes for the liturgy: that liturgy should be a corporate act of worship by all the faithful, not just a clerical elite.

Rather than writing speculative liturgical theology—an activity that would have been discouraged and even censored given the tenor of the times—many liturgists embarked upon a thorough

---

10. This tendency of Catholics at the beginning of the century to idealize the Scholastic period is illustrated by the title of a history of the Middle Ages written by James Walsh, *The Thirteenth, Greatest of Centuries* (New York: Catholic Summer School Press, 1913).

**Liturgical Inculturation**

historical investigation of the Roman Rite before it became encumbered by medieval accretions. The liturgical movement of the first part of the twentieth century was profoundly influenced by these studies. The reform program the movement proposed for Roman Catholic worship was based on the liturgy as celebrated in the basilicas of Rome during the late patristic period and is strongly reflected in Vatican II's document on the liturgy.

Before demonstrating the normative status ascribed to the classic Roman Rite in The Constitution on the Sacred Liturgy, it is helpful to focus on the cultural values embodied in this liturgical model. The best description of these cultural values was offered by the Anglican liturgical scholar Edmund Bishop at the beginning of this century. In comparing the Roman Rite with other Western rites in vigor during the early Middle Ages, Bishop describes "the genius of the Roman Rite," as being "marked by simplicity, practicality, a great sobriety and self-control, gravity and dignity."[11]

In fairness to the liturgical scholars who championed the reform, it is important to note that while they advocated a return to this simple, sober, and dignified Roman style of worship, they were motivated not so much by archaeologism as by a profoundly pastoral concern to promote "full, active, and conscious participation" of the assembly in the liturgical event. The medieval order of Mass was simply too complex and clericalized to serve as a helpful starting point for this enterprise.

### The Constitution on the Sacred Liturgy and Culture

Even a cursory review of The Constitution on the Sacred Liturgy reveals the concern of its framers to return to a simplified, communal, and intelligible order of worship along the lines of the classic Roman Rite. Article 34 of the constitution almost echoes the very adjectives used by Bishop to describe the Roman Rite: "The rites should be marked by a noble simplicity; they should be short, clear, and unencumbered by useless repetitions; they should be within the people's powers of comprehension and as a rule not require much explanation" (DOL 34).

11. Edmund Bishop, "The Genius of the Roman Rite," *Liturgica Historica: Papers on the Liturgy and Religious Life of the Western Church* (Oxford, England: Clarendon, 1918) 12.

**Mark R. Francis, C.S.V.**

"Noble simplicity," "brevity," and "clarity," however, are cultural values that very few people would claim to be normative for all cultures and at all times, especially in regard to ritual. However, this article must be interpreted in the context of the whole document. Clearly, what the council is proposing is a starting point *(terminus a quo)* for liturgical pluralism, which is to be allowed under the umbrella of the Roman Rite. It is conscious that cultural diversity in liturgical expression is not only a possibility but a pastoral necessity. Article 37 states quite plainly that "even in the liturgy, the Church has no wish to impose a rigid uniformity in matters which do not involve the faith or good of the community; rather, the Church respects and fosters the genius and talents of the various races and peoples" (DOL 37).

Nevertheless, a stress on continuity and tradition is also obvious in the liturgy constitution. Although the council noted in article 40 that more radical adaptation in worship could be legitimately called for especially in "mission lands," liturgical change for the sake of change is not a value in itself but must be implemented for a pastoral purpose. For example, article 23 states that "there must be no innovations unless the good of the Church genuinely and certainly requires them; care should be taken that any new forms adopted should grow organically from forms already existing" (DOL 23).

While it is obvious that Vatican II's document on the liturgy opened the door for liturgical change, especially in those areas termed "mission lands," the door was left open in a house that was to remain somehow Roman. Article 38, in speaking of the revision of the liturgical books, calls for "legitimate variations and adaptations to different groups, regions, and peoples, especially in mission lands, *provided that the substantial unity of the Roman Rite is preserved*" (DOL 38, emphasis added).

However, nowhere in the document is this "substantial unity of the Roman Rite" defined. Anscar Chupungco maintains that this phrase should be interpreted in light of article 39, "within the limits set by the typical editions of the liturgical books."[12] While one of the principles of the liturgical reform was a certain elasticity designed to make the renewed liturgy adaptable to local Churches,

12. Anscar Chupungco, *Cultural Adaptation of the Liturgy* (New York: Paulist, 1982) 48.

**Liturgical Inculturation**

the "Roman genius" was still to be recognizable even with these adaptations. Moreover, the more radical adaptation of which article 40 speaks is seen clearly as a concession, almost a necessary evil, since it threatens this "substantial unity of the Roman Rite."

While the council seemed cautious in allowing major changes in the order of Mass, it showed much more openness regarding the possibility of substantial adaptation in the celebration of the other sacraments. Since the Roman ritual itself was never made mandatory throughout the Roman Rite even during the post-Tridentine period, it was much easier for the liturgy constitution to encourage more wholeheartedly the use of the vernacular and the cultural adaptation of the rites of initiation (article 65), the funerals rite (article 81), and even the creation of an entirely new rite of marriage (article 77).

Thus, a quick review of the foundational document of the liturgical reform reveals that there was a concern with culture but that the concept of culture was not defined. This is one of the great weaknesses of the document. While permitting adaptation of the liturgy in view of the cultural context of the assembly, the liturgy constitution also maintained a decided reluctance to pursue an agenda of that which would later be known as "inculturation" lest the "substantial unity of the Roman Rite" be jeopardized.[13] This reluctance is especially obvious in the new order of Mass. I would suggest that the normativity of the Roman Rite as proposed by the council and reflected in the liturgical reform contributes to the separation between liturgy and life and hence liturgy and justice in U.S. culture.

### U.S. Culture and Liturgy

The first step in the liturgical reforms mandated by Vatican II has already taken place. The translation and publication of the various liturgical books has profoundly altered U.S. Catholic worship patterns. The new ritual books are largely faithful to the "noble simplicity," "sobriety," and "dignity" prescribed by the liturgy constitution. The reformed rites are designed to promote the full, conscious, and active participation of the faithful in worship. Why

13. Cf. Aylward Shorter, *Toward a Theology of Inculturation* (Maryknoll, N.Y.: Orbis Books, 1988) 194.

**Mark R. Francis, C.S.V.**

has the liturgy failed to be that source of social transformation for which the pioneers of the liturgical movement so ardently hoped?

There are many possible answers to this question. Mark Searle would contend that the principal cause is a lack of real theological understanding of the liturgical act on the part of both the assembly and the presiders. Despite the efforts of the liturgical movement in English-speaking countries, most Catholics in North America were "ill prepared for the reforms when they came."[14] For this reason, the liturgy was never integrated into other renewal movements within parish life that promoted the *aggiornamento* mandated by the council. Moreover, the clericalism that so distinguished the old order of Mass has now taken another form, one that is just as alienating as its Tridentine counterpart. Because of the very flexibility built into the new rite of Mass, there is a tendency for presiders and others responsible for the liturgy to subject congregations to their "idiosyncrasies" and the "imposition of their personal tastes," thus seriously compromising the objective nature of the liturgical event. Searle sees this as evidence of the susceptibility of the revised liturgy "to the individualism of our culture, rather than becoming, as the promoters of the liturgical movement had hoped, a bulwark against it."[15]

M. Francis Mannion would heartily concur with Searle's assessment of the individualism that now seems to be afflicting the liturgy. In a provocative essay entitled "Liturgy and the Present Crisis of Culture," he states the thesis that "the fundamental reason why liturgy has lost much of its cultural and social power is related to the absorption into post-conciliar American Catholicism of profoundly negative dynamics operative in modern secular culture."[16]

Drawing on recent works in American sociology of religion such as *Habits of the Heart*,[17] Mannion identifies these negative cultural dynamics as "the subjectification of reality," "the intimization of

14. Mark Searle, "Renewing the Liturgy Again," *Commonweal* 115:20 (November 18, 1988) 620.

15. Ibid., 620–621.

16. M. Francis Mannion, "Liturgy and the Present Crisis of Culture," *Worship* 62 (1988) 102.

17. Robert N. Bellah and others, *Habits of the Heart: Individualism and Commitment in American Life* (New York: Harper & Row, 1985).

society," and the "politicization of culture." At the risk of oversimplifying his arguments, I will now summarize these three dynamics.

### The Subjectification of Reality

According to Mannion's reading of sociological studies, modern U.S. culture tends to affirm that life's meaning and values derive from individual experience and do not primarily originate in the shared traditions of society. This "subjectification of reality" opens the public forum to the full reign of consumerism and a "what-is-in-it-for-me?" mentality that judges the worth of any activity, including the practice of religion, on the basis of personal enhancement, psychological or economic. Thus, as Keifer already noted in the previous essay, the experience of religion is privatized to such a degree that common symbols used in the objective liturgical tradition of the Church are no longer able to mediate the religious conceptions and motivations of the gospel, which should serve as an impetus to social transformation.

### The Intimization of Reality

Mannion also describes the U.S. penchant for easy intimacy, which tends to trivialize relationships. The gradual demise of the use of titles like Mr., Mrs., Sir, and Ma'am with strangers and their replacement by first names reflects a culture that prizes intimacy as an absolute value. Unless one is on a first-name basis with another person, the relationship is somehow considered stilted or less than authentic, even if the relationship happens to be with an automatic teller machine. This tendency has an obvious effect on liturgical celebrations, which are by their nature formal, stylized ritual events. Many North Americans expect to experience closeness and warmth in liturgy, much like that of an idealized family. This is impossible, of course, in a large liturgical assembly. Many of the idiosyncrasies in presidential style to which Mark Searle alluded earlier are an attempt to convey this kind of intimacy. Attention to the transcendent dimension of worship becomes almost impossible. In a setting that so prizes human intimacy at the expense of a truly public forum of worship in which it is acknowledged that all who are present are not necessarily personal friends, public and social symbolism loses its power. "Consequently, [liturgy] no longer stands as a model of redeemed society, and for that reason retains

**Mark R. Francis, C.S.V.**

94

little ability to generate enthusiasm for social and cultural transformation."[18]

*Politicization of Culture*

Finally, Mannion sketches the growing politicization of U.S. culture. This process reduces the involvement of individuals within society to "the working out of legal and political conventions by which mutual respect for individual freedom, self-determination, and personal autonomy can be created and maintained."[19] This renders the ability of the faithful to promote the Christian transformation of society singularly problematic, because it "impoverishes the vast complex of human culture, distorts the Christian message, and severely restricts the ability of the liturgy to be an effective agent of social and cultural transformation."[20] When reflected in the liturgy, this politicization often takes the form of promoting a focused ideological agenda at the expense of the only liturgical agenda: the assembly's participation in the paschal mystery of Jesus Christ. Hence the phenomenon of theme Masses for a particular social or political concern, which was well described by Kathleen Hughes in an earlier essay in this book. I would also add that this tendency is one that is present not only on the "loony left," as they say in Great Britain, but is present on both ends of the liberal-conservative spectrum within the Church in the United States. A recent Respect Life campaign in New Jersey, for example, urged preachers, in place of a homily, to read a letter by the bishop that called upon parishioners at Sunday Mass to sign a "Life Roll" stating their opposition to politicians who fail to speak out against abortion.[21] Whether it is a theme Mass to save the whales or an overt call for a particular lobbying effort, this politicization of worship clearly impoverishes the liturgical event. The basis for the Christian social transformation of society must be more than simply a focused political agenda, but the promotion of the common good through personal virtue rooted in our relationship to

18. Mannion, 113.
19. Ibid., 114.
20. Ibid., 119.
21. Mary C. Segers, "Lining up the People in the Pews," *Commonweal* 117:1 (January 12, 1990) 12.

**Liturgical Inculturation**

God through Christ and in the Spirit; a relationship nurtured and celebrated in the liturgy; a relationship that should find expression in all the dimensions of human culture, not just the political.

Toward the end of the article Mannion seems to attenuate somewhat his rather bleak description of the "deleterious dynamics presently operative in liturgical theology and practice."[22] He acknowledges that there is something redeemable in the U.S. cultural tendencies toward subjectivism and intimacy, which, if not raised to a "first principle of theological systems," can promote the very values of liturgical participation and hospitality valued by the liturgical reform. He is less able to see any redeemable aspect to politicization.

### The Dilemma of Inculturation

Mannion's argument is persuasive, and much of what he says rings true. The U.S. culture's exaggerated subjectivism, its overriding concern for intimacy, and the politicization of U.S. society all play a role in sapping the power of the liturgy to promote a truly Christian transformation of society. However, I would take issue with one of his presuppositions—a presupposition about the relationship between liturgy and culture that he holds along with Virgil Michel—a presupposition that is also partially found in The Constitution on the Sacred Liturgy.

Much like Michel, who describes modern society as having lost its moorings and sense of direction, of being neopagan, Mannion has a decidedly negative opinion of U.S. culture. He seems to underemphasize the crucial need for a real dialogue to take place between the faith that we hold in Christ, as expressed in the liturgy, and culture. Basic to his argument is an estimation of the ability of the reformed liturgy to convey the truth about our relationship to God, each other, and the world. Therefore, he seems to contend that U.S. Catholics are at fault if they fail to enter fully into an order of worship that faithfully reflects the values of the liturgical reform, since it is intrinsically capable of promoting both individual holiness and a transformation of society in the United States.

While U.S. culture needs to be critiqued in the light of the gospel, it is imperative that our inherited liturgical forms also un-

---

22. Mannion, 120.

**Mark R. Francis, C.S.V.**

dergo the same scrutiny. We spoke of inculturation earlier as a respectful dialogue between the faith of the Church and the host culture, so guided by the gospel that the essentials of the faith are not compromised but celebrated in the liturgy in such a way that they can truly be claimed by the members of the host culture as their own. A dialogue of this nature still needs to continue between our U.S. cultural reality and the "genius of the Roman rite" which, however hallowed by tradition, still bears the marks of its origin in a time and place that held very different cultural values.

At stake is the ability of the Christian community, assembled in Jesus' name, to see in his story its own story. For the liturgy to be capable of attaining the crucial role ascribed to it in the conciliar documents as the "summit and font of the Church's life," it needs to be expressive of the very people we are, formed by our ecclesial traditions, our national experience, and the way in which we experience God's presence in lives that are lived in fidelity to the gospel. As the African-American bishops so eloquently stated in regard to the liturgy, "All people should be able to recognize themselves when Christ is presented, and should be able to experience their own fulfillment when these mysteries are celebrated."[23] This recognition will be impossible if sufficient attention is not paid to the ways in which North American Christians in the late twentieth century experience and communicate the presence of God. With John Pawlikowski, I agree that "we cannot rebuild the moral ethos of humankind unless we can once again come to experience a living and challenging God through liturgical expression truly reflective of our era."[24] Thus, the demands of inculturation and those of justice follow a parallel course.

## U.S. Culture and the Experience of God

Where and how do people in the United States experience the presence of God? This seems to me to be a basic question in the respectful dialogue between culture and liturgical tradition. The in-

---

23. " 'What We Have Seen and Heard'—A Pastoral Letter on Evangelization from the Black Bishops of the United States," *Origins* 14, no. 18 (October 18, 1984) 285.

24. John Pawlikowski, "Worship After the Holocaust: An Ethician's Reflections," in this volume.

sights of Rabbi Lawrence Hoffman are especially helpful in answering this question. He describes the various ways in which the culture of a given epoch and people profoundly influence the way in which they speak about their experience of God and the ways in which this experience is mediated by the liturgy. Hoffman identifies the underlying cultural values of any given human society with the term "cultural backdrop." He then explains how this cultural backdrop decisively influences the culture's predominant way of conceptualizing God: its "master image."[25]

The cultural backdrop of both the Judaism and Christianity of nineteenth-century Germany, for example, emphasized cultural values such as order, decorum, respect for authority, and social distance of superiors from inferiors. These values are expressed in the liturgy of both the churches and synagogues of the era by an emphasis on the transcendence of God and the distance of the worshiper from the Deity. Nineteenth-century Europe's master image of God, then, was one of a transcendent Deity, majestically enthroned beyond the human world, whose presence was mediated by clergy, the "religious professionals." The United States of the twentieth century holds very different cultural values. Hoffman points out that the U.S. cultural backdrop "was founded on the notion of eradicating the very class distinctiveness on which Europe was based. Here we work to obliterate social distance, using first names, addressing envelopes without particular care for titles, building universally accessible public schools, and jettisoning dress codes that mark off one person from another."[26]

This cultural backdrop makes it very difficult for U.S. Catholics to identify with a master image of God who is viewed *primarily* as transcendent and otherworldly. For the same reasons, it is also difficult for many of us to see our experience of God reflected in the "dignity," "sobriety," and "gravity" of the Roman genius, based as it is on the cultural values of fifth- and sixth-century Rome.

A good example of this "dis-ease" can be found in the way North Americans usually relate to the Roman genius as it is reflected in opening prayers contained in the present Sacramentary.

25. *The Art of Public Prayer: Not for Clergy Only* (Washington: The Pastoral Press, 1988) 153–178.
26. Ibid., 173.

**Mark R. Francis, C.S.V.**

98

Roman presidential prayers are characterized by a rhetorical style influenced by the aesthetic dictates of late classicism, which placed great store on concision and clarity. They manifest an overriding concern to express dogmatic truth with juridical precision and eschew emotion and sentimentality.[27] For this reason they lack poetic imagery and are often experienced as being too short and abstract to involve the assembly in the liturgy. Because of this deficiency, many presiders choose the longer paraphrase of these prayers provided in The Sacramentary simply because they say something the Roman prayers do not. The same problem could also be raised with the Roman canon. Much of its hieratic and stylized language was borrowed from the etiquette of the imperial Roman court, especially the way in which it addresses God. If Catholics in the United States perceive that this is the *only way* we relate as a community to God in the liturgy, we run the risk of turning our worship into a quaint exercise in archaeology and, in the process, drive God from our midst.

However, it would also be naive to assume that liturgical inculturation is simply a matter of dressing the worship of the local community in more familiar garb, in uncritically replacing the Roman genius with the U.S. genius—whatever that genius might prove to be. The American master image of God must also be challenged by the gospel and the experience of the Church's incorporation of the gospel into its liturgical tradition. As Hoffman remarks: "Probably the most satisfying master image is somewhere between absolute transcendence and complete immanence in the philosophical sense of the word: not God as an impersonal force far beyond us, nor God as the inner voice of conscience, but God as friend and comforter, who meets us in the human encounters that matter. When our worship develops ritualized display of those human moments on which we base all hope of meaning, we will have discovered worship that works."[28]

27. *See* Theodor Klauser's discussion of the Roman euchology in his *Short History of the Roman Liturgy,* 2nd ed., trans. John Halliburton (Oxford, England: Oxford University Press, 1979) 37–44.
28. Hoffman, *The Art of Public Prayer,* 177.

**Liturgical Inculturation**

### Dialogue with the Cultures of the United States: A Requirement of Justice

Finally, it is misleading to speak simplistically of the dialogue of inculturation between our liturgical tradition and U.S. culture. It would be more accurate to speak of this dialogue as taking place with the numerous cultures that make up the United States.

A recent article on cultural pluralism in the Archdiocese of Chicago noted that one particular parish on the North Side serves over forty different ethnic groups. From all accounts, this phenomenon is also quite common in many local churches throughout the United States. The ever-growing Hispanic population of this country (itself made up of very diverse cultural groups) and African-American Catholics also need to be brought into this dialogue, for their cultural backdrops and master images of God are quite different from that of the dominant U.S. culture. In fact, the very process of inculturating the liturgy in the United States, taking into account the pluralism and multicultural reality of the people of God, is itself a call to justice. As Thea Bowman points out: "the quest for justice demands that I walk in ways that I never walked before, that I talk and think and pray and learn and grow in ways that are new to me. If I'm going to share faith with my brothers and sisters who are Chinese or Jamaican or South African or Winnebago Indian, I've got to learn new ways, new means, new languages, new rituals, new procedures, new understandings, so I can read my brother's heart, so I can hear my sister's call, and I can live justly."[29]

The inculturation of the liturgy in the United States, though fraught with complexity, could do much to heal the racial and ethnic divisions of this nation and at the same time help those of the dominant culture confront the negative cultural dynamics identified in this essay. This can be accomplished in light of the Christian belief in a God who knows no partiality among the human family, a God who, as Peter reminded the Jewish Christians of Jerusalem, makes no distinction between Gentile and Jew since God purified all hearts by faith (see Acts 15:9). The respectful dialogue of inculturation could also be the single most effective way to realize that

29. Thea Bowman, F.S.P.A., "Justice, Power, and Praise," *Liturgy and Social Justice,* ed. Edward M. Grosz (Collegeville: The Liturgical Press, 1989) 37.

**Mark R. Francis, C.S.V.**

cherished dream of the pioneers of the liturgical movement: making the liturgy "the fruitful source of a wider social growth in Christ, of the penetration of all human contacts and activities with the spirit of Christ."[30]

## For Further Reflection

1. What are the implications for Western Christians of a concept of culture that does not consider Western civilization the standard by which other cultures are evaluated?

2. Our present liturgy is still very much influenced by the "genius of the Roman Rite." What similiarities and differences exist between the cultural values expressed by the Roman liturgy and the cultural values that could be considered typically those of the United States?

3. How do people in the United States experience the presence of God? How might this experience affect the way in which we worship?

4. In your judgment, is inculturation of the liturgy an issue of justice?

30. Virgil Michel, "Nine Years After," *Orate Fratres* 10 (1935–1936) 5.

H. Kathleen Hughes, R.S.C.J.

# The Voice of the Church at Prayer

## Introduction

In the ancient Church, especially in the East, the liturgy was known as *theologia prima,* as distinguished from the more theoretical and speculative formulation of the community's faith, its *theologia secunda.* To distinguish "first" and "second" theology, then or now, is not to suggest an order of priority but to underscore the fundamental relationship between the Church's rich symbolic language when it gathers for worship and its theoretical enunciations when it pauses to reflect more analytically on its experience of God.[1]

In light of this distinction, to speak of liturgy as "first theology" is to speak of evocative and performative language that gives expression to the community's self-understanding: its relationship with God, the demands of that relationship, the community's desires and hopes and fears on its journey as collaborators with Christ in the establishment of the reign of God.

Yet another way to view the relationship of liturgy and more formal theological elaboration is to recall that the first meaning of "orthodoxy" is "right praise." Thus, liturgy is the doxological dimension of theology. Liturgy mediates God's claim upon the human community and invites the community to full and mature encounter with the divine, an encounter that both expresses and contines to enlarge the community's faith. Theological speculation will be enriched by constant dialogue with the community's experience and expression of its faith in the liturgy, and the liturgical experience of faith will be supported, purified, and deepened through dialogue with developed and developing theological elaboration. For fullest interpretation, the Church's *theologia prima* and *theologia secunda* need to be placed in dialogue with each other.

---

1. The authority of the liturgy is captured in the adage *lex credendi lex statuat supplicandi,* attributed originally to Prosper of Aquitaine, who himself simply summarized the thought of his predecessors Augustine, Tertullian, and Cyprian, all of whom regarded the liturgy as the privileged witness to apostolic tradition.

**H. Kathleen Hughes, R.S.C.J.**

Too often, however, the liturgical life of the Church stands in "splendid isolation." It tends to be forgotten or ignored in the process of the development and articulation of the community's beliefs. Such was the case, for example, in the elaboration of the United States bishops' pastoral letter on war and peace, *The Challenge of Peace: God's Promise and Our Response.*[2]

Using this pastoral on war and peace as a case study, the following reflections will attempt to demonstrate the potential richness of the liturgy to augment the community's theological reflection from two perspectives. In the first section the focus will be on the renewed liturgical life of the Church as a *neglected source* in the letter's elaboration of a developed theology of peace, a source that strongly confirms and supports the scriptural and theological foundations for peace advanced in the beginning of the letter. We will be examining what the pastoral letter does not cite, but could add, as the contribution of another sector of the Church's life: the voice of the Church at prayer.

In the second section the focus will shift to the conclusions of the pastoral letter, "The Pastoral Challenge and Response." In this instance it may be argued that the liturgy is an *underestimated means.* This second section will include specific suggestions for the cultivation of a gospel vision of peace as a way of life for believers and as a leaven in society through the recognition of the transformative power of the liturgical life of the Church.

*Liturgy as Neglected Source*

It is clear that there has been a dramatic shift in the voice of the praying Church following the general restoration of the liturgy in line with the mandate of the Second Vatican Council. According to Antoine Dumas, one of the many collaborators in the postconciliar liturgical reform, the criteria that governed the revision of the liturgical texts were truth, simplicity, and *sens pastoral,* a phrase difficult to translate but which might best be rendered "pastoral appropriateness."[3] These criteria dictated that the language of the

2. USCC, *The Challenge of Peace: God's Promise and Our Response* (Washington: USCC, 1983).
3. *See* Antoine Dumas, "Les oraisons du nouveau Missel romaine," *Questions Liturgiques* 4 (1971) 263–270; and "Pour mieux comprendre les textes liturgiques du Missel romain," *Notitiae* 6 (1970) 194–213.

rites reflect not only sound theology and contemporary spirituality but, in addition, the joys and hopes, the grief and anguish of our times, concerns captured by the council Fathers themselves in the Pastoral Constitution on the Church in the Modern World.

Peace, and the quest for justice that will make a stable and authentic peace possible, are surely among the most heartfelt contemporary aspirations, and both have been expressed with clarity in the renewed liturgy. Consider and compare the following prayers, noting in each instance the subtle and sometimes not so subtle shift in the way the praying community names itself, its "enemies," its understanding of God's role, and its own role in the work of building a world of peace, and so on. The prayers on the left are from the English-Latin Roman Missal, 1965 interim translation of the Missal of Pius V; those on the right are from the post-conciliar Missal of Paul VI:

*In Time of War*

O God, you destroy wars and by your power you overthrow the aggressors of those who hope in you. Help your servants who appeal to you, so that we may overcome our belligerent enemies and never cease to praise and thank you. Through Jesus Christ . . . .

*In Time of War or Civil Disturbance*

God of power and mercy, you destroy wars and put down earthly pride. Banish violence from our midst and wipe away our tears that we may all deserve to be called your sons and daughters. We ask this . . . .

*alternative*

God, our Father, maker and lover of peace, to know you is to live, and to serve you is to reign. All our faith is in your saving help; protect us from men [and women] of violence and keep us safe from weapons of hate. We ask this . . . .

*For Defense Against Enemies*

We pray you, O Lord, humble the pride of our enemies and let the might of your right hand crush their arrogance. Through Jesus Christ . . . .

*For Our Oppressors*

Father, according to your law of love we wish to love sincerely all who oppress us. Help us to follow the commandment of your new covenant, that by

**H. Kathleen Hughes, R.S.C.J.**

### For Enemies

O God, you are the lover and guardian of peace and charity. Grant true peace and love to our enemies, forgive them their sins, and let your might guard us against their deceits. Through Jesus Christ . . . .

### For the Defense of the Church

Almighty and eternal God, your hand controls the power and government of every nation. Help your Christians and by the might of your right hand destroy the non-believing peoples who rely on their own cruel strength. Through Jesus Christ . . . .

### For Peace

O God, source of all holy desires, right counsels, and just works, grant your servants that peace which the world cannot give so that we may be obedient to your commands and under your protection enjoy peace in our days and freedom from fear of our enemies. Through Jesus Christ . . . .

returning good for the evil done to us we may learn to bear the ill-will of others out of love for you. Grant this . . . .

### For Persecuted Christians

Father, in your mysterious providence, your Church must share in the sufferings of Christ your Son. Give the spirit of patience and love to those who are persecuted for their faith in you that we may always be true and faithful witnesses to your promise of eternal life. We ask this . . . .

### For Peace and Justice

God our Father, you reveal that those who work for peace will be called your sons [and daughters]. Help us to work without ceasing for that justice which brings true and lasting peace. We ask this . . . .

### alternative

God of perfect peace, violence and cruelty can have no part with you. May those who are at peace with one another hold fast to the good will that unites them; may those who are enemies forget their hatred and be healed. We ask this . . . .

The "new" voice of the Church at prayer is that of a Church desiring and working for peace, a Church no longer self-righteous and vindictive, a Church that recognizes that violence and cruelty are not of God, a Church that fears weapons of hate. The commu-

**The Voice of the Church at Prayer**

nity no longer asks God to lead it in battle and to vanquish its enemies; rather, the community desires to be healed of the violence in
its midst, to return good for evil, and to work for justice, which
alone will bring about a true and lasting peace.

The sample of prayers cited above is from The Sacramentary's
collection of texts entitled "Masses and Prayers for Various Needs
and Occasions," perhaps the most "reformed" prayers of the entire Sacramentary because most clearly expressive of the concrete
human concerns of the twentieth century: the unity of Christians;
the spread of the gospel; the progress of peoples; freedom, secur-
ity, and peace through the wisdom of civil leadership and the integrity of the citizenry. Urgency to establish a world at peace and
to bring the message of salvation to all people is evident throughout this collection of texts. The community of these prayers is not
quietist, asking or expecting God's miraculous direct intervention
in human affairs, but rather recognizing and affirming itself as
God's ambassador of reconciliation for all peoples. The community, through the performative language of its prayer, embraces its
task asking only that its heart be changed to act according to God's
will: to distribute goods more equitably, to bring an end to divisions, to work actively for justice, to be the living presence of
Christ in and for the world.

There is no longer a sense of "we" and "they," whether "they"
referred to non-Catholic or non-Christian "outsiders" or "enemies"
of the faith. Rather, as one new text underscores, the community
understands itself in solidarity with the entire human community:

> Father,
> you have given all peoples one common origin,
> and your will is to gather them as one family in yourself.
> Fill the hearts of all men [and women] with the fire of your love
> and the desire to ensure justice for all their brothers and sisters.
> By sharing the good things you give us
> may we secure justice and equality for every human being,
> an end to all division,
> and a human society built on love and peace.
> We ask this . . . .[4]

4. Mass for the Progress of Peoples, opening prayer.

**H. Kathleen Hughes, R.S.C.J.**

Indeed, the examples could be multiplied, and a fruitful comparison of the older and the contemporary corpus of prayers would yield a rich theology of peace, nonviolence, solidarity as one human community collaborating in the work of reconciliation. While striking and obvious in the texts for various needs and occasions, the same spirit pervades other areas of the Church's new voice of prayer.

An examination of the alternative opening prayers, composed to be more concrete and existential renderings of the Latin originals, shows frequent mention of the community's participation in working and praying for peace. Several prefaces, newly composed for the Missal of Paul VI, speak of peace as the task of today and the promise of tomorrow for those seeking to live in the image of Jesus, *the* witness par excellence of justice and truth. Two Eucharistic Prayers of reconciliation, whose experimental use has now been extended indefinitely because of their strong popularity, demonstrate the community's concern for conversion. The content of these prayers expresses a realism about our situation today "in the midst of conflict and division," as well as the hope that friendship, understanding, mercy, and forgiveness will put an end to estrangement, strife, hatred, and vengeance. In addition, both the *Rite of Christian Initiation of Adults* and the *Rite of Reconciliation* stress, in their introductions, a life in solidarity with others, the shaping of a new moral consciousness, and the necessity of collaboration with others in the extended Christian community in the work of peace, justice, and reconciliation. In each of these instances, the liturgy brings to expression the longings of our age.

As event, the liturgy transcends speculative theology. The symbolic language of worship gives expression to an immediate, radical, and intersubjective experience of the faith of the Church—an elemental expression that, in a sense, comes to full term in theoretical elaboration. The pastoral letter on war and peace perfectly complements this new consciousness of the Church at prayer as expressed in the language of its rites. What remains a curiosity, and a lacuna in the text, is that this pastoral letter never refers explicitly to the community's contemporary language of prayer, articulated in the Missal of Paul VI, nor seems to recognize it as a rich source for theological reflection.

**The Voice of the Church at Prayer**

## Liturgy as Underestimated Means

In the first section of this essay we examined a select number of liturgical texts and noted, in a comparison with earlier texts, that our renewed language of prayer contains a new vision of peace and justice. These prayers also challenge the worshiping community to a new way of being in the world in the face of its violence and injustice. Such an examination was based on the methodological presupposition that liturgy, *theologia prima,* functions as a locus of theology, and that theological reflection, *theologia secunda,* might well incorporate the tradition of the Church's prayer in order to produce a more adequate synthesis.

Such work, however, deals only with texts on a printed page, and one might well question what real difference the celebration of liturgy makes in the daily life of believers. Does the language of the rite actually possess any power to place a claim on participants? Is there any way that the Church's liturgy functions critically within the community? Is there any way that the language of our prayer has the power to effect what is signifies? Is it possible to claim that participation in the liturgy gradually transforms the minds and hearts of the community?

That participation in liturgy might make a difference in the lives of those who gather is a claim that appears consistent with a vision of the power of liturgy articulated by the National Conference of Catholic Bishops on the twentieth anniversary of the promulgation of The Constitution on the Sacred Liturgy: "The liturgy should be the primary school for Christian prayer and spirituality, enabling Christians to live justly, peacefully, and charitably in the world. Often we fail to understand that the celebration of liturgy is the Church's ministry of worship and prayer, calling people to conversion and contemplation, inviting them into communion with God and with each other."[5] But how does it happen?

In this second section we will first examine the way language functions in worship, including its potentially transformative power, and then we will return to the pastoral letter in order to indicate that in the letter the power of the liturgy appears to be un-

5. *The Church at Prayer: A Holy Temple of the Lord:* A Pastoral Statement Commemorating the Twentieth Anniversary of The Constitution on the Sacred Liturgy (December 4, 1983) no. 48.

**H. Kathleen Hughes, R.S.C.J.**

108

derestimated as a means of cultivating a gospel vision of peace in our time.

In speaking about liturgical language, two opposite oversimplifications must be avoided if the real power of the language of prayer to transform our minds and hearts is to be released. The first mistaken notion of the function of liturgical language is that language in liturgy takes the form of assent to doctrine that a certain fact took place in some empirically verifiable way. So, for example, on Easter Sunday, the Church speaks these words:

> God our Father,
> by raising Christ your Son
> you conquered the power of death
> and opened for us the way to eternal life.[6]

As we analyze this prayer, it becomes clear that the level of the surface grammar is misleading. On the face of it, it seems to be a simple declarative sentence. Grammatically, the sentence appears to be a straightforward description of a factual state of affairs: that in some observable way the God of our Lord Jesus Christ raised Christ, that in some verifiable way death is vanquished and eternal life is made available for the community. But such is not the way language functions to produce meaning in the liturgical assembly. When the community gathers for prayer, it is *not* engaged in flat statements of fact.

Above all, in its liturgical language, the community recites the saving acts of God in human history in order to *engage itself* in the telling of its own story and to *stir up its response* in faith. In the very moment when we profess: "God our Father, by raising Christ your Son . . . " the community is engaged in a speech-act: an expression of joy, an exclamation of God's power and sovereignty, a proclamation of divine vindication, and a pledge of loyalty to the one we dare to address so personally.[7] Each time we name God in prayer we use a metaphor that places us in a relation-

---

6. Easter Sunday, opening prayer.

7. Other essays in this collection, particularly those of Barbara Reid and John Huels, address questions of inclusive language. *See also* my essay on the evolution of consciousness regarding inclusive language and our choice of metaphors for naming God, "Singing of God in an Alien Tongue," *G.I.A. Quarterly*, 1:2 (Summer 1990) 41–43.

**The Voice of the Church at Prayer**

ship with God, and simultaneously we say something about ourselves. Each time we place ourselves in relationship with God we also commit ourselves to a way of being in the world while we wait in joyful hope for the coming of the reign of God.

The language of our prayer, no matter what its surface grammar may be, is always self-involving and commissive. Our liturgical language summons us to engage in *speech-acts,* in acts of praise and thanksgiving, in acts of acceptance, in promises and pledges, in confession and commitments.[8]

A second misconception about liturgical language is that it is not really making statements at all but is simply the product of our halting attempts to express our inner attitudes. Again, an example will be helpful. In a prayer cited earlier, "For Our Oppressors," there is a phrase, "We wish to love sincerely all who oppress us." To speak of "a desire to love all who oppress us" certainly implies that the community experiences such a desire, harbors such a hope. But does it? If we claim that liturgical language is an expression of our state of mind and heart, we would also have to acknowledge that sometimes such language does not express what is going on in us. We may feel no such desire to love our oppressors, or, for that matter, we may not feel sorrow or contrition or joy or the myriad other affections of the heart that are expressed in liturgical prayer. We may even, on occasion, feel just the contrary! Would it not be hypocritical to say "Amen" to such a prayer?

Such a conception of language in worship makes of it a kind of progress report on our internal state of mind and heart—an accurate report obviously impossible to achieve when language in worship is, of its nature, public and universal and could not possibly capture the state of mind and heart of each one present. In addition, it would have to be presumed that God is already aware of what is going on in our inner selves and that prayer would be simply a means of repeating information to God that God already knows. One would be forced to ask the question: Why bother to pray at all? Why tell God what God already knows, especially if, in the process, we may be caught in uttering only half-truths?

8. *See* my monograph, *The Language of the Liturgy: Some Theoretical and Practical Implications* (Washington: International Commission on English in the Liturgy, 1983); *see also* A. C. Thiselton, *Language, Liturgy and Meaning,* Grove Liturgical Study 2 (New York: Grove, 1975).

## H. Kathleen Hughes, R.S.C.J.

The point of liturgical language, the point of liturgy, is not for God's sake, as St. Thomas Aquinas pointed out, but for the sake of the community.[9] We come together in the presence of the Holy One; and we respond to God's presence in word and deed *to bring us to reverence;* to allow God, through the liturgy, to make a claim upon us; to place ourselves under the consolation and the challenge of the word; to be transformed, gradually, almost imperceptibly, over time.

In liturgical prayer we are neither primarily assenting to doctrinal statements nor reporting our subjective state of mind. We are engaged in acts; we are doing something in response to Jesus' command to "do this." We are not merely saying something. When we respond "Amen" after the Communion minister says to us, "The Body of Christ," we are at one and the same time saying: Yes, it is true, I believe that this is the Body of Christ; and Yes, I will be the body of Christ, with God's grace. Every Amen spoken in the liturgical assembly makes demands upon us, because every Amen commits us to live in a new relationship with God through the mediation of Jesus Christ and in the power of their abundant and life-giving Spirit.

Such is the potentially transformative power of the Church's public ecclesial prayer. Has this power been recognized in the pastoral letter on war and peace as a chief means of cultivating that vision of justice and peace that the letter proposes?

Toward the end of the pastoral letter on war and peace there is a section entitled "The Pastoral Challenge and Response," a section addressed to the Church as a community of "conscience, prayer, and penance." In this section of the letter, the community is urged to serious study and reflection on the issues raised in the letter, accompanied by prayer and penance. It would seem that the role of prayer is minimized in this presentation, most specificially the role of public, ecclesial prayer to nurture a gospel vision of peace as a way of life and a leaven in society.

At this juncture of our history, faced with the horrors of war and yet confused by the numerous voices and the spectrum of possible legitimate moral options, educational programs undertaken for the formation of conscience are urgently needed. The formation of

9. *Summa theologiae,* 2a–2ae, 91.1.

**The Voice of the Church at Prayer**

conscience envisioned by the bishops of the United States through the study of their pastoral letter will clarify issues and lead to intelligent ethical reflection on the many serious questions raised. In many instances, conscience formation through education may lead to a change of mind in adopting the conscious structures of thought presented in the letter. Yet, in the final analysis, what the Christian community needs more, at this moment, is a change of heart. Perhaps the challenge that needs to be addressed to the community is not only to become a community of "conscience, prayer, and penance," but to become a community of *"prayer, penance, and conversion."*

It is not rational to be a peace Church; it is not rational to love our enemies; it is not rational to turn the other cheek. At root, the pastoral letter is calling for a change of heart, a conversion that is always God's gift and God's initiative. Little we can do will make us either just or peaceful, short of opening ourselves to the God of perfect peace and to the Spirit who transforms hearts.

This suggestion is made not in an attempt to disparage an intellectual approach to the issues of war and peace, nor to set up a dichotomy between conscience and conversion, nor to imply that peace is really only a matter of sentiment rather than of rigorous and thoughtful reflection. It is offered to underscore the biblical understanding of conversion as human response to the utterly gratuitous and gracious intervention of God in human life, a biblical position that the letter itself does state: "All of the values we are promoting in this letter rest ultimately in the disarmament of the human heart and the conversion of the human spirit to God, who alone can give authentic peace."

If the challenge we now face is that of authentic conversion, then the pastoral letter would seem to minimize the role of prayer. It is true that the letter urges us to recognize the power of the Communion rite, to take the exchange of peace very seriously, and to add an intention for peace to the prayer of the faithful. But such suggestions seem to intimate that the Eucharist is made up of a series of elements, some of them more easily adapted to a theme of peace. What may be more helpful to the community is to recognize that when we gather for worship we celebrate not ideas—peace, justice, nonviolence, for example—but a Person, who alone will make us a people of peace. We gather not to express what we

**H. Kathleen Hughes, R.S.C.J.**

112

can, should, or will do for God but what God has done and continues to do for us in the death and rising of Jesus.[10] The effect of sharing in the Eucharist is to allow a claim upon one's whole being and to surrender to the transforming power of the sacrament. Such is true of the celebration of reconciliation and of all the other sacraments as well. The power of sacramental participation, of gathering a community for public, ecclesial prayer, might well have been developed as the letter was disseminated in communities across the country.

The final draft of the pastoral letter included a strong challenge to the community to do penance. The bishops personally assumed the leadership in this area: "As a tangible sign of our need and desire to do penance we, for the cause of peace, commit ourselves to fast and abstinence on each Friday of the year. We call upon our people voluntarily to do penance on Friday by eating less food and by abstaining from meat. . . . Every Friday should be a day significantly devoted to prayer, penance and almsgiving for peace." The bishops note the relationship of penance to conversion of heart in this context.

The witness of tradition suggests other possibilities as well. It has not been uncommon in the history of the Church to set aside days of public prayer and penance. The origins of the rogation days, for example, are found in a city threatened by disaster and in the actions of a bishop who called for prayer and penance that disaster might be averted. The origins of ember days, while partly a response to pagan festivals, were linked to the community's specific needs for which public penance and intercession seemed apt response. Could we not have a contemporary version of these ancient disciplines, days of public prayer and penance not legislated but as invitation, attractive not because of jurisdiction but because of the moral authority of the leaders of our community calling us to our knees? The commentary on the instruction on the liturgical year seems to propose this course of action: "In our time, when all human beings are fully aware of the serious problems of peace, justice and hunger, the exercises of penance and Christian charity that recur with each of the four seasons need to be given back their

10. The transforming quality of worship is taken up more thoroughly in my earlier essay in this volume.

**The Voice of the Church at Prayer**

original value and power." Decisions regarding ember- and rogation-day reinstitution have been left to the episcopal conferences.[11]

It would seem a fitting follow-up to a pastoral letter of the weight and urgency of that on war and peace if the episcopal conference of the United States did seize such an opportunity for public fasting and public prayer in cathedrals and churches across the country at specified times during the year. In addition, the episcopal conference might specify that votive Masses be offered on these days of special public prayer, utilizing some of the very best of The Sacramentary's new prayers in the collection of "Masses and Prayers for Various Needs and Occasions."

"We are called to move from discussion to witness and action." Such are the words of the bishops, used to establish their right to prepare a letter that has political as well as moral dimensions. The same words might well be the response of each Christian who reads this letter and begins the process of discussion and assimilation of its content. The process of study is complex. The issues are profound and not easily assimilated. Nevertheless, even during the process of study, even while our consciences are being formed, we are called to move to witness and action, the witness and action that a community of conversion, prayer, and penance might choose. The value of prayer and penance must never be underestimated in the conversion process. They will be a most authentic means of cultivating a gospel vision of peace among us and a most effective witness to society of the sincerity of our words.

### Conclusion

This essay has focused on one recent document issued in the Church of the United States by its pastoral leaders, *The Challenge of Peace: God's Promise and Our Response,* in order to demonstrate that the community's *theologia prima* is an abundant reservoir for theoretical formulation *and* human transformation. Let us listen more attentively to the voice of the Church at prayer, neither neglecting it as source of systematic theological development nor

11. See "Commentary on the Revised Liturgical Year," *Roman Calendar Text and Commentary* (Washington: USCC, 1975).

**H. Kathleen Hughes, R.S.C.J.**

underestimating it as means of nurturing and deepening the community's self-identity and its cultivation of a gospel way of life.

## For Further Reflection

1. How do you understand the dialogue between the community's *theologia prima* and *theologia secunda?*
2. In comparing the Missals of Pius V and Paul VI, what shifts did you find most compelling in the language of the prayers?
3. What does it mean to suggest that the community's prayer is a "speech-act"?

Edward Foley, Capuchin

# Liturgy and *Economic Justice for All*

*Introduction*

Any discussion presuming a link between liturgy and social justice suggests, for many, a most unlikely marriage of topics. The U.S. Roman Catholic bishops' economic pastoral, *Economic Justice for All,*[1] raises questions that naturally fall within the purview of ethics or moral theology and would clearly benefit from historical reflections and scriptural insights. Approaching the topic of social justice—or more specifically the economic pastoral—from a liturgical perspective, however, might strike the casual observer as quite far-fetched.

This is true, at least in part, because most Roman Catholics think that "liturgy" is a synonym for "Mass." Liturgy thus conceived is fundamentally a rubrical activity relegated to Sunday morning, confined to the sanctuary area and focused on spiritual rather than material or social matters. Though a common perception, this is nevertheless on the verge of defining worship as an act of escape: an obligatory weekly retreat from lived Christianity that makes no room for the grim realities of poverty or unemployment in its holy precincts. Liturgy so defined seems light years removed from questions of economics or social justice.

This apparent gap between this common perception of liturgy and the tough issues addressed by *Economic Justice for All* can and must be resolved by moving toward a more encompassing and authentic definition of liturgy. Such will help us to understand that liturgy is not fundamentally concerned with vesture or worship aids but with mission and justice. It is especially in Jesus that a perfect integrity between liturgy and life is articulated, and so his life will be an important focus in these reflections. An introduction to the meaning of liturgy in the life of Jesus and its continued significance in the early Christian community will then prepare us to consider how our rituals are really corporate rehearsals of our mission. Finally, we will consider how the Eucharist is a particularly

1. NCCB, *Economic Justice for All: Catholic Social Teaching and the U.S. Economy* (Washington: USCC, 1986).

powerful rehearsal of our baptismal call. Such a progression will not only enable us to understand how *Economic Justice for All* relates to liturgy but, more essentially, how liturgy itself is a central metaphor for the Christian quest for justice.

### The Original Link Between "Liturgy" and Life

The original meaning of the word "liturgy" is roughly equivalent to "public service" or "work done on behalf of the people." In ancient Greece, where the term originated, this could have meant producing theater pieces, providing a banquet at a festival, or even exercising one's responsibility to vote. Whatever form it took, those events that were considered to be liturgical presumed some service undertaken on behalf of the wider community. When the word was borrowed by the Jews in their translation of the Hebrew Bible into Greek, the meaning of the term narrowed. Thus, in the Hebrew Scriptures the term "liturgy" is used almost exclusively to designate cultic events involving priests and Levites (as in Exod 28:35). Even here, however, a strong ethical undercurrent remains.

From its usage in the Hebrew Scriptures, various forms of this word found their way into the New Testament, where Jesus himself is called *leitourgos* or "minister of the sanctuary" (Heb 8:2). Despite this overtly cultic reference, the term "liturgy" does not exclusively refer to cultic acts in the New Testament, as was essentially true of the Hebrew Scriptures. Instead, it is successively employed to refer to the duties of state officials (Rom 13:6), the collections for Jerusalem (Rom 15:27), the service of the apostolic envoy (Phil 2:25), and even the proclamation of the gospel (Rom 15:16). It is true that later in the Christian era, this word was again used in a more limited, cultic sense. This, however, can be considered as an unfortunate narrowing of its New Testament meaning.

### Liturgy and the Life of Jesus

It is only in the life of Jesus that the full meaning of the word "liturgy" comes to light. In the course of the Gospels we encounter numerous instances where Jesus prays. He prays in the midst of a gathering of disciples (John 17) and in seclusion (Matt 14:23); before a miracle (John 11:41f.) and after a miracle (Mark 6:46); at the beginning of his public ministry (Luke 3:21) and at the farewell meal with his disciples (Matt 26:26); at the moment of his transfigu-

**Liturgy and *Economic Justice for All***

117

ration in glory (Luke 9:29) and in his final agony on the cross (Matt 27:46). Besides the various passages that depict Jesus praying there are also a number of texts that present Jesus' teaching about prayer. Here we learn that prayer is to be unceasing (Luke 18:1), confident (Matt 18:19), from the heart (Mark 11:23), and always centered on the one Jesus called "Father" (Matt 6:9).

What is most striking about this impressive testimony concerning prayer, however, is neither its frequency nor variety. Rather, what is notable is the absolute integrity between the way Jesus prayed and the way he lived. Jesus centered his prayer on the one he called "Father" because he centered his life on the same. He was able to pray and to preach the word because he lived the word—he was the Word. Jesus could challenge others to pray without ceasing because his own life was a single, ceaseless prayer. Communion with God, personal mission, and service to others were not unrelated elements in Jesus' life but different facets of a single reality.

Our contention that prayer in the life of Jesus was not a retreat from life or mission but a rehearsal of mission is underscored in Luke's accounts of Jesus' baptism (3:21), his selection of the Twelve (6:12), and his teaching of the "Our Father" (11:1). In each of these instances a moment of mission or instruction is wedded to an experience of prayer. So, too, was the whole of Jesus' mission and teaching one with his prayer.

### Jesus' Liturgical Legacy

This gospel memory of Jesus as the one who perfectly integrated union with God, personal mission, and human service is echoed in the New Testament instructions on prayer and discipleship for the early Church. It is especially Paul who understands prayer as an unceasing Christian experience (Rom 1:9). This constant commitment to prayer, however, does not exempt anyone from vigorously working for the kingdom (2 Thess 3:6-12). Paul well comprehends the essential link between how one prays and how one lives: Thus he rejoices when blessing and service are joined (Rom 15:27), and he erupts in anger when some dare to enter into cultic worship while ignoring the needs of others (1 Cor 11:17-32).

It is this fundamental link between liturgy and work for the kingdom, perfectly fused in the example of Jesus and reiterated by

**Edward Foley, Capuchin**

118

Paul, that defines authentic worship and establishes the Christian agenda. It is an agenda that demands an uncompromising union of ethical living and common prayer and presumes at least the desire for an ethical life as a prerequisite for genuine worship. The Christian ideal is given classic expression in the early moments of the Acts of the Apostles. Here the Lukan summary of the primitive Christian experience inextricably links common life and common worship (Acts 2:42-47). It is this same ideal—once and for all established in Jesus—that continues as the true "liturgical" standard for every age.

The U.S. Roman Catholic bishops demonstrated their understanding of this connection between liturgy and life in the message accompanying *Economic Justice for All:* "Our faith is not just a weekend obligation, a mystery to be celebrated around the altar on Sunday. It is a pervasive reality to be practiced every day in homes, offices, factories, schools and businesses across our land. We cannot separate what we believe from how we act in the market place and the broader community" (no. 25). The pastoral itself echoes these insights when it calls for "a deeper awareness of the integral connection between worship and the world of work" (no. 329). It is only such a perspective that prevents liturgy from degenerating into a rubrical spectacle and preserves it, instead, as the enacted belief of the Church.

### Liturgy as a Rehearsal of Justice

Now that we have introduced a more encompassing definition of Christian liturgy and illustrated the intrinsic connection between worship and Christian living—especially as revealed in the life of Jesus—it is necessary to explore how liturgy can be considered a rehearsal of the Christian mission. More specifically, we will attempt to illustrate how Christian liturgy is both an expression of an impetus for justice and is in itself a just act. Such a discussion will prepare us to further consider how the Eucharist is a special rehearsal of our mission in justice.

### Liturgy as Fount and Summit

The first document of the Second Vatican Council, The Constitution on the Sacred Liturgy, states that "the liturgy is the summit toward which the activity of the Church is directed; at the same time it is the fount from which all the Church's power flows" (CSL 10, DOL 10). Worship thus conceived occupies a place at the very center of the Christian experience. This central place is reaffirmed by the constitution when it continues, "the aim and object of apostolic works is that all . . . should come together to praise God in the midst of his Church" (CSL 10, DOL 10). This is liturgy as summit and summation of the Christian mission. Consequently, all that we do—all ecclesial energy expended in the proclamation of the gospel—finds its purpose and fulfillment in the gathering of the baptized to give thanks and praise.

Besides this expressive power, however, the constitution also notes that liturgy has what might be considered a creative or generative power. This is to say that worship not only announces what has been accomplished but also proclaims what is yet to be achieved: it is not only a summation but an introduction. Thus our common prayer is just as much about our future as it is about our present or the past. Liturgy does not proclaim salvation in Christ as a completed event but engages us in the ongoing work of salvation; it not only reveals the Church to be holy but directs us to new ways of holiness. Accordingly, the constitution admits worship's power to inspire the faithful to become of one heart in love and prays that they may grasp by deed what they hold by creed (10). This is liturgy as fount and summit of the Christian life.

These two facets of Christian worship—one expressive, the other creative—lead us to the heart of worship's power. They also begin to reveal why we can call Christian worship a rehearsal of our mission in Christ. Liturgy, authentically understood and lived, is not an empty statement about a distant God or ideal human relationships; it is, rather, a symbolic activity: what the bishops in *Music in Catholic Worship* call "vehicles of communication and instruments of faith" (7).

The act of worship integrated with human life, therefore, has the potential to create the reality it signifies. Consequently, we are not only informed of our incorporation into the body of Christ but, through Christian initiation, we are in fact incorporated; we are not only assured that Christ is made present through the consecrated bread and wine but are ourselves transformed into his body and blood. Liturgy in this fuller sense is not simply informational. Rather, it is formational and transformational.

**Edward Foley, Capuchin**

120

This is what it means to call liturgy a "rehearsal" of the Christian life. Rehearsal, in this sense, is not simply a dramatic enactment of some long-finished historical event. Nor is it an imperfect repetition of some act in order to get it right. Rather, it is a continual reentry into and further appropriation of a rich and inexhaustible reality. Rehearsal so imagined is neither artificial nor preparatory; it is, rather, ritual engagement with the truth. To experience again, for example, a performance of Arthur Miller's classic *Death of a Salesman* is thus a rehearsal: a fresh confrontation with the questions of meaning and success that gnaw at our national conscience. The annual commemoration of the birthday of Martin Luther King is a personal and collective rehearsal of his challenge and his dreams. Analogously, our entry into the Christian mysteries is a rehearsal of the call offered to us in faith as well as a foreshadowing of what our response is to be.

It is in this sense that liturgy can further be understood as a rehearsal of justice. "Justice" is traditionally defined as giving to others what is their due. Christian worship is, in turn, giving God what is God's due—*dignum et iustum est*—for this is right and just. Liturgy is consequently a paradigmatically just act. Besides directing our attention to the Holy One, worship further links praise with human care and service: encouraging us to support each other in faith, to be reconciled, and to share peace. Therefore, baptism, marriage, and all other liturgical acts rehearse just relationships by recognizing the dignity of others in Christ. Liturgy is not an escape from the social ills that confront humankind—just as it is not a way of holding God at bay. Instead, worship catapults us into the social arena, where the kingdom is to be proclaimed and served.

### Eucharist and the Economy

Our journey from a broad definition of liturgy to the acknowledgment of worship as a just act finally leads us to a consideration of Christian Eucharist. *Economic Justice for All* recognizes that there is an intrinsic link between Eucharist and the world food problem today: "The problem of hunger has a special significance for those who read the Scriptures and profess the Christian faith. From the Lord's command to feed the hungry, to the Eucharist we celebrate as the Bread of Life, the fabric of our faith demands that we be creatively engaged in sharing the food that sustains life. There is no more basic human need" (282). If Christian liturgy is a rehearsal of who we are to be as followers of Jesus, then the example of Jesus who fed the hungry, nourished the outcast, and was recognized in the breaking of the bread compels us to attend to the cries of the hungry.

More than calling for charity to the hungry, however, the celebration of the Eucharist also seems to offer a critical reflection on the economy itself. As Enrique Dussel has demonstrated, Eucharist presupposes that people have bread and wine or a staple food and festive drink—both of which are "works of human hands."[2] Eucharist, therefore, presumes the existence of an economy. More than this, Eucharist also presumes that people have some basic control over the economy and are free to give their produce back to God. Specifically, the Eucharistic gesture of "offering" assumes that we have bread and wine or their cultural equivalents to share.

But what happens when the produce is not free to offer or when there is not enough food to satisfy basic human needs? Is it possible to celebrate Eucharist when some do not control the fruit of their labor or even have the opportunity for work? When the promise of the earth becomes perverted and workers can no longer feed their families, much less offer from their earnings to God, then the potential for authentic Christian Eucharist is greatly diminished.

Dussel would go even further and suggest that the example of Jesus demands not only the ability to give produce back to God but also the freedom to share with the poor to whom the kingdom is promised. Eucharist at its core, therefore, rehearses a just economic system in which gifts can be offered to God and human hungers satisfied. This is the presumption of the Church's worship, ritually enacted in the offering of the produce and praise and the sharing of Communion. The Eucharist thus rehearses not only the messianic banquet of the next life but an authentic Christian banquet in this life. To the extent that such is not provided, one can question our capacity to fully celebrate Christian Eucharist.

2. Enrique Dussel, "The Bread of the Eucharistic Celebration as a Sign of Justice in the Community," *Can We Always Celebrate the Eucharist?* eds. Mary Collins and David Power, *Concilium* 152 (New York: Seabury, 1982) 56–65.

**Edward Foley, Capuchin**

## Conclusion

In his book *On Liturgical Theology* Benedictine liturgist Aidan Kavanagh notes that "the liturgy of a church is nothing other than that church's faith in motion on certain definite and crucial levels."[3] Worship in this perspective is not the fulfillment of a Sunday morning obligation, an elaborate artistic endeavor, or even a moment of cosmic appeasement. The U.S. Roman Catholic bishops have acknowledged that the economic arena is one of the chief places where we live out our faith. Furthermore, our public worship is the central place where such faith is rehearsed. It is only by maintaining a connection between these two—between the altar and the marketplace—that our faith can truly be put into motion. Only then, in the example of Jesus, will authentic worship be rendered "in spirit and in truth" (John 4:23).

### For Further Reflection

1. Our worship is described by official documents as having the power both to express and to create the justice of God's reign. Reflecting on your own experience of liturgy, why is it that many leave the Eucharist unaware of its challenge to live justly?

2. How do you understand the liturgy as a "rehearsal" for living the Christian life?

3. Can the Eucharist really be celebrated when there is great economic disparity in the worshiping community?

3. Aidan Kavanagh, *On Liturgical Theology* (New York: Pueblo, 1984) 8.

Barbara Reid, O.P.

# Liturgy, Scripture, and the Challenge of Feminism

## Introduction

It is at table that our true colors show most clearly. Intended to be the very sign of unity, the Eucharistic table more often becomes the arena in which our deepest theological, personal, and pastoral differences come into the open. What Christians really believe about inclusion, equality, and justice becomes evident in who is at home in the liturgical assembly, in what is said and done there, and in who performs what roles. The way we celebrate liturgy reveals most clearly our operative images of God, ourselves, and one another. This essay focuses on how our attitudes toward women and men are manifest in liturgical expression and will sketch a biblical basis for a feminist vision of a Church of equal disciples.

## Feminism

Many people shy away from the term "feminism" because it conjures up for them distasteful images of angry, men-hating women. However, the same people might be quite committed to values such as equal pay for women and men in the same jobs, equal opportunities for women and men in education, and so on. Although there are several different kinds of feminism, a working definition is this: a commitment to the humanity, dignity, and equality of all persons to such a degree that one is willing to work for changes in structures and in relationship patterns so that these occur to the equal good of all.[1] Feminism, according to this definition, does not advocate replacing male domination with female domination. Rather, it works for the liberation of all. Feminism does not deny differences between the sexes; but differences are recognized precisely as differences, not as indicators of inferiority or superiority. As applied to the Church, feminism advocates a Church of equal disciples. It seeks the full use of the God-given

1. Joan Chittister, "Yesterday's Dangerous Vision: Christian Feminism in the Catholic Church," *Sojourners* (July 1987) 18.

gifts of all the baptized members, women and men alike. Christian feminists are women and men who are committed to the vision of Jesus and to the elimination of sexism in the Church and in society as a work of justice.

### Biblical Basis for Feminism

Feminism is not simply a secular liberation movement that has caught on in religious circles. There is a firm biblical basis for the vision espoused by Christian feminists. It is true that the Bible was written from a predominantly patriarchal perspective. That is, it was written primarily by men, about men, and for men. Women's experience is minimal and marginalized. When a woman is included in the Bible, she is usually defined in terms of the man to whom she belongs. However, many feminists believe that a liberating message for women can be found through new methods of biblical interpretation. The following are some examples.

### Images of God

For the majority of Christians, the traditional image of God has been "loving father." There are some fifteen references to God as father in the Old Testament (e.g., Deut 32:6; Ps 68:6; Isa 63:16; Jer 3:4), and "father" is the most frequent designation for God in the New Testament. In particular, it is the usual way in which Jesus addresses God in the Gospels (e.g., Mark 14:36; Matt 11:25; Luke 23:34; John 17:1). Jesus also teaches his disciples to address God as father (Matt 6:9; Luke 11:2). That the early Church continued to address God as "Abba," "Father," is evident from Galatians 4:6 and Romans 8:15.

A careful look at the Scriptures, however, reveals quite a wide variety of images of God, many of them feminine. There are a number of times when God is shown as giving birth and as mothering. In the Book of Deuteronomy, for example, God speaks through Moses, reminding the Israelites not to forget "the God who gave you birth" (Deut 32:18).[2] The prophet Isaiah speaks of God's anguish over Israel as "a woman in labor, gasping and panting" (Isa 42:14). Isaiah also consoles Israel with the words, "Can a

2. All Scripture quotations are taken from the NAB unless otherwise indicated.

**Liturgy, Scripture, and the Challenge of Feminism**

mother forget her infant, be without tenderness for the child of her womb? Even should she forget, I will never forget you" (Isa 49:15). And further, "As a mother comforts her son, so will I comfort you; in Jerusalem you shall find your comfort" (Isa 66:13). The psalmist describes reliance on God, "I have stilled and quieted my soul like a weaned child. Like a weaned child on its mother's lap, [so is my soul within me]" (Ps 131:2). Job 38:28-29 balances parental images of the Creator: "Has the rain a father; or who has begotten the drops of dew? Out of whose womb comes the ice, and who gives the hoarfrost its birth in the skies?"

There are instances in which God is portrayed as a midwife. The psalmist says to God, "It was you who drew me from the womb and soothed me on my mother's breast. On you was I cast from my birth, from the womb I have belonged to you" (Ps 22:9-10, NJB). In Isaiah 66:9 God says to Zion, "Shall I bring a mother to the point of birth, and yet not let her child be born?"

God is also spoken of in nonhuman metaphors. God is likened to a rock (Deut 32:15), a consuming fire (Deut 4:24), and a lion (Hos 5:14). In several instances, God is likened to a mother eagle who incites her nestlings forth by hovering over her brood, spreading her wings to receive them, bearing them up on her pinions and giving them refuge under her wings (Deut 32:11-12; Ps 91:4).

Jesus, too, uses other images than "father" when speaking of God. In the parable of the shepherd who searches for the one lost sheep (Luke 15:1-7), the shepherd exemplifies God's attitude toward repentant sinners. In just the same way, the woman who searches for the one lost coin (Luke 15:8-10) represents the way God acts. Jesus also uses feminine metaphors for himself. When he laments over Jerusalem, he likens himself to a mother hen: "How many times I yearned to gather your children together as a hen gathers her brood under her wings, but you were unwilling!" (Luke 13:34; similarly Matt 23:37). In the Gospel of John, as Jesus' "hour" of his passion, death, and resurrection approaches, Jesus compares his coming travail and the grief of his disciples to that of a woman in labor. He explains, "When a woman is in labor, she is in anguish because her hour has arrived; but when she has given birth to a child, she no longer remembers the pain because of her joy that a child has been born into the world" (John 16:21).

**Barbara Reid, O.P.**

126

All of these images are attempts by the biblical writers to describe what God is like, yet no image adequately expresses who God is. God is like a loving father, a birthing and nursing mother, a midwife, a steady rock, a mother eagle who hovers over her brood, a woman who searches for the lost. But God is *not* any of these. All of our language about God ultimately falls short of the reality of God's being. God is more than our words can express. Yet the language we use to speak about God is immensely important because a curious thing happens with the human metaphors we use for God. The imaging works in both directions! When we use predominantly male images for God, then being male becomes equated with being God-like. Women, then, are not like God, are less holy than men. But this theology is flatly contradicted by the creation stories, to which we will now turn.

### Creation of Human Beings

There are two stories of creation in Genesis 1–2. In the first account, woman and man are created simultaneously; male and female are both created in God's image (Gen 1:27). It is the second account, Genesis 2:18-24, that is often interpreted in a way that places woman in a secondary position and that justifies male domination of women. Genesis 2:18-24 has been understood to tell of the superiority of man over woman because man was created first, and because woman was created from man. People have seen in Genesis 2:18 the divinely prescribed role of woman as "helpmate" to man. Feminists have taken another look at this story and see quite a different picture.

It is important to keep in mind the nature of the stories in Genesis 1–11. These are stories of primeval events, not of actual occurrences. They are the way that the ancient biblical writers tried to explain why their world was the way it was. Both accounts of creation agree that the creation of human beings was a deliberate plan of God (Gen 1:26; 2:18). Woman is not an afterthought. In fact, when one looks carefully at the structure of Genesis 2, the following pattern emerges: a deficiency is stated, followed by God's response to alleviate it. In verse 5, there is no shrub or herbage of the field, no rain, and no human to work the land. So God proceeds to make a garden (v. 8), a stream of water to water the whole surface of the ground (v. 6), and a human being (v. 7). Part

**Liturgy, Scripture, and the Challenge of Feminism**

of the divine plan of creation in Genesis 2 is that things keep improving. Following this pattern, the creation of woman in verses 22-23 is God's way of addressing the need for another like the first human being (v. 18). Indeed, the exclamation of the man, "This one at last!" (v. 23) shows the creation of woman to be the climax of the story.

The idea that woman is subordinate to man because she is derived from him, taken from his rib, must also be reexamined. Two things about the word "rib" may shed some light on Genesis 2:21. The idea of "rib" for the creation of woman may reflect a word play in Sumerian. In that language, *ti* means both "rib" and "to make live." If the author of Genesis 2:21 wanted to make that association, then derivation of woman from man was not what the story intended to convey. Furthermore, the Hebrew word for rib, *sela'*, everywhere else in the Old Testament means "side." So in Genesis 2:21, the woman is taken from the man's side, a notion that speaks more of equality than subordination. In addition, if one argues that woman is subordinate to man because she is made from him, then one must argue that man is subordinate to the clay of the ground, because he is made from it (Gen 2:7)! Clay and rib are merely the raw materials God uses for the creation of human beings.

What of woman's role as "helpmate" for man (Gen 2:18)? The Hebrew word *'ezer,* usually translated "helpmate," occurs over twenty times in the Old Testament. In the majority of those instances, it refers to the strength or salvation that comes from God. For example, the psalmist prays, "The LORD answer you in time of distress; the name of the God of Jacob defend you! May he send you help [*'ezer*] from the sanctuary, from Zion may he sustain you" (Ps 20:2-3). The notion of "power" or "strength" stands behind the word *'ezer.* And the next word in Genesis 2:18, *kenegdo,* means "corresponding to him." So in Genesis 2:18, God's intention in creating the woman is to make for the man "a power like his own" or a "strength corresponding to his." This suggests that God's design for human existence is that relations between male and female be marked by mutual strength, partnership, support. The exclamation of the man in 2:23 shows that he recognizes the woman as "a power equal to his own." The man announces their very identity, saying that woman is "bone of my bone and flesh of

**Barbara Reid, O.P.**

128

my flesh." Bone and flesh are used together in the Old Testament to describe a person in his or her totality. It describes the range of possibilities from might to frailty. In other words, the man says that woman is strong like him, and weak like him.

When Genesis 1 and 2 are read together, they explain two basic things about human beings: Created male and female, they are like God and are in relationship with God (Gen 1); created male and female, human beings are in relationship with one another (Gen 2). This is God's plan (1:26; 2:18) and it is very good (1:31; 2:23).

### The Origin of Sin

What happened to the idyllic portrait of Genesis 1–2? The next chapter of Genesis tries to explain sin and suffering in human existence. A traditional interpretation of Genesis 3 is that woman was the weaker of the two and that she easily succumbed to temptation. Having fallen herself, she then becomes the temptress for the man and ensnares him. In the end, God's prescription for restoring order in the world is for man to rule over woman.

Feminist scholars offer a different interpretation.[3] Looking at the narrative dynamics in Genesis 3:1-7, we find it difficult to support the idea of woman as the weaker of the sexes. In the dialogue with the serpent, it is the woman who is the spokesperson, even though the man is present (v. 6 reveals that the man is with her all along). She is intelligent, informed, and perceptive in the way she discusses theology with the serpent. She acts independently, thinks and decides for herself. In contrast, the man is silent and passive. He is not reluctant when the woman gives him the fruit. He does not theologize, he simply acquiesces. The first episode of Genesis 3 shows two different but equally culpable ways of human disobedience. Both the man, in his acquiescence, and the, woman in her action, are responsible for sin.

In the second scene (vv. 8-13), both hear YHWH God in the garden. God interviews the man first. In his responses, it becomes evident that the unity between him and the woman has been destroyed. He answers only for himself: "I heard . . . . I was afraid. . . . I was naked. . . . I hid" (v. 10). He is evasive and

3. The following is from Phyllis Trible, *God and the Rhetoric of Sexuality. Overtures to Biblical Theology* (Philadelphia: Fortress, 1978) 105–139.

**Liturgy, Scripture, and the Challenge of Feminism**

defensive in answering God. He betrays his woman and tries to blame God: "The woman whom you put here with me—she gave me fruit from the tree, and so I ate it" (Gen 3:12). The woman confesses more quickly, without blaming God or implicating her companion. She simply states, "The serpent beguiled me and I ate" (v. 13, NJB). Both man and woman are responsible for the introduction of sin into the world, and both admit it before God. Woman is not the source of evil, nor is she the tempter. That is the role of the serpent.

The consequences of human disobedience are then described (vv. 14-19). The harmony of God's creation is now disrupted. The distinctions in creation now result in opposition. What had been made for delight now ends in pain and alienation. The divine, human, animal, and plant worlds are all adversely affected. None of this is God's original intent; it is the result of human choice, for which both man and woman are responsible. Man's rule over woman (v. 16) is part of the disorder and is already in place by the end of the story. The woman has disappeared from the scene. God speaks of the man having become "like one of us," and God sends him forth from the garden (vv. 22-24).

*The Vision of Jesus*

In addition to a rereading of the stories of human origins, Christian feminists also find a liberating message for women in the vision of Jesus and the way he interacted with women. In all four Gospels, Jesus is concerned with women as well as men. Many of those healed by Jesus are women: Simon's mother-in-law (Mark 1:29-31), Jairus' daughter (Luke 8:40-42, 49-56), the woman with a hemorrhage (Luke 8:43-48), the woman bent for eighteen years (Luke 13:10-17). Jesus touched and was touched by women (Luke 7:38; 8:54; 13:13), even those considered unclean (Luke 8:44-45). Women received Jesus' forgiveness (Luke 7:36-50). Jesus had close women friends, such as Martha and Mary (Luke 10:38-42; John 11:1-44; 12:1-11). He taught women (Luke 10:38-42), and he engaged in theological discussions with women (Mark 7:24-30; John 4:4-42; 11:17-27), even though it was against Jewish custom to do so (John 4:27).

**Barbara Reid, O.P.**

130

Jesus' disciples include women as well as men. The crowds who followed him consisted of both men and women (Matt 14:21). Mary Magdalene, Joanna, Susanna, Mary, Salome, and many other women followed Jesus from Galilee (Mark 15:40-41; Matt 27:55; Luke 8:1-3), and it is they who remain faithful to the end. These women witnessed Jesus' crucifixion (Mark 15:40-41; Matt 27:55-56; Luke 23:49; John 19:25) and his burial (Mark 15:47; Matt 27:61; Luke 23:55). They were the first to discover the empty tomb and to be given the commission to proclaim the resurrection (Mark 16:1-8; Matt 27:1-8; Luke 24:1-11; John 21:1-2, 11-18). Two of the Gospels recount that it is to the women disciples that the risen Jesus first appears (Matt 28:9-10; John 20:11-18). Women belong to the community of believers that is gathered in Jerusalem awaiting the promised Spirit (Acts 1:13-14).

Women not only follow Jesus but they exemplify the ministry of a disciple. In the Gospels Jesus' mission is described in terms of serving, *diakonein:* "For the Son of Man did not come to be served but to serve and to give his life as a ransom for many" (Mark 10:45; similarly, Matt 20:28; Luke 22:27). Jesus instructs his disciples that such service is the mark of anyone who wants to share in Jesus' mission, especially those who aspire to greatness or positions of leadership (Mark 9:35; Matt 23:11; Luke 22:26-27). Ministering *(diakonein)* to others' needs is the basis on which a Christian will be judged (Matt 25:44). In all four Gospels, the only followers of Jesus who are said to serve *(diakonein)* are women: Simon's mother-in-law (Mark 1:31; Matt 8:15; Luke 4:39); Mary Magdalene, Joanna, Susanna, Mary, Salome, and the other Galilean women (Luke 8:1-3; Mark 15:41; Matt 27:55); and Martha (Luke 10:40; John 12:2). Other characteristics of disciples, such as prayerfulness and faithfulness, are exemplified by such women as Elizabeth, Mary, and Anna (Luke 1–2), the persistent widow (Luke 18:1-8); and the widow who gives her all (Luke 21:1-4).

Women were also prominent in ministry in the Pauline communities. Prisca, along with her husband Aquila, was a close co-worker of Paul (Acts 18:24-28; Rom 16:3-4). Mary, Tryphaena, Tryphosa, and Persis worked hard in the service of the gospel (Rom 16:6, 12). Euodia and Syntyche were leaders in the Philippian community and had struggled at Paul's side in promoting the gospel (Phil 4:2-3). Women such as Phoebe of Cenchrae served as

**Liturgy, Scripture, and the Challenge of Feminism**

deacons (Rom 16:1-2). Junia[4] was notable among the apostles (Rom 16:7). Women heads of house churches included Prisca (1 Cor 16:19; Rom 16:5), Nympha (Col 4:15), and Lydia (Acts 16:11-15, 40).

In sum, feminists draw out part of the New Testament portrait that has been overlooked by patriarchal interpreters. The Gospels show Jesus not only in the company of the Twelve, but also of women. Women are recipients of Jesus' teaching, healing,and forgiveness. They actively follow Jesus and participate in his mission. Women are model disciples and ministers not only in the Gospels but in the Pauline letters as well.

### Feminist Interpretation of Scripture

There is no one method used by feminist interpreters of Scripture. In the examples given above, several methods are operative. One approach is to search for feminine symbols and images, such as feminine metaphors for God, and to exalt those as a model for present-day women. Another technique is to reinterpret stories that have traditionally been told from a patriarchal perspective, for example, the stories of the creation of human beings and the origin of sin in Genesis 2–3.

One insight of feminists is that many Bible stories yield a different message when seen through the experience of women. No interpreter comes to a text without all the presuppositions that form his or her particular worldview. One's nationality, sex, social status, race, marital status, age, religious tradition, all affect how a person reads and interprets the Bible. Some feminists concentrate, then, in articulating the stories of the Bible from a woman's perspective. At times such a task results in bringing to the fore women in the tradition who may have been overlooked by male interpreters. At other times the task involves reconstructing women's experience from scant clues and silences in the text.[5]

---

4. *See* B. Brooten, "'Junia . . . Outstanding Among the Apostles' (Romans 16:7)," *Women Priests: A Catholic Commentary on the Vatican Declaration,* eds. L. Swidler and A. Swidler (New York: Paulist, 1977) 141–144, for evidence that the name in Romans 16:7 is a woman's name.

5. *See,* for example, Elisabeth Schussler Fiorenza, *In Memory of Her: A Feminist Theological Reconstruction of Christian Origins* (New York: Crossroads, 1984).

**Barbara Reid, O.P.**

There are also feminist approaches that are valuable for dealing with texts in Scripture that do not give a positive image of woman and that cannot be reinterpreted in a liberating manner. Stories such as that of the abuse and murder of the concubine in Judges 19 or the sacrifice of the daughter of Jephthah in Judges 11:29-40 are told not to perpetuate such atrocities toward women but to pronounce judgment on them and call for repentance.[6]

Another approach to texts that advocate the inferiority or subordination of women (e.g., 1 Cor 14:34-36; 1 Tim 2:11-15) is to understand them in their historical context and to reinterpret them in light of changing times and circumstances. Such reinterpretation is most faithful to the biblical tradition. The Bible is not a static body of revelation that is simply passed on from generation to generation. It is a living tradition, a partner in a believer's active encounter with God. Jesus is a good example of one who knew his Jewish tradition well but reinterpreted it for his day (e.g., Matt 5:17-48; Mark 2:23-28; 7:1-23). Similarly, the Apostle Paul, a Pharisee who knew the Law and his tradition inside and out and who kept it blamelessly (Phil 3:5-6), radically reinterpreted it all in light of his experience of Jesus (Phil 3:7-11). Followers of Jesus have, in subsequent centuries, reinterpreted biblical traditions such as Paul's approval of slavery (1 Cor 7:21-24; Phlm). In the same way, feminists urge Christians today to understand as historically conditioned any biblical text in which women are regarded as subordinate to men and to reinterpret it in a theological framework that advances the dignity and equality of all believers.

## Liturgy

The perspective from which we interpret Scripture becomes evident in our liturgical celebrations. The language and symbols we use in our readings, preaching, hymns, and prayers, as well as the assignation of ministerial roles, reveal clearly our concepts of God, self, and others. For many Christian feminists, there is a distressing gap between their theology and their experience in the assembly. For those who are new to the feminist perspective, changes in

6. *See,* for example, Phyllis Trible, *Texts of Terror: Literary-Feminist Readings of Biblical Narratives.* Overtures to Biblical Theology (Philadelphia: Fortress, 1984).

**Liturgy, Scripture, and the Challenge of Feminism**

traditional language, symbols, and roles can be confusing and up-
setting. A movement to feminist consciousness is actually a conversion process that demands a shift in one's whole worldview. The
translation of feminist insights into liturgical expression must be
preceded by education and explanation with sensitivity to the positions of people at all points of the continuum.

*Language*

The language that we use in our readings, hymns, preaching, and
prayers plays a crucial role in how we perceive God, ourselves,
and others. The way one is named, or whether one is named at all,
has a profound effect on one's identity. Language both says what
one's world vision is and shapes one's worldview. The use of language is not a trivial issue. It matters whether one uses "man" or
"human being." Increasingly, the English-speaking world is recognizing that woman is not included in the word "man" and that
"brothers" does not mean "brothers and sisters." Our language
must not perpetuate the attitude that man is the paradigm and that
woman is "other." Thus, the language used both in addressing the
assembly and in referring to believers must express the reality that
both women and men are created in God's image.[7]

A commitment to the use of inclusive language in our liturgies
requires concerted effort on the part of all liturgical ministers. The
music ministers must examine their choice of hymns for the images
of God they contain and for the language used of believers. In
some instances musicians may need to question the appropriateness
of continuing to use a particular hymn. In other cases substitutions
for exclusive language can be announced at the beginning of the
celebration. Similarly, those who prepare the prayers of intercession need to formulate both the prayers and the response in language that is inclusive. Lectors, too, must prepare their readings
ahead of time and be alert to the language used. They should be
aware that the translations of the Bible approved for liturgical
proclamation, the RSV, NJB, and NAB, have all been revised in recent years, with some attention given to translating inclusively

7. *See* the guidelines prepared by the ICEL, "Statement: The Problem of Exclusive Language with Regard to Women," *Doctrine and Life* 32 (1982)
318–322.

**Barbara Reid, O.P.**

134

words that refer to people. A lector should consult these newly revised versions, or the *Lectionary for the Christian People*[8] for help on the language with which to proclaim the word. Such endeavors are not "changing the Bible." Rather, they reflect more accurately the biblical writers' intent in modern-day language.

Preachers have a particularly important role. The language and images they use and the perspective from which they interpret Scripture is the model they offer for the congregation. Homilists might ask themselves whether they always speak of God as "he." Do they ever speak about the feminine images of God or do they reinforce the dominant image of God as "father"? Preaching with other divine metaphors than "father" does not say less about God or take away a precious image. Rather, it says more about God; it expands a narrow perception of God who cannot be contained by a single metaphor. Preachers also have an opportunity to expound on the role of women disciples who figure often in the gospel readings. They can help rectify the false impression that the "twelve apostles" were the only ones who followed Jesus and shared his mission. Another important role of the preacher is to help reinterpret those passages that place women in an inferior position. For example, when "Wives, be subordinate to your husbands" (Eph 5:21) is proclaimed, the homilist should not skirt it and preach on the gospel instead. Silence is generally interpreted as tacit approval. Rather, the preacher should use the occasion to explain the cultural setting of the Greco-Roman household from which this admonition comes. The homilist might pose the question of whether other structures that are emerging today in both family and Church better model the reciprocal love and obedience required of all members of the household or Church community.

### Roles

Another indicator of our commitment to a Church of equal disciples is that of roles: Who does what in our liturgical gatherings. Does the assigning of liturgical roles bespeak a theology that regards all the baptized as holy? Is full use made of the gifts of all the members, women and men alike? Women should be visibly ac-

8. Gordon Lathrop and Gail Ramshaw-Schmidt, eds. (New York: Pueblo, 1986). 3 vol.

tive in all those liturgical ministries currently open to them: lector, Eucharistic minister, hospitality, preparing the table, musician, preaching and presiding in retreat settings, at wake services, services of the word, and Communion services. As for those roles presently denied women, such as presiding and preaching at Eucharist, believers must study the Scriptures and tradition, attentive to the movement of the Spirit in our day, and may respectfully question our current restrictions. Keeping the dialogue open on the question of the ordination of women is not being disobedient to the 1977 Vatican Declaration on the Admission of Women to the Ministerial Priesthood. Quite the contrary! The document itself concludes with the admission that the biblical argument on this topic needs more study. For Rome to revise a position in light of later discussion is certainly not without precedent in our tradition.[9] A revision of restrictions on ministerial roles for women, however, should not be based on the lack of men to perform such ministries, but rather should proceed from a theology of woman created equally in God's image, fully redeemed, and equally sharing in the gifts of the Spirit.

*Conclusion*

Feminism, as a commitment to work for changes in structures and in relationship patterns for the humanity, dignity, and equality of all persons, is a vision that presents believers with tremendous challenges. Our Scriptures and tradition support such a vision. At the same time they call us to reinterpret, to make the word living and active for our day. The way we celebrate at the liturgical table is probably the best litmus test for the degree to which we are really committed to eliminating sexism from our midst. Our language, symbols, and distribution of roles in the liturgical assembly must express that we are a Church of equal disciples.

**For Further Reflection**

1. What images of God, women, and men are predominant in contemporary worship?

2. Do you believe that sexism is a sin?

9. *See* the collection of essays edited by Carroll Stuhlmueller, *Women and the Priesthood: Future Directions* (Collegeville: The Liturgical Press, 1978).

**Barbara Reid, O.P.**

3. In your experience, are the ministerial gifts of women valued equally as those of men?

4. What most needs to change in our liturgical practice in order to be most faithful to Scripture and tradition?

John M. Huels, O.S.M.

# Liturgy, Inclusive Language, and Canon Law

As more people become sensitized to the powerful symbolic effect of language in shaping culture, ideas, and even one's perception of self,[1] there has likewise developed an acute awareness of the issue of inclusive language, that is, language that upholds the equality and dignity of all people. The use of inclusive language, in its broad sense, refers to the attempt to correct references that are perceived to be racist, sexist, clericalist, and anti-Semitic, or that discriminate against those who are disabled. However, the most pressing liturgical concern now is commonly thought to be the remedy of past discrimination against women, whether overt or subtle, within the official texts of liturgy. "The way one is named within the worshiping community—and whether one is named at all—could affect the way one lives the Christian life. The failure of much of liturgical and theological language adequately to recognize the presence of women seems effectively to exclude them from full and integral participation in the life of the Church and this exclusion can prevent the whole Church from experiencing the fullness of Christian community."[2]

Many presiders and liturgy committees have responded to this new consciousness of gender-specific language by altering the biblical and liturgical texts as they are proclaimed, prayed, and sung in worship to reflect the value of inclusivity. Where, for example, the liturgical or biblical text addresses its audience as "brethren" or "brothers," persons sensitive to the effect of language on the assembly commonly substitute the words "brothers and sisters." Or where words like "man," "mankind," and "he" are used to refer

1. The science of anthropology has contributed greatly to the appreciation of the power of language. *See*, e.g., *Language, Thought, and Reality: Selected Writings of Benjamin Lee Whorf* (Cambridge, Mass.: M.I.T. Press, 1956); and Malcolm Crick, *Explorations in Language and Meaning: Towards a Semantic Anthropology* (London, England: Malaby Press, 1976).

2. Advisory Committee to the ICEL, "Statement: The Problem of Exclusive Language with Regard to Women," *Eucharistic Prayers for Study and Comment by the Bishops of the Member and Associate Member Countries of ICEL* (Green Book) (Washington: ICEL, 1980) 64–65.

**John M. Huels, O.S.M.**

to both men and women, inclusive terms such as "people," "persons," "humanity," "all," "we," "one," "they," and the like are substituted.

However, some Catholics, clergy and laity, although possibly supportive of the use of inclusive language in other contexts, consider such unauthorized changes in the liturgy as a direct violation of canon law.[3] Their position is justifiable by a literal reading of canon 846, §1 of the 1983 Code of Canon Law: "In celebrating the sacraments the liturgical books approved by competent authority should be faithfully observed; therefore no one on personal initiative may add, remove or change anything in them."

The aim of this essay is to demonstrate that canon 846, §1 does not prevent liturgical ministers from changing certain kinds of masculine words in the officially approved liturgical texts to make them inclusive. The first section of the essay points to the use of inclusive language as a matter of justice and, consequently, to the implication that its use in the liturgy should be regarded as favored or even required by the Church's law. Second, there is a consideration of the "mind of the legislator" to establish how the competent Church authority views the issue of using inclusive language without express authorization. The next two sections examine the historical and theological contexts of canon 846, §1. This context reveals that the law does not intend to exclude liturgical ministers from making minor adaptations in the texts of the liturgy, provided these changes are in keeping with the nature and purpose of the liturgy itself.

The question of "God" language will not be addressed here because of its complexity. Masculine titles given to God, such as "Father," "Son," and "Lord," are steeped in biblical and theological significance, and they cannot be facilely changed in the liturgy without creating other problems.[4] In recent years, liturgists and

3. It is difficult to know how widespread this view is, but the experience of this writer indicates that it is a recurring question and one that troubles some liturgy presiders and some members of the faithful. It is also perplexing for diocesan officials who do not want to exclude the use of inclusive language but who do not know how to justify it legally.

4. Among these are canonical and liturgical problems. Canonically, one need only note the role that certain masculine titles for God have in the sacramental forms. The words "Father," "Son," and/or "Lord" occur in the ordination formulas for deacons, presbyters, and bishops. The word "Lord" is

other scholars have been studying the question of how God is addressed in the public assembly.[5] More study and dialogue is needed, in concert with Christians of other denominations, before general consensus on this issue will be achieved.

## Inclusive Language as a Justice Issue

The Second Vatican Council affirmed the Church's belief in the dignity and equality of all members of the body of Christ. The Dogmatic Constitution on the Church states: "In Christ and in the Church there is no inequality arising from race or nationality, social condition or sex."[6] This teaching is codified in the Church's constitutional law in canon 208 of the Code of Canon Law, the first canon in the section on the rights and obligations of all the

---

pronounced twice in the sacramental form for the anointing of the sick. The Trinitarian formula—Father, Son, and Holy Spirit—is constitutive to the sacramental forms for baptism and penance. Only the supreme authority of the Church, the pope or the college of bishops, may alter the sacramental forms (can. 841). Their utterance is necessary for the validity of the sacraments.

Liturgically, the words "Father," "Son," and "Lord" frequently are found in prayers and greetings that call forth a response from the assembly: "The Lord be with you"; "This is the word of the Lord"; "Through Christ our Lord"; "In the name of the Father, and of the Son, and of the Holy Spirit." They are standard utterances of ritual intended to evoke a common response: "And also with you"; "Thanks be to God"; "Amen." When other words are substituted by the minister, members of the assembly are often confused and participation suffers.

5. In a brief but thoughtful article, Kathleen Hughes and Ron Lewinski sketch some important principles for adapting the language of the liturgy. They recognize that all adaptations demand knowledge, time, and energy, and thus "it is important to exercise great restraint and care in this moment of transition. We need always to remember we are proclaiming the faith of the church to which our communities must be able to say Amen." *See* "Inclusive Language in the Liturgy," *Liturgy 80* 18 (July 1984) 14–15.

Gail Ramshaw has written extensively on the subject of God language in the liturgy. Some useful studies include her *Worship: The Search for Liturgical Language* (Washington: The Pastoral Press, 1988); *Christ in Sacred Speech: The Meaning of Liturgical Language* (Philadelphia: Fortress, 1986); "Naming the Trinity: Orthodoxy and Inclusivity," *Worship* 60 (1986) 491–498; "*De Divinis Nominibus:* The Gender of God," *Worship* 56 (1982) 117–131.

Another balanced discussion of the issue is found in Mary Collins, "Naming God in Public Prayer," *Worship* 59 (1985) 291–304.

6. LG 32.

**John M. Huels, O.S.M.**

faithful: "Among all the faithful, in virtue of their rebirth in Christ, there is a true equality of dignity and action; all cooperate in the building up of the Body of Christ in accord with each one's own condition and function."[7]

Since men and women enjoy equal dignity in the Church, Christians are bound in justice and by law to support efforts that promote equality between men and women and to avoid whatever diminishes the authentic equality and dignity of the baptized. Such efforts include the proper use of inclusive language in the liturgy and in other contexts. In a 1989 document of the bishop-presidents of six national episcopal commissions of the Canadian Conference of Catholic Bishops, the promotion of inclusive language is explicitly recognized as a justice issue. "As Christians, we are called to witness to the fundamental equality and dignity of all people. This involves diverse actions for social justice which protect and promote human life and dignity. One relatively simple but effective action is the use of inclusive language. . . . Using inclusive language is one way of emphasizing the Church's responsibility to take a stand against one of the widespread forms of discrimination found in our society."[8]

Canon 222, §2, also part of the Church's constitutional law, obliges all the faithful to promote social justice, and several other canons in the code are devoted to justice issues and the Church's teaching on the dignity and equality of persons.[9] On the basis of these laws and teachings, one could argue that the use of inclusive language in the liturgy is not only desirable, it is obligatory as well. To the extent that inclusive language is a matter of justice affecting the dignity and equality of Christians, all Catholics are bound to promote its use, since all are bound to promote social justice.

7. *See* Sharon Holland, "Equality, Dignity and Rights of the Laity," *The Jurist* 47 (1987) 103–128.

8. "To speak as a Christian Community: Pastoral Message by Bishop Members of the CCCB Pastoral Team on Inclusive Language," Canadian Conference of Catholic Bishops document, no. 614 (July 28, 1989) 2, 4.

9. Can. 222, §2 states: "The faithful are also obliged to promote social justice and, mindful of the precept of the Lord, to assist the poor from their own resources." *See also* cans. 287, §1; 528, §1; 747, §2; 768, §2. For a study of these and other pertinent canons *see* Terence T. Grant, "Social Justice in the 1983 Code of Canon Law: An Examination of Selected Canons," *The Jurist* 49 (1989) 112–145.

**Liturgy, Inclusive Language, and Canon Law**

## The Mind of the Legislator

A primary rule in canonical interpretation is to attend to the *mens legislatoris*—the mind of the legislator—in attempting to understand any legal text (can. 17). This does not mean the interpreter must try to guess what are the private and subjective intentions of the legislator, whether pope, diocesan bishop, council, or other legislative official or body. It does not matter what the legislator might personally think about inclusive language or any other issue. Nor does it matter whether the legislator is perceived to be conservative or progressive on such questions. What is significant in the art of canonical interpretation is the "mind" of the legislator that is recoverable from objective data. This could include such factors as the historical situation that gave rise to the law, the law's theological underpinnings, its relation to other legal texts, its application and enforcement by Church officials, and the way it is understood in the customs and practices that have grown up in the Christian communities.[10]

On the issue of inclusive language, the legislator in question is primarily the conference of bishops. The episcopal conference of each nation or region is the competent authority for overseeing the preparation of translations of liturgical and biblical texts (can. 838, §3; 825). Since the question of using inclusive language is largely a matter of the translation and adaptation of the original languages into the vernacular, it follows that one should look to the views of the episcopal conference of each nation to determine the "mind of the legislator" on this question.[11]

---

10. On the interpretation of canon law, *see The Art of Interpretation: Selected Studies on the Interpretation of Canon Law* (Washington: Canon Law Society of America, 1982). On the interpretation of liturgical law, that is, the canons and other laws of the Church regulating the liturgy, *see* John Huels, *Liturgical Law: An Introduction,* American Essays in Liturgy 4, series ed. Edward Foley (Washington: The Pastoral Press, 1987); and Huels, *One Table Many Laws: Essays on Catholic Eucharistic Practice* (Collegeville: The Liturgical Press, 1986) ch. 1.

11. It must be noted that the legislative competence of episcopal conferences is restricted in the law. According to can. 455, all conference decrees must be submitted to the Apostolic See for review *(recognitio)* before they can be promulgated. Although this review in effect constitutes a kind of approval of the legislation by higher authority, the conference itself, not the Holy See,

**John M. Huels, O.S.M.**

142

In 1975 the bishops from English-speaking episcopal conferences who make up the Advisory Committee for the International Commission on English in the Liturgy (ICEL) expressed their concern regarding discriminatory language in liturgical texts: "The Advisory Committee recognizes the necessity in all future translations and revisions to avoid words which ignore the place of women in the Christian community altogether or which seem to relegate women to a secondary role."[12]

In 1980 the Advisory Committee issued an expanded statement establishing principles for the use of inclusive language in all future translations of liturgical texts. Not only does the statement address future translations, it also approvingly acknowledges that individual presiders and others have already been changing the official vocabulary in present liturgical texts that were translated before the principles of inclusivity had been enunciated: "Sensitive Christians have begun to remedy the problem of liturgical language that is discriminatory toward women by careful choice of a vocabulary which includes all people." The statement later adds that whenever women and men are together in the assembly, they are to be addressed as "brothers and sisters" or with other inclusive phrases, even if the authorized text says "brethren" or something else.[13]

The "mind" of the National Conference of Catholic Bishops of the United States (NCCB) on the issue of inclusive language, judging from its liturgy committee's actions and its own voting history on liturgical language, appears to be fully in accord with ICEL policies. A March 1, 1985 statement of the chairperson of the Bishops' Committee on the Liturgy is highly supportive of the use of inclusive language. Observing that the exclusive language used in liturgical texts translated before 1975 "now grates on the ear," the statement notes that the NCCB changed the institution narrative in the Eucharistic Prayers from "for all men" to "for all," and it ap-

---

is the true canonical legislator for its own decrees. *See* Frederick R. McManus, "The Scope of Authority of Episcopal Conferences," *The Once and Future Church: A Communion of Freedom,* ed. James A. Coriden (New York: Alba, 1971) 129–178.

12. Minutes of the Advisory Committee meeting, August 1975, quoted loc. cit., n. 2 above, p. 64.

13. Ibid., 66–67.

plauds efforts made by ICEL since 1975 to use inclusive language in its new translations and original texts.[14]

At the time of this writing, the Bishops' Committee on the Liturgy and the NCCB Committee on Doctrine are jointly preparing "Criteria for the Evaluation of Inclusive Language in Biblical Translations Proposed for Liturgical Use." The draft text says that language that addresses and refers to the worshiping community ought not use words or phrases that deny the common dignity of all the baptized. It explains that some words formerly were understood to be inclusive generic terms, such as "men," "sons," and "brothers," but today they are often perceived to refer only to males. "Therefore, these terms should not be used when the reference is meant to be generic."[15]

The National Conference of Catholic Bishops of the United States and other English-speaking conferences are committed to the use of inclusive language in the liturgy. The mind of the legislator is clearly supportive of such language. The problem is that most liturgical texts now in use were translated before 1975 when ICEL adopted its original statement on inclusivity. If a minister changes these texts before new translations are authorized, it might seem at first sight that canon 846, §1 is being violated. Moreover, canon law requires that all translations of liturgical texts prepared under the auspices of the conference of bishops are to be reviewed by the Holy See (can. 838, §§2, 3). Since the canons of the code represent papal legislation emanating from a higher-level authority than the episcopal conference, one could object that the "mind" of the episcopal conference on this issue cannot circumvent the literal wording of canon 846, §1, which prohibits all changes in the liturgical texts by individuals. Therefore, to be fully convincing, a legal justification for the use of inclusive language must take account of the meaning of this canon.

14. Chairman of the Bishops' Committee on the Liturgy, March 1, 1985, "The Revised Grail Psalter," *Thirty Years of Liturgical Renewal: Statements of the Bishops' Committee on the Liturgy,* ed. Frederick R. McManus (Washington: USCC, 1987) 247–251.

15. Seventh draft, May 30, 1990, unpublished, p. 10.

**John M. Huels, O.S.M.**

### Historical Context of Canon 846, §1

The deepest meaning and purpose of a law is rarely evident from the literal words of the legal text but may often be uncovered by studying its context. A standard rule of canonical hermeneutics is to look to the context of a law to understand its meaning (can. 17). The context includes not only the law's place and role within the document or text of laws itself but also its broader context, especially its historical and theological contexts.

The historical context sheds light on the circumstances that first gave rise to the law and its subsequent development in the course of time. Laws are often made in a dialectical context. A need in the ecclesial society arises (perhaps an abuse needs to be corrected), and a law is enacted in an attempt to respond to this need (to eradicate the abuse). However, laws by nature tend to be stable, and they often outlast their original purpose. Circumstances change with the progress of time, and old laws must be understood in new ways if they are to continue to be of service to the community. Otherwise they become obsolete. While technically remaining in force, such laws have little or no positive role to play in the life of the contemporary community and can even be harmful when attempts are made to enforce their literal meaning.

Canon 846, §1 is not a new law. It has a history. It is based remotely on statements of Pope Pius XII in his 1947 encyclical, *Mediator Dei,* and more proximately on a statement from Vatican II's Constitution on the Sacred Liturgy. Pius XII taught that "the sovereign pontiff alone enjoys the right to recognize and establish any practice touching the worship of God. . . . Private individuals, therefore, even if they be clerics, may not be left to decide for themselves in these holy and venerable matters."[16] Vatican II stated in a similar vein that "no one, even if he be a priest, may on personal initiative add, remove, or change anything in the liturgy." This statement in the Constitution on the Sacred Liturgy, article 22, §3, is even more restrictive than canon 846, §1; it applies to all liturgical rites, not just the sacraments, and unlike the canon, it

---

16. *Mediator Dei,* November 20, 1947: *AAS* 39 (1947) 544; English trans. in R. Kevin Seasoltz, *The New Liturgy: A Documentation, 1903–1965* (New York: Herder and Herder, 1966) 123.

**Liturgy, Inclusive Language, and Canon Law**

specifically mentions that not even priests may make changes in the liturgy.

In examining the context of the restrictive statement of Pius XII in *Mediator Dei,* attention should first be called to the mentality of rubricism. "Rubricism" is a term used pejoratively for the approach to the liturgy before Vatican II. It was then widely assumed that good liturgical celebration required only the exact adherence to the many detailed laws, called "rubrics," printed in the liturgical books to guide the correct performance of the rites. Any deliberate infringement of a rubric was considered sinful; commentators on the liturgy would distinguish those rubrics which bound under penalty of mortal sin from those which bound only under penalty of venial sin. In this context, to assert that no one, not even clergy, could change anything in the liturgy was to say nothing more than what was common teaching and practice of the time. This same context certainly does not exist today. With the liturgical reforms of Vatican II, the rubricistic mentality, though evidently still alive in a few, is hardly the prevailing approach anymore toward the liturgy and liturgical law.

In looking further at the historical context of *Mediator Dei* in 1947, one finds that the restrictive statement about private persons not making changes in the liturgy was intended by Pius XII to be a reassertion of the exclusive authority of the pope over the liturgy, its laws, and liturgical change and experimentation. The modern liturgical movement was growing strong by the 1940s. *Mediator Dei* affirmed this movement and gave it new impetus; it was largely a positive document. However, the encyclical also manifested a fear that the movement might get out of control, hence the Pope's insistence on the rule that all liturgical change had to be authorized by the Holy See.

Although some important liturgical changes were introduced by Pope Pius XII,[17] key reforms in the order of Mass that affected the greatest number of Catholics did not come about until the pontificate of Paul VI, who had the task of implementing the conciliar agenda. Clearly, the Church had changed between *Mediator Dei* in 1947 and 1963, when the Constitution on the Sacred Liturgy was

17. *See* John Huels, "Participation by the Faithful in the Liturgy 1903–1962," *The Jurist* 48 (1988) 608–637.

**John M. Huels, O.S.M.**

promulgated. A new historical context had developed, one in which Church authority no longer felt threatened by the liturgical movement but instead gave it official approval and adopted its major objectives. Many practices that previously had been considered grave abuses, such as Mass in the vernacular with priest facing the people and Communion from the cup, were strongly encouraged or even required after the council. With an entirely changed context, canon 846, §1 calls for a different kind of interpretation than it would have been given in 1947 when a rubrical mentality prevailed and the liturgical movement was suspect.

Vatican II vindicated the liturgical movement. Many liturgical reforms that Pius XII did not adopt were authorized by the council and instituted by Pope Paul VI. Since the historical context had changed so greatly from 1947 to 1963, why was it necessary to include the restrictive-sounding statement against changing anything in the liturgy in article 22, §3 of the Constitution on the Sacred Liturgy? What is the historical context at Vatican II that gave rise to this statement?

The likely answer lies in the dialectical nature of the council. On all issues the council Fathers tried to achieve the broadest possible consensus, and this resulted in many compromises. Statements introducing significant reforms were placed alongside statements from the Councils of Trent and Vatican I and popes of that era. Certainly evidence of this kind of compromise can be seen in article 22 of the Constitution on the Sacred Liturgy, which, in its first and second paragraphs, ushered in one of the most significant liturgical reforms of the council, namely, the decentralization of authority over the liturgy. Unlike *Mediator Dei,* which contained a forceful assertion of the exclusive authority of the Holy See over the liturgy, the Constitution on the Sacred Liturgy partially restored the powers that bishops had enjoyed over the liturgy before Trent.

Following this major change in Church discipline stated in paragraphs 1 and 2 of article 22, paragraph 3 contains the restrictive statement against unauthorized liturgical innovations that harkens back to Pius XII in *Mediator Dei.* In the dialectical context of the council, doubtless a key purpose of such a statement was to reassure the conservative minority who did not want to change anything and who feared abuses if authority over the liturgy were to be extended to the bishops.[18] The restrictive third paragraph thereby helped bring about the consensus that ultimately resulted in the nearly unanimous favorable vote on the constitution as a whole.

The restrictive statement of Vatican II about not changing anything in the liturgy on one's own authority must be considered in the historical situation at Vatican II, namely, a dialectical context that resulted in many compromises to achieve the broadest possible consensus. Assuredly, this purpose for the restriction is no longer operative today. The council achieved virtual unanimity among participants on the objectives of the liturgical reform; the most vociferous opponents of the liturgical reforms have now been discredited and their leaders excommunicated.[19] Therefore, if canon 846, §1 is to be properly understood today, it must be interpreted within an entirely new context. This context is that of a new liturgy and a new spirit or attitude in applying liturgical law.

*Theological Context of Canon 846, §1*

Church laws frequently have some kind of theological underpinning—scriptural, doctrinal, moral, liturgical, or other. An adequate interpretation of Church law requires that the interpreter attend to the possible theological foundations for the law. Any interpretation of a liturgical law that ignores the theology behind the law is not a good interpretation. It is not faithful to the law's true meaning and spirit. It becomes mere legalism, a kind of canonical literalism akin to biblical fundamentalism.

All Church laws dealing with the liturgy must be understood within the overall context of the goals and principles of the

18. *See* Joseph A. Jungmann, "Constitution on the Sacred Liturgy," in *Commentary on the Documents of Vatican II*, vol. 1, ed. Herbert Vorgrimler (New York: Herder and Herder, 1967) 19–20.

19. Archbishop Marcel Lefebvre, the late leader of the Catholic traditionalist movement, Bishop Anthony de Castro Mayer, and the four priests they ordained bishops without authorization from the Holy See were all automatically excommunicated at the time of the ordination on June 30, 1988, in virtue of cans. 1382 and 1364, §1. The excommunication was publicly declared by a July 1, 1988 decree of the Congregation of Bishops. The decree also warned all priests and faithful not to assent to the actions of the schismatic Lefevre lest they, too, incur the penalty of excommunication for committing an act of schism. *See Communicationes* 20 (1988) 166.

**John M. Huels, O.S.M.**

reformed liturgy. Canon 846, §1 of the code and article 22, §3 of the Constitution on the Sacred Liturgy cannot be properly understood in isolation from the theology underlying the rest of the constitution, the postconciliar liturgical documents, and the revised liturgical books. This context reveals that the aim of the liturgy is to build up the body of Christ by prayerful and meaningful liturgical celebrations whereby God's people can participate fully in the liturgy in keeping with their ecclesial roles and their unique culture and customs.

What is true of the liturgy must also be true of liturgical law, which is intended to support the aims of the liturgy. Liturgical law, like all canon law, is promulgated by Church authority for the good of the Christian community. The purpose of liturgical law must be seen as supporting authentic and positive experiences of worship for the entire community. If a law is interpreted in a concrete situation without this good of the actual community in mind, it is a poor interpretation because it is not faithful to the law's spirit and purpose.

The Constitution on the Sacred Liturgy itself, in article 11, indicates that this is the proper methodology for interpreting and applying liturgical laws: "Pastoral ministers must be vigilant that in the liturgical celebration not only are the laws for liceity and validity observed but also that the faithful participate in it knowingly, actively, and fruitfully." In other words, the exact and literal fulfillment of the rubrics and other laws ought not to be the only consideration of the liturgical minister but, rather, how the law can be understood and enfleshed in ways that enhance the worship experience of the assembly. This is the purpose of liturgical law; this is its theological foundation. One's interpretation of the law and one's fidelity to it must always be within this context. Mere rubrical precision without fidelity to the spirit and purpose of the liturgy is no longer an adequate response to liturgical law.[20] Fidelity to the spirit of the law and the interpretation of the letter of the law in light of its spirit is the "new way of thinking" about canon law that Pope Paul VI challenged the Church to assume.[21] Anyone

20. See Thomas Richstatter, *Liturgical Law: New Style, New Spirit* (Chicago: Franciscan Herald Press, 1977).

21. See Ladislas Orsy, "The Meaning of *Novus Habitus Mentis:* The Search for New Horizons," *The Jurist* 48 (1988) 429–447.

**Liturgy, Inclusive Language, and Canon Law**

who approaches canon 846, §1 with the prevailing ecclesial mentality and liturgical theology of the 1940s cannot possibly find an adequate interpretation of this canon for the Church of the 1990s.

What, then, does canon 846, §1 mean in light of the new liturgy? What does it mean to say that in the celebration of the sacraments no one on personal initiative may add, remove, or change anything found in the liturgical books? In light of the liturgical reforms since Vatican II, it clearly does not mean a return to rubricism. Rather, it expresses the Church's concern that its sacramental celebrations be authentic experiences of Catholic worship, that its principal liturgical actions express the unity of Christ's body. Given the new context for this law, minor adaptations in the texts used at liturgy to make them more inclusive are by no means against the intent and spirit of canon 846, §1. On the contrary, because the purpose of the law is to promote the good of the community, the use of inclusive language best upholds the spirit of the law. In many places today the use of language that excludes women is considered offensive and rude. Instead of assisting the liturgy's goal of building up the body of Christ, ministers who use exclusive language at worship may unwittingly contribute to a sense of division and alienation among a significant part of the assembly.

Canon law, when interpreted in accord with its deepest spirit, does not exclude minor adaptations in the texts of the liturgy that are consistent with the liturgy's nature and ritual structure and that truly enhance the unity and prayerfulness of the celebration. Sometimes, however, liturgy planning and celebration fall victim to the latest fad or ideology as those in charge attempt to impose their ideas on the liturgy and the community. This causes resentment among those in the assembly who believe that the Church's liturgy is being abused or manipulated. They feel angry or indifferent rather than challenged and motivated. Even the promotion of a worthwhile social justice concern can do more harm than good if it appears to be an imposition on the liturgy instead of emanating from the liturgy itself.

If changes in the liturgy made by individual ministers cause frequent upset and divisiveness in the community, very likely they are not good adaptations. Also, if changes made by individuals offend against the liturgy's nature, ritual structure, and purpose, they are not good adaptations. They are abuses.

**John M. Huels, O.S.M.**

The principal purpose of canon 846, §1 is to avoid liturgical abuses so that everywhere in the world the sacraments of the Church are authentic expressions of Catholic faith and practice. The canon does not preclude good adaptations that support and enhance the worship experience. Knowing the difference between a good adaptation and an abuse often requires broader horizons than the merely canonical. Liturgical planners and ministers should be knowledgeable about Scripture, theology, and liturgy if they are going to be making adaptations, even minor ones. In addition to such knowledge, they must also have a respect for and sensitivity to their community that enables them to judge whether their adaptations will have the desired effect, whether such adaptations will indeed create better liturgical celebrations and contribute to the assembly's conversion of heart and moral action.

*Conclusion*

A good case can be made for asserting that the use of inclusive language in the public prayer of the Church is a matter of justice and, to the extent that this is true, that all Catholics are bound to promote its use just as they are morally bound to promote all matters of social justice. Bishops in the United States, Canada, and other countries have endorsed the value of using inclusive language in the liturgy. The episcopal Advisory Committee of the International Commission on English in the Liturgy has encouraged individual ministers to change liturgical texts in certain cases to make them inclusive.

Canon 846, §1 of the Code of Canon Law states that no one on personal initiative may add, remove, or change anything in the liturgical books when celebrating the sacraments. This may, at first sight, appear to prohibit individuals from using inclusive language when the official texts do not. However, when the historical and theological contexts of the canon are uncovered, it becomes clear that the spirit of the law, if not its letter, actually favors the use of inclusive language. The purpose for inclusive language in the liturgy is related to the deepest purpose of the liturgy itself, namely, the building up of Christ's body, the Church, as it is manifested concretely in local worship assemblies.

Most liturgical texts presently in use were translated into English before the principle of inclusivity was adopted by the ICEL Advisory Committee in 1975. However, ICEL is currently undertaking a thorough revision of the translations of the Latin texts of the order of Mass and is composing original English prayers for the Mass. Moreover, the Bishops' Committee on the Liturgy of the United States episcopal conference is in the process of preparing a second edition of the Lectionary. Sensitivity to inclusive language as well as to God language is a major value and goal of these efforts. The completion of these projects and their subsequent approval by competent ecclesiastical authority should contribute greatly to the goal of equality between men and women in the language of the liturgy.

**For Further Reflection**

1. Why is the use of inclusive language in the liturgy considered to be a matter of social justice?

2. What does "mind of the legislator" mean? What is the mind of the legislator regarding the substitution of inclusive language in the liturgy for language that is perceived to be exclusive?

3. How do the historical and theological contexts of 846, §1 shed fuller light on this law's proper interpretation?

**John M. Huels, O.S.M.**

Paul J. Wadell, C.P.

# What Do All Those Masses Do for Us? Reflections on the Christian Moral Life and the Eucharist

*Introduction*

In December 1983 Stanley Hauerwas, then a professor of Christian ethics at the University of Notre Dame, came to Catholic Theological Union at Chicago for a lecture. In a discussion that evening with some of the faculty, Hauerwas was asked what he thought about the U.S. bishops' recently released pastoral, *The Challenge of Peace.* Hauerwas responded that he was deeply impressed with the document but regretted that the bishops had not asked more of American Catholics. He wished the pastoral had gone beyond making pacifism an option for the American Church but had affirmed it instead as one of the distinct characteristics of a people who pledge to live the truth we find in Jesus. When the questioner suggested American Catholics would never accept pacifism, Hauerwas, a Methodist, responded, "You Catholics go to Mass all the time. Never underestimate what all those Eucharists do for you."

What do all those Eucharists do for us? It is an arresting question and one that goes to the heart of the connection between liturgy and the Christian moral life. For too long Catholics have made too sharp a distinction between what we do when we worship and how we live everyday. We presume praising God is one thing and living morally is something else; however, while it may be fitting to distinguish our communal prayer from our everyday behavior, it is misleading and dangerous to separate them entirely. Liturgy and Christian morality share a common goal: Both want to tutor us in the truth of Jesus so we can become as much like God as we possibly can. The strategy of Christian worship and the strategy of the Christian moral life are one. They seek to bring God fully to life in us and in our world. They work to remove all the things that obstruct the full flowering of God, whether that be in our hearts, in our relationships, or in the structures and institutions of society. As Enda McDonagh notes in *The Making of Disciples,* this is what is at stake in liturgy and moral life: the emergence or obstruction of the real God in God's own world.[1]

Liturgy and ethics seek the liberation of God into every aspect of our lives, our world, and creation. God fully alive, healing and redeeming us, binding us up and making us whole, is the steady focus of the Christian life. What needs to happen if God is to come fully to life in us? It is this question more than any other that illumines the connection between liturgy and Christian morality, and in this essay we shall explore it in two ways. First, we shall consider the Christian moral life as the ongoing endeavor of learning and being disciplined in the language of God, and we shall consider the Eucharist as a primary context for achieving this. Secondly, we shall speak of Christian morality as a training in right vision and examine how the Eucharist might help us achieve this.

### Christian Ethics as Learning the Language of God

Learning to be moral is something like learning a language. A language is a system of communication that grows up around a common life. We talk to one another because there is something we want to share. In the same way, the Christian moral life is a system of communication that grows up around the core conviction that for us Jesus is Lord. If this is the most compelling fact of our lives, then it is something we want to understand, to live, and to share. The Christian moral life is nothing more than the ongoing endeavor to live from the good we call Jesus, a good that bonds us together and reminds us of who we want to be. This is why we can speak of Christian morality as a community's conversation about the purpose and goal of its life. To have a language is to have a way of life. To be a Christian is to be given the language of God that comes to us in Jesus and to embrace a way of life we call discipleship. As we speak this language of God we are formed in it, and as we live it we become one with it. In this respect, the goal of the Christian moral life is to become articulate in the Word we call Jesus; in fact, so eloquently that we are his presence in the world. Why might this be?

1. Enda McDonagh, *The Making of Disciples* (Wilmington: Michael Glazier, Inc., 1982) 59.

**Paul J. Wadell, C.P.**

In *What Ethics Is All About* Herbert McCabe describes the Christian moral life as a community's endeavor to master the startling, scandalous language of God.[2] As McCabe sees it, Christian morality begins in God's communication of a Word to us. As John writes in the prologue of his Gospel, "In the beginning was the Word." In the beginning God speaks, God delivers a message, and the message has a name: Jesus, the Logos, the Word of Life. Every language is a matter of someone speaking and others trying to respond. In Jesus, God speaks to us. Our task is to hear the Word, to receive it into our lives, and to respond; however, we are to respond not in our native tongue, but in the often confounding language of God. To enter the Christian moral life is to allow the Word we call Jesus to become the grammar of our lives.

Jesus is the center of this new language because Jesus is not only a revelation about God but is also God's revelation about ourselves. Jesus can be seen as a word in two ways. He is the self-communication of God to us, but he is also God's disclosure of the meaning of our life and our world. Jesus articulates God, he bespeaks God, indeed he is the utmost explication of God. It is in and through Jesus that we come to know the heart and soul of God. But Jesus also articulates us to ourselves. When we look to Jesus we see who we most genuinely are. We see the kind of life that brings us to fullness. We see the attitudes, values, and behavior that enable human flourishing. More than anything, we see the radical and redemptive truth we are called to live. In the Word-made-flesh we fathom the truth about God and the truth about ourselves. This is why we can say that Jesus is not only a person to follow, Jesus is also a new language to learn. In Jesus a new language is spoken in our world, and it is nothing less than a dazzlingly new way of life. To live it is to be redeemed.

Thus, the Christian moral life is the steadfast commitment to learn the language of God that comes to us in Christ, to embody it, and to witness it to the world. We are to speak to others in the language in which God has spoken to us; we are to be the presence of Christ because we want to invite everyone to the same life and peace and joy that God has shared with us. We have found

2. Herbert McCabe, *What Ethics Is All About?* (Washington: Corpus Books, 1969) 126–173.

**What Do All Those Masses Do for Us?**

freedom and life in Christ, and we want others to know that same liberating passage from all that spells death to resurrection life. To do so, we must become adept in the Word. We must become fluent in the language of God. Our most basic moral challenge is to move from being stutterers of the Word to being eloquent proclaimers of the Word, for we know there is no other way to enter the life of God. Language and life go together for us. Just as it was through Jesus that God entered our world, so it is through Jesus that we pass into the life of God. Our goal is reunion with God, but what the Christian moral life reminds us is that we make our way back to God by following and imitating the one who is the Word of God; in other words, we enter the life of God through Jesus, the language of God. Jesus gives us access to God; that is why the language of God must become our own.

### The Language of God: Crossing Over to Something New

But that is not easy. As soon as we try to learn the language of God we discover how different it is. God's language is unlike any we have tried to speak before. It not only twists our tongues, it also changes our hearts. In Jesus, God invites us to see life in a revolutionary way. The divine language is so new and so different that when it is spoken in Jesus it sounds utterly strange to our ears. Not only do we fail to understand it, we are also threatened by it; we find the language of God too much for us.

We cannot learn the language of God by measuring it against other languages and other ways of life. We can only learn this language if we realize it involves nothing less than dying to one understanding of life and taking up another. Jesus involves us in something qualitatively different, which is why we must see discipleship as a fresh, clean start. As every disciple knows, following Jesus entails a break with the past and a reevaluation of everything we once considered important. If we stay with the language of God we recognize that at some point we have crossed over to a new way of seeing and thinking. We have undergone a conversion that marked the start of a new vision of the world. We are not in life as we once were; in fact, we are so different that the only way to capture the change is to confess that in Christ we have become a new creation. We have broken through to new life, we have become part of God's revolution. It is not so much a change of place

**Paul J. Wadell, C.P.**

156

as a change of person. We have arrived at different ways of evaluating and appreciating. We have come to a very different understanding of what is reasonable and expedient. In learning the language of God, we have entered God's revolution of love.

It is nothing less than catastrophic. Learning the language of God involves us in an ongoing transformation of how we think about everything. The language of God upends us. It explodes our sense of value and goodness and possibility because it takes its meaning from a God who calls us to question what we customarily accept and challenges us to embrace what we never before imagined. Christian ethics involves us in something startlingly different because it does not commence with our language but with God's language. In Jesus God speaks a language that affirms trust instead of betrayal, a language that seeks community instead of division, a language that works for generosity and service instead of domination and violence. Jesus speaks in a different tongue, a tongue that says all destructive powers will not prevail, a tongue that says power resides not with the language of death but with the language of life and love and mutuality, the language of peace, forgiveness, and healing. With the language of God the center has shifted; a new world has begun.

But it is not, at least initially, a world of which we want to be a part. We like to think we are faithful disciples and at one with Jesus, but for much of our life Jesus is more a scandal than a friend. One of the most confounding ironies of the Christian story is that God comes to offer us life, but we respond by putting God to death. The language of God is the promise of new and never-ending life, but strangely enough it is a promise we reject. We say we want the life and hope Jesus brings, but when we have the chance to embrace it we turn away. At least initially, we are scandalized by the ways of God. Jesus comes to commence a revolution from death to Easter life, but the revolution is rejected. The world that needs the Word spurns the Word. Jesus is the language that frees us for life, but he is not a language we readily embrace; indeed, as the cross starkly testifies, Jesus is the language we try to silence, the Word we put to death. From the cross we see that the strange thing is the continuous thing: In Jesus God's love becomes our life, but that life is refused. We need the language of God, but we choose to remain with the language of death. In the shadow of

**What Do All Those Masses Do for Us?**

the cross we see that God offers to reconstruct the world according to perfect love, but we kill such love because we fear it. McCabe explains this well:

> After the crucifixion, to interpret the defect of the world as sin, to interpret it, that is, as involving the rejection of the Father's self-giving, is the same as to say that given the sin of the world, the crucifixion was bound to happen. It is to say that this is the kind of world we have, a crucifying world, a world doomed to reject its own meaning. In so far as a man calls men to a deeper kind of humanity, in so far as he offers them, not just in theory but in practice, a more human mode of communication, he will be rejected by mankind. The openness of love becomes the vulnerability of the victim. If you love enough you will in the long run be killed. . . . The Son of God did not come to us in order to be crucified, but since he comes to be a totally loving, totally human being, it was inevitable that he would be crucified. At least we can see this now by hindsight. What he came to do was to bring a new life, a new form of human communication out of this crucifying world. His resurrection means that this is possible.[3]

### The Eucharist: Encountering and Learning the Language of God

What might all this have to do with the Eucharist? If the above analysis is correct, it suggests we have to be trained in the language of God, and one place that that can occur is in the Eucharist. To change from being a person who crucifies the Word to being a person who lives it implies a drastic remolding of the self, and the Eucharist should help us achieve this. If the moral life is a matter of learning and appropriating the language of God, a language we first not only resist but work to destroy, then the Christian life involves a total reconstruction of the self from the deadly ways of sin to the life-giving ways of God. That is exactly what it means to become a disciple, and the Eucharist is a most fitting place for learning and growing in discipleship. To be a disciple is to submit ourselves to being disciplined in the surprising, often confounding, ways of God. We encounter those ways in the Eucharist when we listen to the Word of God and take that Word to heart. It is thus that God comes fully to life in us.

3. Ibid., 132–133.

**Paul J. Wadell, C.P.**

What do all those Eucharists do for us? Can we possibly celebrate them for a lifetime and remain the same? Hopefully not. To celebrate the Eucharist is to step into a story that illumines the meaning and direction of our life. The saga of creation, covenant, redemption, and restoration is not a narrative we are to view from afar, but precisely the story that governs our understanding of reality and our sense of what our being in the world involves. It is not so much that we bring our world to these stories of God we find in the Scriptures, but that we let the stories constitute and shape our world. These are not incidents from a far-off past to which we occasionally turn, but the stories by which we want to know and understand life now. Put differently, it is not our experience that led to the creation of these stories, but the stories—the Hebrew Scriptures and the New Testament—that indicate what our experience in the world most truly involves.

To be a Christian is to place our life in the center of a story of God we want to make our own. We do not inhabit this story passively; rather, we strive to appropriate it. We want to embody its viewpoints and perspectives; we wish its values and vision to be our own. We want to grow so at home in the saga of Israel and Jesus that it gradually reformulates not only our reading of the world but also our understanding of ourselves. In short, in Eucharist we place ourselves in the narratives in light of which we are to comprehend everything. We grasp rightly what these stories entail when we realize we are not to use them to help us understand bits and pieces of life otherwise opaque, but when we see that these stories of God's dealings with the world collectively describe the drama every life is. This is what George Lindbeck means when he says, "A scriptural world is thus able to absorb the universe. It supplies the interpretative framework within which believers seek to live their lives and understand reality. . . . It is the text, so to speak, which absorbs the world, rather than the world the text."[4]

We are to see ourselves in these stories. We are to read the world by them. When we hear the account of God's offer of covenant to Israel and Israel's infidelity, we are not to listen nostal-

4. George Lindbeck, *The Nature of Doctrine: Religion and Theology in a Postliberal Age* (Philadelphia: Westminster Press, 1984) 117–118.

gically but to see the story as a grammar of our experience now. Or when we see Jesus forgiving sins and setting people free, we are not to project that healing into an out-of-reach past but are to realize Jesus summons us to repentance and new life today. To gather in Eucharist is to enter once more into the narratives we take to be normative for our lives. It is the story we not only want to live, but the story we also want to work on us, to change us, to turn us inside out from sin to resurrection life. As Lindbeck puts it, "To become a Christian involves learning the story of Israel and of Jesus well enough to interpret and experience oneself and one's world in its terms. A religion is above all an external word . . . that molds and shapes the self and its world, rather than an expression or thematization of a pre-existing self or of preconceptual experience."[5]

What do all those Eucharists do for us? They mold and shape our self, they fashion us in the attitudes and virtues of Jesus. However strange these stories of God might first seem to us, and however resistant we initially may be to them, we enter them and struggle to let them change us because we know their endless chorus of sin and restoration chronicles what must happen to us if we are not to end up with a life we ultimately regret.

*The Eucharist: A Summons to Participate in the Life of Christ*

It is through the constant rehearsal of the stories of God in the Eucharist that we learn to love the language of God. Liturgy puts us in touch with the common memories of a people. But to remember is not to look back; rather, it is to bring the past to bear on the present in order to shape life a certain way. Remembering is an act that makes pivotal past events contemporaneous. Remembering is an act of belonging, for to remember is to recall and appropriate the stories and traditions we want to illumine our lives; it is to say that here in this history is where we stake our lives. In Eucharist we pledge to do our lives in memory of Jesus, but that remembering is no abstract, intellectual exercise. To remember Jesus in Eucharist is to make Jesus the one in whom and through whom we want to live now. What makes the Eucharist such a dangerous ritual is that it releases Jesus from the confinement of the

5. Ibid., 34.

**Paul J. Wadell, C.P.**

past so that he can live in us now, calling us from sin, challenging us, working the rehabilitation we long resist.

The Eucharist, if celebrated properly, should never be nostalgic consolation for us. What it is and should be is a summons to participate in the life of Christ. To remember Jesus in Eucharist is to be a member of his followers today. To do our lives in memory of him is to become part of his life, death, and resurrection. The remembering constitutive of the Eucharist releases Jesus into the present. What celebrating the Eucharist does is allow Jesus to relate to us redemptively every day of our lives. As Enda McDonagh puts it, "In Christian liturgy, the primary events are the life, death and resurrection of the primary person, Jesus Christ, but not as an isolated person or remote past figure but as the fount and head of a people brought into being and continuously shaped by him and these events."[6] Or as he says more pointedly, "Remembering in Christian liturgical terms is sharing. Person and events are not merely recalled but participated in."[7]

To celebrate Eucharist is to let Jesus be the paradigmatic shaping event of our lives, and that always entails some kind of surrender. There is a dual handing over in the Eucharist. In Christ God is handed over to us, a surrender captured beautifully in Graham Greene's poignant reflection that "we have a God we can hold in our hands." But there is something stunted and incomplete about any Eucharist that is not completed by the surrender of ourselves unto God. Eucharist involves mutual surrender. God surrenders God's being to us in Christ, but likewise are we through Christ to surrender ourselves to God. Put differently, if in the Eucharist we can hold God in our hands, it should also be true in the Eucharist that God draws us into the divine embrace. The giving and the taking, that is the heart of Eucharist, and we celebrate it profoundly only when God's offer to us is met by our offer to God.

What becomes of us if we make this oblation week after week? We become a new creation. With the Eucharist, to remember is to reform. In the gradual, piecemeal surrender of ourselves to God we are remade in the goodness of Christ. All those Eucharists should make us godly, not instantaneously, but cumulatively if we

6. McDonagh, *The Making of Disciples*, 39.
7. Ibid., 39.

**What Do All Those Masses Do for Us?**

enjoy enough of a history with this sacrament to submit to the conversion every Eucharist implies. It is here that liturgy and Christian ethics converge, for if the purpose of the Christian moral life is to tutor us in the language of God, the Eucharist is the ritual activity by which that language is heard, practiced, and eventually embodied. The strategy of the Eucharist, like the strategy of Christian morality, is to let God come fully to life in us. Anyone who has taken discipleship seriously knows this is not easily achieved, but anyone who has prayed and worshiped wholeheartedly knows that through the Eucharist we can loosen the grip of sin in our lives and come to shine in the loveliness of God. This is why Christian morality and the liturgy ultimately are one, and why the Eucharist is the most morally charged event in the Christian life. Through the Eucharist we not only change, we become godly—we take on "the mind and heart of Christ"—and Christian morality wants nothing less.

### The Importance of Vision in the Christian Moral Life

There is a second way we can consider the relation between Christian morality and the Eucharist, and that is to speak of the Eucharist as a training in moral vision. What might this mean? It may be best to begin with an example. There is a scene in John Steinbeck's novel *East of Eden* in which Samuel says to the Chinese servant Lee, "You are one of the rare people who can separate your observation from your preconception. You see what is, where most people see what they expect."[8]

Samuel is right: Lee is rare. Most of us see not what is, but what we expect to see or need to see. And while that may be normal, it has moral consequences because what we do not see may be what we need to see in order to be good. There is a tight connection between our perceptions and our behavior because how we act in a situation turns largely on how we see it. Ordinarily we think of morality solely as a matter of acting; however, it is also a matter of seeing. Vision and virtue go together because we cannot act rightly unless we first see rightly. This is why a situation misperceived gives birth to misguided behavior. In the moral and spiritual life we need conversion not only in what we do, but also in how we

8. John Steinbeck, *East of Eden* (New York: Bantam Books, 1975) 187.

**Paul J. Wadell, C.P.**

see. Could the Eucharist play a role here? What might all those Eucharists we celebrate do for our moral vision? A second way of capturing the moral importance of the Eucharist is to speak of it as the ritual activity through which a people's vision is cleansed and healed. More strongly put, through worshiping together in Eucharist we should gradually take on God's view of things. That may sound outlandish, but it is exactly the moral vision required if we are to attain the special goodness Christians call holiness.

### Fantasy as a Problem in the Moral Life

The problem, however, is that seeing things as God does is often the last thing we want to do. There is a stubborn tendency in each of us to distortion. We do not want to see things as they really are, but as we need them to be. Instead of reverencing the world, we twist it to meet our needs. Instead of respecting other people, we manipulate them to fit our plans. This is why Iris Murdoch says the basic moral challenge is to "pierce the veil of selfishness" in order to see the world as it really is.[9] We cannot possibly become good unless we learn to see rightly, but that is a nettlesome challenge for all of us because, at least occasionally, fantasy is stronger than the truth.

We tend to think that the enemy of the moral life is weakness of will or malicious intentions, but far more often, Murdoch contends, it is fantasy. She describes fantasy as "the proliferation of blinding self-centered aims and images"[10] and suggests it is often what masters our hearts. People lost in fantasy have a dangerously skewed reading of the world. They are so absorbed in themselves that they have lost all grasp of what is real; they are too deceived to be good. To fantasize is to drown in illusion. A person of fantasy is someone who has withdrawn from what is real. He or she has retreated into a dream world of soothing images, a world turned wholly to their needs. Unable to respect the preciousness and uniqueness of what is not themselves, they seek refuge in a fortress of delusions. They see everything—other people, creation, all of life—not for what it is, but only for what it can do for them,

9. Iris Murdoch, "The Sovereignty of Good over Other Concepts," *The Sovereignty of Good* (London, England: Routledge & Kegan Paul, 1970) 93.
10. Ibid., 67.

**What Do All Those Masses Do for Us?**

which is why fantasy is manipulative and self-serving; it is the imposition of ourselves and our needs on reality.

Fantasy is neither harmless nor benign. If we see the world through the lens of fantasy our actions will reflect it, whether we are individuals, communities, or nations. We can only choose and act within the confines of what we see, but what if what we see is not what is? How we behave in a situation turns on what we think is going on. If we see one way instead of another our behavior will reflect the difference. But if our actions are the work of fantasy, then what we do, however unintentionally, will at best be flaccid and at worst bring harm. If what we see is not what is, we misfire in our desire to do good. Virtue is born from vision, and that means a splendid moral action is rooted in a truthful grasp of reality. It is not fantasy we need but enlightenment.

### A Story of a Woman with Uncanny Perceptions

We cannot separate our behavior from our perceptions. An example of this is chronicled in *An Interrupted Life,* the diary of Etty Hillesum, a young Jewish woman who lived in Amsterdam during World War II and met her death in Auschwitz. Etty had an uncanny ability to shape the perfect deed. She always seemed to know how to do exactly what needed to be done, but her virtuosity was not luck; rather, it was the work of a kind and loving gaze upon the world.

One day in the early years of the war Etty sees her old college professor, Bonger, walking near the skating rink by her home. Immediately she senses something is wrong. Etty sees not the gruff, confident Bonger she knew in the classroom, but a man who looks broken and frightened. Without any hesitation Etty shapes the perfect deed. She goes out to Bonger, puts her arm around him, and begins to walk with him. "And he, fearless Bonger, was suddenly as defenseless as a child, almost gentle," Etty writes, "and I felt an irresistible need to put my arms round him and to lead him like a child and so, with my arm round him, we walked on across the Skating Club. He seemed a broken man and good through and through."[11]

11. Etty Hillesum, *An Interrupted Life* (New York: Washington Square Press, 1981) 23.

**Paul J. Wadell, C.P.**

164

Etty performs the flawless gesture. In every situation we are invited to respond in a fitting way. Etty's gift was knowing how to respond to the shape of all the situations she encountered, but she could act well because she first perceived well. As the incident with Bonger testifies, Etty knew how love was meant to be practiced because she could recognize the grace hidden in every situation. No indiscriminate responder, Etty shaped each deed according to what the situation required. In doing so, Etty reminds us of the relationship between love and goodness and justice, and our perceptions. In order to do good, to love rightly, and to act justly, we must first perceive the shape of the situation before us and what it demands. If we are locked in fantasy and illusion, love, justice, and goodness are impossible for us because we misconstrue the nature of other people and our world. It is only when we see clearly the relation we have with other people and all of life that we can grasp what love, goodness, and justice truly are.

### The Eucharist: Learning to See with the Eyes of God

Can the Eucharist help us achieve this? Might it be a setting for nurturing the kind of vision requisite for goodness? There are many ways to speak of the moral importance of the Eucharist, but in light of our reflections we can describe it as a training in right vision, the ritual activity by which a people who acknowledge their blindness come before God to have their vision healed. What can and ought to happen through our celebration of the Eucharist is that our misperceptions are eased as we are formed into a people with a new and more truthful vision. In celebrating the Eucharist we should be lured gradually from the self-protective but deadly grasp of fantasy into enlightenment.

Consider the rhythm of the Eucharist. We begin by praising Christ for the divine mercy shown to us. At the opening of the Eucharist our posture is not one of self-assurance but of trust in God. This posture of trust is important because it provides the opening necessary for the Word to enter. We render ourselves available to the one in whom everything is rightly seen. There is in the Eucharist a movement from confession to reception. What begins in acknowledgment of God's mercy culminates in transfiguration. This opening of ourselves to Christ is how our tainted vision starts to be restored.

**What Do All Those Masses Do for Us?**

Through the Eucharist we can learn to "pierce the veil of selfishness" and see the world as it is because, however painstakingly, we take up a new center. No longer absorbed in ourselves, we are more and more absorbed in God. Unlike fantasy, the Eucharist cultivates a profound contemplation that is not a retreat from reality but a deeper and more intimate entry into all that is not ourselves, particularly the ultimate otherness of God. Through the Eucharist we respond to the call for a more radical engagement with the world, other people, and God. In this way the Eucharist edges us beyond the limited and often prejudiced boundaries of our own perceptions.

All this has to happen if we are ever to become good. What this analysis suggests is that moral and spiritual growth hinge on our liberation from fantasy, and that must happen if we are ever to touch the goodness, love, and holiness for which we are made. In order to become good our usual ways of seeing and thinking must be overturned. The Eucharist can play a vital role in this transformation because when the Word is received and freed in us it works a radical perceptual change. All those Eucharists do make a difference because by taking on the Christ who comes to us in bread and wine our whole orientation to reality ought to be altered. If we are open to the Christ we consume we will begin to read the world through his eyes. No longer clinging to fantasy, we are nudged closer to the point of view of God. Everything starts to look different to us because it is no longer seen through the falsifying lens of fantasy; rather, it is all seen through the one we say is the light of the world.

How so? In celebrating the Eucharist we not only open ourselves to the Word, we are also changed according to the Word. When we begin the Eucharist we confess that our vision is corrupted; however, we come to the Eucharist because we know it is in Christ that our vision is restored. This restoration occurs not by Christ working apart from us but by Christ working graciously within. Our ability to see and act rightly is proportionate to our likeness to Christ, and through the Eucharist this likeness should be acquired and enhanced. All those Masses do make a difference.

In his *Summa theologica,* Thomas Aquinas calls the Eucharist food for the soul and says "this sacrament does for the life of the spirit all that material food and drink does for the life of the body,

**Paul J. Wadell, C.P.**

166

by sustaining, building up, restoring and contenting."[12] But there is a crucial difference between food for the body and food for the soul. When we eat a meal, Aquinas observes, the food we consume is digested and assimilated into our bodies to nourish and strengthen us. It is not we who are changed according to the food, but the food that is changed according to us. But with spiritual food it is different. When we eat the Body and drink the Blood of Christ, it is not Christ who is changed according to us, but we who are changed according to Christ. Feeding on Christ, we are transfigured in Christ. As Aquinas puts it, "Spiritual food changes man into itself. This is the teaching of Augustine in his *Confessions*. He heard, as it were, the voice of Christ saying to him, 'You will not change me into yourself as you would the food of your flesh; but you will be changed into me.'"[13]

Again we see the moral life and the liturgy converge. To be moral we must act rightly, but we cannot act rightly unless we have acquired the kind of moral vision capable of genuine goodness. Morality begins with the cleansing of our vision, and the Eucharist can be an important context for achieving this, because through the proclamation and reception of the Word, the darkness of fantasy is scattered by the light of the one through whom everything is truthfully and lovingly seen. When we eat the Body and drink the Blood of Christ we take on everything about him, we consume him entirely, his attitudes, his outlook, his values. To eat the Body and drink the Blood of Christ is to take Christ to heart, it is to allow Christ to affect every dimension of our lives, including our viewpoints and perceptions; these too must be subject to conversion, otherwise our worship is dishonest. We should not underestimate the cumulative effect of all the Eucharists we celebrate because to feed on Christ is to be changed by him. It is a transfiguration, the acquisition of a new and redeemed self, a self better able to view the world with the eyes of God. To seek that is not to hope for too much; on the contrary, it is what ought to happen from a lifetime of taking Jesus to heart.

12. *Summa theologica*, III, 79, 1.
13. *Summa theologica*, III, 73, 3.

**What Do All Those Masses Do for Us?**

## Some Conclusions

What do all those Masses do for us? In this essay we have seen that the Eucharist is the most morally charged moment of our lives. We may not customarily think of it that way, but is it not true that there is nothing more moral than encountering the God who wishes to redeem us? Christian morality and Christian liturgy converge in the goal of liberating God to fullness in ourselves and in our world. The full flowering of God in each of us describes a people wholly redeemed. But how does such a drastic reconstruction of the self take place? We considered two ways.

First, we examined the transformation that comes to us when we devote ourselves to learning the language of God that is Jesus. It is not a language we immediately embrace because God speaks in a way that challenges our world, judges our sinfulness, and calls us to leave death behind. There is much in each of us that resists the Word that must become our own. But that is precisely why the Eucharist is so important in the Christian moral life. Through the Eucharist God enters our world and we enter God's. We not only listen to the stories of God, we become part of those stories, we let them guide and govern our lives. Through the Eucharist we are broken into the language of God. We hear the Word spoken to us, we grapple with it, eventually we take it to heart. The transfiguration we undergo is leaving behind the features of sin and taking on the features of Christ; that is what it means to be redeemed.

The second way we spoke of the moral importance of the Eucharist was to consider it a setting for achieving the kind of vision and enlightenment necessary for virtue. Morality is ultimately about how we practice our lives. It concerns behavior, it focuses on everyday activity. As Christians we know we are to practice love and justice; we are to embody the virtues that not only enable us to do good but also allow us to become good. Morality issues in right action, but we noted that right action is born from a contemplative vision of the world. We cannot act rightly unless we first see rightly; however, we do not acquire vision by opening our eyes, we acquire it by changing our hearts. Sin affects how we see. Sin turns us to fantasy, skewing our vision so that we twist everything to ourselves. Like any sin, fantasy is never benign because its harvest is always injustice, whether that be to other people, nations, or the environment. This is why we said becoming good de-

**Paul J. Wadell, C.P.**

168

mands a cleansing and healing of vision, it requires enlightenment. And we suggested the Eucharist can be important here because by opening our hearts to Christ we are gradually assimilated to the one in whom all things are seen for what they truly are; in short, through the Eucharist we should acquire God's view of the world.

What do all those Masses do for us? They should make us a new creation. They should help us live a paschal life. No one should be able to celebrate Eucharist and remain the same. If that happens something is wrong, the power of the Eucharist is being thwarted. What should happen is that through the Eucharist all of us are freed from sin for God. And that means we are free for life, free for peace, free for a happiness and joy we have never tasted before. It is the joy of God fully alive in us. When that happens everything we are is worship, everything we do is good.

### For Further Reflection

1. What are some ways you see the liturgy shaping or influencing your understanding of the Christian moral life?

2. Do the ways we celebrate Eucharist now enable us to experience it as an important setting for growth and development in the Christian moral life?

3. What does it mean to you to speak of the Christian moral life as "the challenge to learn the language of God"? Why is the language of God so difficult to learn?

4. If we live the language of God we call Jesus, what kind of witness do we give to the world? What is it we have to offer the world?

Gilbert Ostdiek, O.F.M.

# Liturgical Catechesis and Justice

### Introduction

It is no secret that concern for justice has all too often in recent times suffered the fate of the marginated in the meeting halls and workplaces of catechists and liturgists. In discussing the social dimensions of catechesis in Asia in 1967, participants in the International Catechetical Study Week held in Manila that year reported: *"The liturgy* which has the possibility of instructing the Christian community does not seem to inspire a consciousness of the needs of social justice."[1]As regards catechesis itself, the report went on to note the heavy investment of personnel and resources in the sacramental catechesis of children, with no comparable investment in communicating the social teaching of the Church on a wide scale.

The problem cannot be dismissed as being peculiar to the Asian context. Fifteen years later and half a world away, John Egan drew attention to that same split between liturgy and social justice in our own experience of the liturgical renewal.[2]

These commentators, however, are not just bearers of bad news. They are also voices in a steadily growing chorus raised to insist that there is an intrinsic and essential connection between liturgy and justice, between catechesis and justice, and that good pastoral practice must restore that connection.

The purpose of this essay is to add yet another voice to that chorus.[3] Toward that end, the essay will offer a series of reflections, first on justice, then on liturgy and justice, and finally on liturgical catechesis and justice.

---

1. Cited in Michael Warren, ed., *Sourcebook for Modern Catechetics* (Winona, Minn.: St. Mary's Press, 1983) 63; emphasis theirs.

2. John Egan, "Liturgy and Justice: An Unfinished Agenda," *Origins* 13, no. 15 (September 22, 1983) 246–253.

3. I gratefully acknowledge the insights and help that Jeanette Lucinio, S.P., assistant professor of religious education and a faculty colleague, has contributed to the preparation of this essay.

*Justice*

The words "justice" and "social justice" have many meanings in everyday usage, from a socially accepted ethical norm that requires that we give people their due, to the legal system that protects such rights through law and the courts, to the moral conviction that leads people to commit themselves to lobbying and working for the rights of the poor and marginated. These meanings share a common presupposition rooted in the Latin origins of the word *(jus),* that justice has to do with rights and with law. This essay will take a slightly different tack, drawing a working understanding of justice from the biblical vision.

Though the Scriptures have no precise equivalent for our word "justice," *sedeq* and its cognates bear something of the meaning of "justice" or "righteousness." Several dimensions of the biblical usage pertinent to this essay can be named here without extensive explanation.[4]

First, justice is not an abstract concept or reality. Though the Hebrew root *sdq* literally means "a decision rendered," the biblical usage is concerned less with law and legal judgments than with relationships. Righteousness is a quality of the relationships between humans, or between humans and God, and is ultimately, therefore, a quality of the persons themselves. Justice binds them together in mutual fidelity and concern.

Second, justice has more to do with action than with being. A typical biblical phrase is "to do justice," "to exercise righteousness." Justice requires the partners in a relationship to show compassion in supplying the needs of the other, thereby preserving the relationship. The relationship need not be as intimate or close as that of family, kin, or neighbor; in Jesus' parable of the Good Samaritan, those who share our humanity and are in pressing need can lay a claim on our care. It was especially incumbent on the kings of Israel to act justly, and most of all toward the poor and the powerless.

Third, though justice is oriented to others and to action in biblical usage, it has overtones of inner personal integrity. Mercy and compassion are hallmarks of the way of living of those who are

4. *See,* e.g., Albert Descamps, "Justice," *Dictionary of Biblical Theology,* ed. Xavier Leon-Dufour (New York: Seabury, 1973) 281–286.

just, and when they are unjustly accused and called to account, the righteousness of their life and actions will be vindicated. Judgment does not render them just; it reveals the justice that is theirs.

Rooted in an inner personal integrity, fidelity, and mercy, justice is a way of being and acting that focuses on serving the needs of others. Such justice is not peculiar to humans alone; it is characteristic of God as well.

*The Justice of God*

In Israel's long experience, God is one who remains faithful to the covenant, who always acts to save the people. "Just deeds" and "acts of mercy" became shorthand ways to name the deeds by which God delivered the people (e.g., Judg 5:1; Mic 6:5; Dan 9:16; 1 Sam 12:7). In this usage, justice is attributed to God and becomes equivalent to salvation. The experience of the "just ones," the "suffering righteous," was particularly important in bringing about this shift in vocabulary. Only God can save them and vindicate their justice; indeed, the innocence of these "just ones" lays a claim on God's saving intervention on their behalf. And so, rather than simply being something they do, their justice is now God's gift of deliverance.

The God of Israel, however, is not only a God who does justice but also one who is just. Justice is frequently paired with fidelity, mercy, and compassion in describing this God. These qualities take on a special prominence in Jesus' teaching about the God who makes the rain to fall and the sun to shine on the just and unjust alike (Matt 5:45). No human being is excluded from these most basic forms of God's care.

God's justice is manifest not only in judgment and mercy; it is also revealed and embodied in the law God gives. This brings the biblical vision full circle. For the Jews, to follow and observe the Torah is to do justice, the justice of God. But God's justice is shown first of all toward the poor and the powerless, as the prophets clearly saw. Any who would do the justice of God, particularly those who represent God in positions of power, are called to exercise God's care for the poor. The prophets dreamed of a final time when empty cult would give way to justice surging like a tidal wave (Amos 5:24), when God would send a messiah-king who

**Gilbert Ostdiek, O.F.M.**

172

would "judge the poor with justice" (Isa 11:4), one whom the people would name "the Lord our justice" (Jer 23:6).

### Jesus, the Just One

For Christians, the justice of God finds its fullest revelation in Jesus, named the Just One (Acts 3:14; 7:52; Jas 5:6; 1 Pet 3:18; 1 John 2:1). This title, always associated in the Christian Scriptures with the death of Jesus, serves to underline that he is the "innocent suffering one." But is that the only meaning of this title? Is there not also an echo of the deep and abiding sense of justice, the commitment to do God's will in service of others that marked his preaching, his way of acting, his entire life?

The reign of God is central to the preaching of Jesus. His Sermon on the Mount portrays a God of the kingdom who is an indiscriminate God, a God whose saving invitation is extended to all. The parable of the great feast describes a realm for all to share, rich and beggar alike. Any who would belong to that kingdom must seek not only the kingdom but also "God's way of justice" (Matt 6:33). Jesus' injunctions about seeing all who are in need as our neighbors with a claim on our care, forgiving without limit, and praying for persecutors are all of a piece with that vision of the reign of God.

The deeds of Jesus are no different in spirit. From the very beginning of his public ministry, he chose the prophetic vision of God's anointed one sent to heal and to save as his mission statement (Luke 4:16-22). True to this call and to the message he preached, he excluded from his healing ministry no one who was in need. The inclusion he practiced in all his deeds of caring for the poor and outcast is mirrored and summed up most of all in his indiscriminate meal practice and in the charge leveled against him: "This man welcomes sinners and eats with them" (Luke 15:2).

Inclusion, however, was never coercion. Characteristically, Jesus taught by way of parables, inviting his hearers to leave behind their prejudices and presumptions and to look at their life situations in a new way. Parables do not prescribe how one is to act; they open up new insights, which in turn inspire new questions and a need to search for new answers. Jesus' actions, as well, are an invitation to human and religious wholeness: restoring sight invites faith; table sharing calls to pardon and reconciliation; healing of leprosy opens onto thankfulness and fidelity to the law. All the words and deeds of Jesus are marked by this respect for persons and their freedom.[5]

Jesus was, in all he taught and did, the Just One. And so, his death could not convict him of injustice; rather, in death he was revealed as the Just One, and God vindicated him and raised him up. But his justice was not simply that of a good human being. As Paul later intimates, what is revealed in him is the justice of God (see Rom 1:17; 3:21-26). Furthermore, God has made him "our justice" (1 Cor 1:30). "For our sakes God made him who did not know sin, to be sin, so that in him we might become the very holiness [justice] of God" (2 Cor 5:21). For Paul, then, Christ is both the justice of God and our justice; for the baptized, being in Christ is being in the justice of God.[6] What remains for the Christian is to follow this way of justice, that is, to give expression in action to the justice that has been received in baptism.

In sum, the Scriptures depict a God of justice whose care is extended to all, who acts to liberate the oppressed and to defend the poor, and whose will it is that all act in that same way. That portrayal is heightened in the teaching and works of Jesus, who uniquely personified the justice of God and was given, in death, the title of the Just One. Those baptized into him as followers of his new way are called to do justice, to manifest in their words and deeds the justice of God revealed in Christ. Action on behalf of justice is thus not something Christians can take or leave; it is a constitutive element of the gospel and of the Church's mission to follow it and to preach it.[7] Neither can justice be something peripheral to the liturgy, the "source and summit" of Christian living (CSL 10, DOL 10).

---

5. See Mark Searle, "Serving the Lord with Justice," *Liturgy and Social Justice,* ed. Mark Searle (Collegeville: The Liturgical Press, 1980) 30.

6. See Klaus Berger, "Justice," *Encyclopedia of Theology: The Concise Sacramentum Mundi,* ed. Karl Rahner (New York: Seabury, 1975) 790.

7. See the Synod of Bishops, Second General Assembly (1971), "Justice in the World" no. 6, *The Gospel of Peace and Justice: Catholic Social Teaching Since Pope John,* ed. Joseph Gremillion (Maryknoll, N.Y.: Orbis Books, 1976) 514.

**Gilbert Ostdiek, O.F.M.**

174

*Liturgy and Justice*

In reflecting on the connection between justice and liturgy, it may be well for us to begin with several reminders about liturgy.

First and most importantly, liturgy is the action of the risen Lord. He is present and active in the assembly as its liturgist (see Heb 8:2), leading the assembly through the presider and liturgical ministers, speaking in the proclamation of the gospel, and performing saving deeds in the celebration of the sacraments (CSL 7, DOL 7). The central event celebrated in the liturgy is the dying and rising of Christ. That moment of his dying and rising, as suggested earlier, summed up and gave final expression to his whole way of life, his "being for others." The liturgical renewal is slowly leading us to understand this great truth, that the crucified and risen Christ is present and acting in the entirety of the liturgy.

Next, the renewal has taught us that the liturgy is also the action of the entire assembly (CSL 7, DOL 7), not just of its public functionaries. Gathered in assembly, the baptized are invited to make Christ's action their own, to become one with the risen Lord as he continues to proclaim the coming of God's reign and to bring it about through his great act of giving himself in service of others. As Paul so aptly puts it: "It is through him that we address our Amen to God when we worship together" (2 Cor 1:20).

Such solidarity with Christ in celebrating the liturgy is not without consequences. The teaching of Vatican II on liturgy as source and summit is normally read to place liturgy at the center. It cuts the other way as well. The world in which we live and its needs are to be brought to the liturgy, as the restored prayer of the faithful attests. And the prayer after Communion and the dismissal of the renewed liturgy are gradually forming an awareness that those who take part in the liturgical remembrance of the Lord's words and deeds are sent back out into the world on mission, to be the leaven of the gospel and the test case for God's reign. Liturgy without gospel living is empty and pretentious. Those who celebrate the death and resurrection of Christ must join him in doing the justice of God and become with him the advocates and agents for the inbreaking of God's reign. Liturgy without action on behalf of justice is incomplete and unfinished. But how are we to be sensitized to that connection?

**Liturgical Catechesis and Justice**

## Liturgy for Justice

The first strategy that comes to mind is to make the connection overt in the liturgy itself. In times when there is great public awareness of injustice or when those committed to its redress gather to take action, we find it easy to introduce the theme of justice into our celebrations through the homily, the prayer of the faithful, and the choice of prayers and readings "For Peace and Justice" from the materials in the back of The Sacramentary and Lectionary.

This strategy has its merit and ought not be neglected. One of the functions of effective liturgy is to so tell the story of Jesus and his work for the coming of the kingdom that we are able to name both its presence and its absence in our world and, by his grace, to open ourselves to conversion and transformation at those points in our individual and collective lives where we have kept God's reign at bay. All liturgy ought to have what Searle calls a parabolic potential, that is, the potential "to subvert all human perspectives and to offer us a way of seeing the world from the vantage point of God's justice revealed in word and sacrament."[8]

But this strategy of doing liturgies for justice has its risks as well. As experience of the last decades teaches us, it is very easy to impose themes on the liturgy from without. Themes that seem artificial or that seem to be someone else's "cause" are easily dismissed as foreign and having no claim on our commitment. What is needed, then, is another strategy that bonds liturgy and justice in a more constant and integral way.

## Liturgy That Does Justice

Mark Searle offers us a starting point for such a strategy when he writes: "The liturgical assembly, then, is the place where justice is proclaimed, but it is neither a classroom nor a political rally nor a hearing. It is more like a rehearsal room where actions must be repeated over and over until they are thoroughly assimilated and perfected—until, that is, the actors have totally identified with the part assigned to them."[9]

8. Searle, "Serving the Lord," 31.
9. Ibid., 32.

**Gilbert Ostdiek, O.F.M.**

What is at stake here is the formative power of the liturgy itself. If it is of the very nature of liturgy to rehearse the justice of Jesus over and over so that we can identify with him and make his way of living our way, then what we need most of all is a liturgy that does justice. An unjust liturgy would contradict itself; it would form us not in the ways of the Just One, as liturgy claims to do, but in the unjust ways of the world.

In the Catholic tradition of examining one's conscience, perhaps a series of questions inspired by official documents on the liturgy can direct our attention toward areas that might prove basic to doing liturgy justly.

• Does our style of celebrating the liturgy not only tolerate, but positively enable and promote the presence and active participation of the faithful, which is their baptismal right (CSL 11, 14, DOL 11, 14)?

• Do we distribute the roles of ministry in the assembly rather than hoard them in the hands of a few (CSL 28, DOL 28)?

• In planning liturgy do we give the spiritual good of the assembly preference over our personal outlook (GIRM 313, DOL 1703)?

• Do we adapt the liturgy to the life circumstances, needs, and desires of the people, as all the rites now require, so that the experience of their daily lives and cultures can be named and transformed in the celebration?

• Do we set aside all distinctions, divisions, and classifications in our celebrations (EACW 32), and do we so word our prayers that all in the assembly, of whatever gender, race, or way of life, are included in our common prayer rather than left outside, on the margins?[10]

• Are our prayers of the faithful truly the responsible prayer of a priestly people offered for the needs of the Church and the world and its oppressed, rather than self-serving petitions (GIRM 45, DOL 1435)?

• Do we fashion and use symbols so that they are fully and authentically human and thus draw us and our world into the holi-

10. *See* ICEL, "Sexism in Liturgical Language," *Doctrine and Life* 32 (1982) 318–322. *See also* Barbara Reid, "Liturgy, Scripture, and the Challenge of Feminism" in this volume.

ness of God, or do we settle for a minimalism in our symbols (EACW 14)?

• Do we by our prayerfulness and sense of God's presence open up our symbols, especially the fundamental ones of bread and wine, water, oil, the laying on of hands, so that people can appreciate their meaning (EACW 15)?

• Do our seating arrangements facilitate full involvement of the assembly by clear lines of sight and access to its ministers, its central actions, and especially to one another (EACW 68), and do the seating arrangements indicate that those who minister not only lead the assembly but are clearly part of it (EACW 69)?

• Are presiders and liturgical ministers truly servants of the assembly (EACW 37) rather than its masters?

• Are our worship spaces, liturgies, and liturgical ministries truly accessible to all persons who are disabled (EACW 57)?

• Do our celebrations clearly communicate that no other symbol is more important than the assembly itself (EACW 28–29)?

These questions are only a sample. The point is this: If at any time we have to answer no to questions such as these, our liturgy is not yet a liturgy that does full justice. A liturgy that excludes, denies, oppresses, or treats unjustly and without respect our persons, our full baptismal status, our humanity, our life situations and cultural traditions, is, by that very fact, a "pedagogy of oppression."[11] Only a liturgy that does justice can form us in the ways of justice and inspire in us that fundamental consciousness of the needs of social justice that can be brought to full term in catechesis.

### Liturgical Catechesis and Justice

In keeping with recent ecclesial documents, catechesis is taken here as a ministry of the word, and more specifically as the continuation of evangelization.[12] Qualifying it as liturgical catechesis

11. For an extended discussion of this topic, *see* Tissa Balasuriya, *The Eucharist and Human Liberation* (Maryknoll, N.Y.: Orbis Books, 1979); Mark Searle, "The Pedagogical Function of the Liturgy," *Worship* 55 (1981) 332–359.

12. *See,* e.g., Vatican II, Decree on the Church's Missionary Activity, no. 17, and Decree on the Pastoral Office of Bishops in the Church, no. 14; the Sacred Congregation for the Clergy, *General Catechetical Directory* (Washington:

**Gilbert Ostdiek, O.F.M.**

can mean any of a number of things: catechesis *about* liturgy, where liturgy is the subject matter; catechesis *framed* by liturgy, where the catechetical sessions incorporate prayer and appropriate forms of celebration; catechesis *through* liturgy, where the liturgy itself is understood to have a formative power and to be the "first" catechesis; and catechesis *from* liturgy, where liturgical experience serves as a primary source for catechesis.[13] The last two aspects are of the most significance for these reflections.

From this perspective, liturgical catechesis begins with the celebration itself and presupposes that people truly experience the presence of God in the liturgical assembly, making them and their lives holy in God's sight. If this experience is lacking or if our liturgical actions and symbols block us off from it, liturgical catechesis can only talk about a meaning that is extrinsic to the actual experience of the liturgy. Liturgy is formative, by contrast, when it effects an "opening up of our symbols, especially the fundamental ones of bread and wine, water, oil, the laying on of hands, until we can experience all of them as authentic and appreciate their symbolic value" (EACW 15). When that happens, catechesis is in an ideal position to help people name and reflect on what they have already experienced in the liturgy. Good liturgical catechesis starts from the liturgy itself.

The highly symbolic way in which liturgy communicates is the key in shaping how liturgical catechesis is to proceed. Just as God's saving presence became enfleshed in Jesus of Nazareth and in all that he said and did, so, too, that saving presence continues to take on human embodiment in the assembly and in what it says and does. "The most powerful experience of the sacred is found in the celebration and the persons celebrating, that is, it is found in the action of the assembly: the living words, the living gestures, the living sacrifice, the living meal" (EACW 29). Liturgical symbols function by inviting participants to "see beyond the face of the person or the thing, a sense of the holy, the numinous, mystery" (EACW 12).

USCC, 1971) 17–18; NCCB, *Sharing the Light of Faith: National Catechetical Directory for Catholics of the United States* (Washington: USCC, 1979) 31–36.

13. *See* my *Catechesis for Liturgy: A Program for Parish Involvement* (Washington: The Pastoral Press, 1986) 7–21.

**Liturgical Catechesis and Justice**

In response to this symbolic, enacted character of the liturgy, liturgical catechesis will be less concerned with information and analysis than with helping people to dwell with delight in the symbols and to explore with both mind and heart the hidden and unspeakable mystery of God and themselves experienced there. For that reason, liturgical catechesis instinctively chooses to follow an action-reflection paradigm. Such catechesis begins with the story of people's experience, engages them in naming and reflecting on that experience in the light of the longer Christian story, and draws from that dialogue of stories an understanding of how they are to continue to live out their discipleship. Perhaps the best example of such a model of catechesis is to be found in the restored catechumenate. From personal stories elicited and listened to in the precatechumenate to the protracted telling of the great stories of the tradition during the catechumenate, through the reflective time of enlightenment to the time of mystagogy when the newly baptized dwell in their experience of the Easter sacraments and take their place in the life and ministry of the community, the catechumenate constantly alternates between action and reflection. This kind of approach is especially important if we are to develop the connection between liturgical catechesis and justice.

What, then, are some strategies for naming and exploring that connection?

*Liturgical Catechesis for Justice*

The first strategy is to make justice an explicit concern of liturgical catechesis. When the liturgy is a liturgy for justice, it openly proclaims justice in the readings, prayers, and homily, and it invites the assembly to action on behalf of justice. In such cases liturgical catechesis can easily become a catechesis for justice. Taking its cue from the call to action inherent in the biblical vision of justice and the liturgical rehearsal of Jesus' dying and rising, such catechesis will have as its primary aim to cultivate and nourish our sense of call and commitment to doing justice. At other times that call is not so apparent in the words and symbols of the liturgy, leaving liturgical catechesis a much more difficult task of listening and discerning what doing the justice of God in our world would mean. In either case, liturgical catechesis for justice will help people come to full awareness of that call.

**Gilbert Ostdiek, O.F.M.**

But there is another side to our liturgical symbols. Not only do they serve to connect us with the mystery of the God who is just and who calls us to a way of justice in Jesus; our symbols also bear the traces of unjust human action. Sharing bread and cup speaks of table fellowship, inclusion, and being "for others." It also speaks of exclusion, enmity, and oppression of others. Children are not the only ones who fight with food; peoples and nations also use food as an economic weapon and a tool of oppression.[14] Bathing someone in water means new life, belonging, and being entrusted to the care of others; it also portends death and the uncaring ways in which society washes its hands of the unwanted. Anointing with oil can also mean graduating the young into the ranks of the initiated without having to listen to them seriously; it can mean offering a healing presence to the sick without providing the larger ministry of care and companioning that gives anointing its full meaning. Laying on of hands can also symbolize pardon without the need for reconciliation and power that masquerades as service. The point is that the human symbols used in the liturgy have a dark side as well and often serve the cause of human injustice. Honest liturgical catechesis will also challenge us to listen with our hearts to hear the cries of the poor, which echo faintly in our symbols but are often drowned out in the more positive meaning we find in them.

Like liturgy for justice, liturgical catechesis that takes justice as its theme has its limitations. In espousing the cause of justice first experienced in the liturgy, it can, like liturgy for justice, become preoccupied with the subject of justice but neglect to act with justice. Another strategy is needed to provide that balance.

### Liturgical Catechesis That Does Justice

Thomas Groome offers us the rationale for such a strategy when he writes: "The Christian faith community must educate for justice and do so justly because the central theme in the preaching and

---

14. Joseph Grassi, *Broken Bread and Broken Bodies: The Lord's Supper and World Hunger* (Maryknoll, N.Y.: Orbis Books, 1985); Enrique Dussel, "The Bread of the Eucharistic Celebration as a Sign of Justice in the Community," *Can We Always Celebrate the Eucharist?* ed. Mary Collins and David Power (New York: Seabury, 1982) 56–65; Edward Foley, "Liturgy and *Economic Justice for All,*" in this volume.

life of Jesus was the reign of God. . . . Because the ultimate purpose of Christian religious education is to lead people out *(e-ducare)* toward the reign of God, it must educate justly and for justice."[15]

But how can liturgical catechesis educate justly? What would it look like? Liturgical catechesis that is just will manifest a number of qualities, some particular to it and some common to all catechesis.

First, liturgical catechesis, as the name implies, presupposes collaboration between those engaged in the twin ministries of liturgy and catechesis. Healthy modeling of interdependence and mutual concern for each other by these two ministerial cadres will not be lost on either worshipers or learners.

Second, liturgy and liturgical catechesis would both be seen as part of a larger, continuous pastoral ministry. Early accounts of two sacramental celebrations in the community, that is, the breaking of the bread in the Emmaus story (Luke 24:13-35) and the baptism on the first Pentecost (Acts 2:1-41), both illustrate a process in which evangelization, catechesis, liturgy, and mission go hand in hand. A process of pastoral care marked with ritual events accompanies those who are on their way to faith and discipleship. What this means, concretely, is that good pastoral practice assumes that there will be collaboration and coordination of liturgy and catechesis not only in practical matters such as scheduling but also in more important issues of the content and style of both.

Third, out of respect for the learners, as suggested earlier, liturgical catechesis best follows an action-reflection paradigm. Such an approach starts with the actual experience of the liturgy and respects the importance and uniqueness of that experience for each. It empowers people (1) to name and reflect on their experience, (2) to dialogue out of that experience with the experience of the past believers enshrined in the tradition, and (3) to make responsible decisions about how they will live out the implications of the liturgy in their lives. Such catechesis treats the learners and their freedom with full respect.

Fourth, as with all catechesis that educates justly, just liturgical catechesis attends to climate and environment, to ensure that

15. "Religious Education for Justice by Educating Justly," *Education for Peace and Justice,* ed. Padraic O'Hare (San Francisco: Harper & Row, 1983) 72 and 75.

**Gilbert Ostdiek, O.F.M.**

catechetical methods are enabling, that inclusive language prevails, and that interdependence replaces competition.[16]

Fifth, liturgical catechesis, like all catechesis, recognizes that its task is to foster mature faith and practice. Adult believers are as deserving of such catechesis as children, and the catechesis will, in justice, make use of the experience of adults and enable them to play a central role in their own education.

Finally, liturgical catechesis will remain especially attentive to the symbolic nature of liturgy. If the liturgy is truly just, using authentic symbols that honestly speak to people in their world and opening up the symbols to the experience of God that lies within, the catechetical process will then continue that opening-up process in a reflective context.[17] Catechesis is itself a ritual process that communicates nonverbally by how it is accomplished. Done justly, it will remain fully consonant with a just liturgy.

*Conclusion*

This essay has focused on the intrinsic connection between liturgy and liturgical catechesis on the one hand, and the justice of God revealed in the life of Jesus and made the standard for the reign of God on the other. If both liturgy and liturgical catechesis are done not only *for* justice but *with* justice, we will have laid a firm foundation for forming and instructing the Christian community in an awareness and habitual practice of a justice that truly announces and introduces the reign of God.

**For Further Reflection**

1. What concrete words or actions of the liturgy hurt you and make you feel excluded? Which make you feel accepted and included? Are there ways in which your community's liturgies

16. *See* Jeanette Lucinio, "The Pastoral's Challenge to Religious Education: The Living Word," *Economic Justice: CTU's Pastoral Commentary on the Bishops' Letter on the Economy,* ed. John Pawlikowski and Donald Senior (Washington: The Pastoral Press, 1988) 95–111.

17. *See* my "How Do Initiatory Symbols Come Alive for Adults?" *Before and After Baptism: The Work of Teachers and Catechists,* ed. James Wilde (Chicago: Liturgy Training Publications, 1988) 97–113.

make others, particularly those of other cultures or social classes, feel either welcomed or unwanted?

2. Do any biblical passages come to mind to help shed light on what you and others experience in such liturgies?

3. How can you work to improve the justness of your community's liturgical celebrations and liturgical catechesis?

**Gilbert Ostdiek, O.F.M.**

Anthony Gittins, C.S.Sp.

# The Dance of Life: Liturgy and Ethics in Cross-Cultural Perspective

*Scandal and Shame: An Unfolding Dishonor Roll*

Since the word "billion," and more recently "trillion," moved from the pages of comic fantasy to those of the national press, from describing the incalculable to talking about the budget, the previously unimaginable "million" has been stripped of its emotional power, domesticated, and put in its lowly place. That's a pity, when a million represents more than enough people to fill Chicago's Soldier Field stadium fifteen times over, and when a million represents hundreds of thousands more days than all those elapsed between the day of Jesus' birth and the day this page is read.

And since the rather esoteric word "genocide" has become merged in Western minds with the evocative and specific "holocaust" *(shoah)* for which it was primarily coined, the impact of other atrocities may be somewhat blunted by comparison. And that's a tragedy too, when hundreds of people can permanently "disappear" from the streets of South American towns with hardly a protest from the world beyond; when, in three days in 1989, tens of thousands of civilians, including babies, can be tied with wire, disemboweled, and machine gunned on the order of a Rumanian dictator; and when hundreds of thousands of Indian citizens can be scarred, maimed, and killed in an industrial accident that does not call down immediate and universal opprobrium on the industry.

Atrocity, then, has by no means vanished from the face of the earth. But though the public and grandiose obscenity of the railroads of death and the extermination camps of northern Europe half a century ago will necessarily point the accusing finger for generations to come, calling both Christians and religion itself before the bar of justice, there remain still other millions to be adequately accounted for, and still other forms of genocide as yet only partly exhumed for the scrutiny and judgment of anyone concerned about the putative "absence of God" in human affairs.

**The Dance of Life**

185

A case in point would be the ten or twelve million Africans shipped from their sparsely populated continent to feed the insatiable cultural appetite of worthy burghers, yeomen farmers, and God-fearing Christians. Up to two million died of suffocation, disease, or heartbreak on board ship; probably more than twice that number perished before transshipment—hunted down, incarcerated, starved and beaten to death.[1] Yet even this must be a serious underestimate; for when the figures are in, arguably fifty million people "exchanged hands" in a travesty of trade and an attack of cultural dementia and Christian doublethinking of epochal and international proportions.

Perhaps four million people constituted the cargo of ships bound for Brazil to replenish the stocks of human labor; elsewhere the indigenous populations were simply exterminated or replaced by Europeans. There are no surviving indigenous people in Uruguay; the country is populated by whites and their descendants. And, across the globe, the last native Tasmanian died almost a century ago. Having been reduced by 90 percent from their original two thousand, the surviving two hundred died within a generation; all were gone by 1880.

And this sorry tale continues indefinitely: Up to the present day, 39 out of every 40 Brazilian Indians have been alienated from their land, "detribalized" and killed, reducing numbers from 1.2 million to a mere 30,000. Before that, they had been reduced from at least several millions by the Portuguese colonists who organized hunting expeditions and massacres. And those whose communities escaped flintlocks and machetes were not immune to flu and measles.

Also in the present century, in 1915, Turks massacred Armenians in numbers still not computed, much less broadcast: hundreds of thousands for sure, perhaps the million and a half the Armenians claim.

There could almost be an alphabet of atrocities: *A, B, C, D,* Amin, Bokassa, Ceaucescu, Duvalier. Nor should we forget Stalin, the Khmer Rouge, the I.R.A., and many a legitimately elected government's "covert action"; all have contributed some of the

---

1. The story is told in many places. An excellent and accessible treatment is found in Basil Davidson, *Black Mother: Africa and the Atlantic Slave Trade* (Harmondsworth, England: Penguin Books, 1980).

**Anthony Gittins, C.S.Sp.**

more colorful chapters to the sagas of the murdered millions and of genocide. These atrocities happened at the hands of Christians and other "religious" people as often as not; and contemporary people who would call themselves "believers" or "religious" are heir to a whole litany of outrages, epitomized for many by the Holocaust, yet by no means limited to it.[2]

But the world is much wider than the Northern Hemisphere, and religious experience is far more comprehensive than that of Christians alone. And it should be acknowledged that news does not spread uniformly or with equal impact. So questions about the place—or specifically the absence—of God, should certainly be posed not only in the shadow of the *Shoah* but in the context of the experience of *all* who suffer and continue to search, across cultures and down the ages. They too are surely part of the canvas on which humanity has left its mark; they too should not have suffered alone and unknown, unacknowledged and unsung.

### The Universal Search for Meaning: Analysis and Synthesis

Wherever Christianity has spread, new ethical problems and moral dilemmas have taken root: to flower—sometimes speedily and prolifically, sometimes belatedly and morbidly—and to demonstrate in a thousand new strains the interaction of native ambience and foreign organism. But reflections by Christians themselves about the universal meaning of suffering and the justice of God, about the experience of an imperfect ethos, yet the commitment to an enduring worldview,[3] should not be understood as exhausting human wisdom or as assuring a noble response by those who have pondered the issue: every culture—and probably every generation—must address for itself the "ultimate questions."[4] Only thus are new and precious insights produced.

Our present concern, then, is not so much to suggest what Christianity may have to offer universally by way of synthesis be-

2. *See* John Pawlikowski, "Worship After the Holocaust," in this volume.

3. The *ethos* is the stuff of daily experience, the way things actually are; and the *worldview* is the right order of things, the way things should be in a perfect world. *See* Clifford Geertz, "Ethos, World View, and the Analysis of Sacred Symbols," in his *Interpretation of Cultures* (New York: Basic Books, 1973) 126–141.

4. A useful introduction is John and Denise Carmody's *Religion: The Great Questions* (New York: Seabury, 1983).

**The Dance of Life**

tween liturgy and its response to the call of justice, as to acknowledge that other cultures and religious traditions too have always had problems to face, and that some of their wisdom might need to be learned or remembered by Christianity and applied in its own continuous struggle for meaning and relevance. Western understanding and mainstream Christian theology are well enough represented in this book, but much wisdom and many broad streams of religious praxis remain unknown or untapped.

The starting point of many contemporary reflections—including some in the present volume—is the dichotomy between liturgy and life, and the need for healing. But from the outset we should identify such a separation as a distortion of liturgy (in the broad sense of the celebration of life in its totality, or public worship), and we should try to call to mind worlds in which liturgical performance is not so distorted but is clearly a dramatization of the fundamental ethical concerns of life. So it might be helpful to recall that analysis—separation—is not the only useful social process; synthesis—conjoining—can be equally illuminating and often no less creative.

### Anthropological Approaches to Religion and Life

Anthropological textbooks used to fall neatly into chapters under the section heading "Social Institutions." An institution was defined minimally as "a standardized mode of coactivity." Economics was considered an institution in this sense, as were politics, kinship, and religion (sometimes glossed as "belief and thought"). But then the reader was informed that religion was not *necessarily* "institutionalized." So, contrary to the sceptics who were persuaded that an absence of institutionalized structures bespoke an absence of religion itself, one should not expect always to see a three-dimensional structure or even an organic bureaucracy. People certainly had a system that could be called "belief and thought," even though it might be articulated rather differently from the systematic formulations and social organization of religion in the West.

Social institutions, then, do not necessarily need to be institutionalized at all; frequently they are embedded in the social fabric, in the way people act and relate both formally and informally in predictable and somewhat routinized or structured ways. Thus, marriage in some cultures may not be recognizable to a canon law-

**Anthony Gittins, C.S.Sp.**

188

yer or a British judge, if such people are looking to recognize in another culture what they take for granted as normal and normative in their own. But to other people, marriage not only exists, it is inseparable from behaviors they would classify as "economic" or "political" or "religious."

To search for freestanding, narrowly defined, or discrete social institutions is thus often futile, and these may be chimeras in the mind of the searcher. Very many people live quite contentedly in a world of agglutinating or embedding social institutions; or, less technically, where relationship or relating are acknowledged values. To such people, it is obvious that choosing and settling with a spouse, producing and rearing offspring, and growing into domestic stability are part of an *integrated process,* as it is that expressing ritual behavior ("doing liturgy"), pointing out common social and ethical concerns, invoking sanctions or asking forgiveness, are themselves inextricably bound up, indissoluble, and embedded in the social fabric of their lives. It is surely likely that some of the moral dilemmas and alien forms that have rooted in the native soils of lands visited by Western Christianity have been due to the unhealthy institutionalization of that religion, which has then—not infrequently—been transplanted injudiciously and at the expense of the indigenous life that thrived before being contaminated or struck down.

It is sad yet unsurprising that many—not all—religious and social revolutionaries foisted by Europe upon the rest of the world, unmindful of the good, the stable, and the enduring in the cultures encountered, besotted with the sourer fruits of Medieval ecclesiology and Enlightenment bombast, should have dispensed some of the least enriching of their patrimony while failing to identify the treasures on display before them. And it is surely regrettable that having sometimes propagated a version of the Christian religion that effectively separated liturgy from life and ritual from relevance, those sowers of missionary Christianity should have left the reapers to gather a harvest less than abundant, and blighted with unattractive thorns and tares.

## Disjunction and Dysfunction

A Church set apart from the world, or over against it, is doomed to formalize or dramatize a liturgy disassociated from real life; far from being "the Church's ritual enactment of the relationship between God and the world,"[5] liturgy then becomes a husk, an appendage, a bauble. Now the separation of Church and state, whether by fiat or by gradual process, is something peculiar to a world in which people think in terms of opposition and exclusion rather than complementarity and inclusion. In such a world, so long as it is possible to think of or to conceive of "Church" in a separate context from "state" or of "religion" abstractly separated from "politics," then it is possible to persuade people that such a situation actually exists. And if it is possible to carve out, to delimit, to define areas of control peculiar to each, then it is possible for people to grow up actually believing that religion and politics have nothing to do with each other. But however persuasive Western thinking might be, and however jealously Western democracies might guard their itemized and analytically distinguishable constitutional freedoms, it is nevertheless incumbent upon us as reflective subjects to know that there are *other* ways of interpreting reality and *other* ways of understanding relationships, both between persons and between institutions.

The separation of the gospel from culture is one of the sadder signs of our times, as Vatican II noted in the Pastoral Constitution on the Church in the Modern World: "The split between the faith which many profess [religion] and their daily lives [politics] deserves to be counted among the more serious errors of our age. . . . Therefore, let there be no false opposition between professional and social activities [political behavior] on the one part, and religious life [religion] on the other" (*Gaudium et spes*, no. 43).

Bold words these, and timely. But we need to acknowledge that institutionalization, whether of religion, politics, economics, or anything else, leads to a radical disjunction between social realities and relationships that are characteristically in conjunction in other cultures. We are aware, from personal experience, of the anonymity or contractual nature of many economic arrangements; we know the frustration of looking for someone to help us and of failing to find a flesh-and-blood person within a bureaucratic system,

5. *See* Ralph Keifer, "Liturgy and Ethics: Some Unresolved Dilemmas," in this volume.

**Anthony Gittins, C.S.Sp.**

especially when we are left holding a muzak-piping telephone or are ordered to the far end of a line of people. We bemoan the lack of person-to-person relationships in a world of plastic cards and computer chips. But the more the world in which we live worships at the altars of efficiency and progress, the more dehumanized will people continue to feel and the more will they suffer the separation (at least initially: we can even get used to discomfort) of what should be joined. We are creatures of our subculture, socialized into a world of more-or-less shared meanings and taught to respond in ways that will prove intelligible to others and produce efficiency and progress. And our own particular way-of-being-in-the-world characterizes our relationships, our religion, our worship.

### A Syllabus of Errors

If the opposition decried by Vatican II is to be dissolved, the solution will have to be at the sociocultural level of reintegration and not simply left to individual initiative. But the historical record indicates something of the difficulty of such a program: sociocultural change is often too slow for the reformers, and individual initiative, however inspired, may be quickly stifled.

At the beginning of the eighteenth century, and reacting against the sad and disappointing legacy of a missionary religion in decline after two centuries, there arose a prophet in the Kingdom of the Kongo in West Central Africa. Donna Beatrice confronted and preached directly against the Catholic Church, accusing it of failing to produce an integrated religion to which the people could respond, and declaring that Jesus had been born in Africa, had chosen African disciples, and was thus, in modern terminology, "incarnated," "contextualized," and "embedded" in African culture in a way never disclosed and certainly not imitated by foreign missionaries. Not surprisingly, her message spread rapidly, and with it her fame. Not surprisingly either, she soon came into confrontation with expatriate missionaries and with the code of Christian orthodoxy. Her efforts to reintegrate religion and life, belief and action, liturgy and ethics, in ways compatible with a holistic African approach to existence were an embarrassment to the king and a scandal to the missionaries. Pedro IV's royal attempts to set her free were unavailing; the powerful God-fearing Capuchins succeeded in having her condemned. She was burnt at the stake, along with the alleged father of the child she claimed to be born of the Holy Spirit; and the baby was immolated for good measure.[6]

This "final solution" was in 1706. But by 1968 it was reported that there were now six thousand independent Churches in Africa, and the number was rising.[7] And characteristic of many of them is the figure of a prophet preaching against irrelevance, the disjunction of Christian belief and practice. Also, new liturgical forms have developed more suited to an African community of worshipers no longer tolerant of foreign or imposed liturgies. Holocausts, big or small, are rarely the "final solution."

### Learning from Mistakes

But whether we consider the case of independent Churches in Africa, cargo cults in Melanesia, sects in Europe, *santería* or *candomble* or *umbanda* or *voodoo* in the African-American world, or new religious movements globally, we should be impressed by their efforts to rediscover (and re-create) meaning in worship in worlds raped of meaning and to use liturgical forms as an extension of their commitment in the real world of struggle and injustice. And perhaps we should also look for the antithesis of this: a distancing or removal from the cares and concerns of a world gone mad, or maybe a withdrawal into fatalism or private grief. And this leaves us with several considerations.

In the first place, there appears to be something in the nature— or at least, and certainly, in the nurture—of the human person-in-society that creates liturgical activity as an expression of concerns about the discrepancy between the way things are and the way things are expected to be (the ethos and the underlying worldview) in order to emphasize and address that discrepancy in the conviction that it is both worth doing and possible to effectuate.

Secondly, a community that gathers for common liturgical action of an expressive and instrumental nature (to worship or give glory,

6. For the history of an inculturated Catholic Church in the Kongo, *see* J. Thornton, "The Development of an African Catholic Church in the Kingdom of the Kongo, 1491–1750," *Journal of African History* 25 (1984) 147–168.

7. David Barret, *Schism and Renewal in Africa* (Nairobi, Kenya: Oxford University Press, 1968).

**Anthony Gittins, C.S.Sp.**

192

and to cajole or persuade) will be a relatively homogeneous community, united in common convictions about values, torts, sanctions, and meanings; otherwise it will collapse on itself, or break up centrifugally. The corollary of this is that where a community has already fragmented, whether geographically or philosophically, a common liturgical action will become undesirable and ultimately impossible.[8]

And thirdly, if the split between liturgical action and ethical concerns and priorities is allowed to widen, it will result in empty liturgies and formalism, or perhaps the creation of an otherworldly piety or a spiritualized religion, detached from the concerns of flesh-and-blood people. Such a split may be a step toward irreligion or impiety.

## Countercultural Witness

In a secularized, pluralistic, individualistic, and rational world, the only way for a vital, integrated relationship to be maintained between liturgical action and ethical sensitivity may be for it to be enfleshed in a countercultural and an "unnatural" environment. One abiding function of religious systems is to account for, though not necessarily to justify, the status quo of its own ethos.[9] Religion is characteristically conservative, espousing and perpetuating meaning systems even after the conditions that gave rise to them have changed. Christianity not only coexisted with the Nazi Holocaust but with African slavery; it presently coexists with millions of starving people in a world of plenty, with nations steeped in militarism, and with more than half its members suffering public discrimination. Current patriarchalism and a catalogue of other "isms" are at odds with the teachings of Jesus and of the magisterium. The story needs no further elaboration.

In such a world, a prophet, radically and permanently committed, may attract the attention of an otherwise self-interested society and self-focused culture; prophets, formally or informally so-called, may gather their clientele and create new *ad hoc* communities. But prophets always risk being silenced or killed by agents of the dom-

---

8. A good example of this phenomenon is the Navajo "sings" or curing rites, described by Geertz, *The Interpretation of Cultures,* 104–105.

9. Ibid., 140 and 126–141, *passim.*

inant culture—religious or secular—in the name of good order or orthodoxy. So a Camillo Torres or a Martin Luther King, an Oscar Romero or a Dorothy Day, a Ghandi or a Bonhoeffer, or a supernumerary Jesuit in El Salvador may be variously described as traitor, heretic, prophet, or martyr. And a Church that tries to be monocultural in a multicultural world (whether in terms of classic patriarchalism, the dominant culture of capitalism or fascism or racism or sexism, or a leveling out of cultural differences) will soon fail to be understood as relevant to a huge portion of its constituents and will re-create and underscore the disjunction between its liturgical rites and the ethical concerns of those constituents. A Church committed to the idea of monoculturalism will fail to address the ethical needs and perspectives of local cultures and of minorities existing on the margins. Hence a statement such as the following may be dangerous and naive if, in practice, the emphasis is placed on "the unity of the human race" at the expense of the "particular features" (to which a formal bow does seem to be made), and if it conceals a failure to learn the lessons in the charred bodies of many a Donna Beatrice: "Little by little, a more universal form of human culture is developing, one which will promote and express *the unity of the human race* to the degree that it preserves *the particular features* of the different cultures" *(Gaudium et spes* no. 54, emphasis added).

If, at the local level, within the vernacular or autochthonous liturgies, the link between performance and ethical concern is not uncovered, identified, and respected, then any external imposition—whether with honeyed words or gentle promises—will not only fail the test of relevance but will effectively drive a wedge between what was previously linked and bonded: liturgy and ethics. Is it not the case that the Basic Christian Communities of Latin America have proved so popular and so successful because of their perceived relevance and their ability to link liturgy and ethical concerns? And is it not the same success—differently interpreted—that has caused much of the opposition from within and without the Church? The Basic Christian Communities, produced as the fruit of the Spirit by the reflective action of liberation theology, can trace their existence, just as much as can the independent Churches of Africa, to what has been perceived by their members as "a failure in sensitivity, the failure of missions at one small

**Anthony Gittins, C.S.Sp.**

point, to demonstrate consistently the fullness of the biblical concept of love, as sensitive understanding toward others as equals."[10]

These Latins and Africans know themselves to be struggling to maintain a sense of the relevance of their religion to their daily life, or their liturgy to their ethical concerns. And in order to do so they have, perforce, become countercultural, insofar as they challenge both the conservatism of established religion and the values of the dominant culture. Without romanticizing cultures less familiar than our own, perhaps we have still much to learn about the relationship between liturgy and life.

### Meaning and the Threat of Chaos

Religion is centrally concerned with the problem not only of suffering and injustice but of meaning; unless different religious systems persuade their adherents that life is not totally chaotic and meaningless, they cannot subsist. To this end, religious symbols, rituals, and ceremonies converge to create and restore order in disorder, life amid death, joy in sadness, and so on.[11] Some of the tensions and paradoxes addressed in liturgy are synthesized in a poignant Javanese poem:

> We have lived to see a time without order
> In which everyone is confused. . . .
> One cannot bear to join in the madness,
> But if [we] do not do so
> [We] will not share the spoils,
> And will starve as a result.
> Yes, God: wrong is wrong.
> Happy are those who forget.
> Happier yet those who remember and have deep insight.[12]

If the conjunction of liturgy and life, ethical issues and worship, serves to maintain a modicum of social and cosmic order or to acknowledge its inherent precariousness, then the disjunction must open the floodgates to the danger of social breakdown, through the privatization of religion or the pursuit of individual self-interest

---

10. Barret, *Schism and Renewal in Africa*, 156.
11. Robin Horton, "A Definition of Religion and Its Uses," *Journal of the Royal Anthropological Institute* (1960) 201–225.
12. Quoted in Geertz, *The Interpretation of Cultures*, 106.

and cosmic chaos, through a pervading sense of meaninglessness or a failure to establish a shared universe of meaning. An anomic—empty, lawless, normless—world is one that threatens to spin uncontrollably, one in which people succumb to feelings of hopelessness, one in which present trends (whether to local violence to persons or things or global destruction) are perceived to be irreversible.

There may be occasions in the life of everyone—the person living within a tightly knit worshiping community as much as the person without formal religious affiliations—when chaos threatens to break through; if *my* child dies or disaster strikes *my* life, my response is rather more focused than when *people* die or when disaster strikes *others*. But there is characteristically religious reaction to such vicissitudes: "the formulation, by means of symbols, of an image of a genuine order of the world which will account for, and even celebrate, the perceived ambiguities, puzzles, and paradoxes in human experience."[13] The religious response, the response that synthesizes ethical concerns and acts of worship, is, according to Geertz, "a matter of affirming, or at least recognizing, the inescapability of ignorance, pain, and injustice on the human plane while simultaneously denying that these irrationalities are characteristic of the world as a whole."[14]

### Liturgy Engaged with Life

A series of examples may serve to illustrate both the intimate relationship between ethics and liturgy in their broadest perspectives and the potential disasters that follow from the split between them. And if these examples serve to generate discussion and controversy—thereby, some enlightenment—my purpose will have been served.

> One quiet, bright morning, as dawn breaks over a village in West Africa, the paramount chief stretches a rope-like liana vine along the ground and between the mud houses until he has effectively divided the village in two. Though he is acknowledged to be unpredictable, senile, and something of a figure of fun (behind his back), nobody is laughing now. People come and stand, serious faced and reverential

13. Ibid.
14. Ibid., 108.

**Anthony Gittins, C.S.Sp.**

at their doorways as the chief, preoccupied and stooped, passes slowly by. Reaching the last house he straightens, stands to one side of the liana vine, and then, ungainly and unbalanced and perhaps un-sober, he jumps laboriously across it in an act that heals the separation and symbolically joins the sundered village. In turn, all the people follow suit; tension is relaxed and harmony restored to a community that for weeks has been paralyzed by witchcraft accusations. The chief acts not as the figure of fun but as the presider over a broken, hostile, suspicion-ridden people.

Here is a liturgy, performed by chief and people united as a total community, along with unseen ancestors and supreme being, specifically addressing the ethical issues of selfishness, hostility, violence and death that are the associates of witchcraft, and explicitly focusing on them in order to dissolve them in the rekindled sentiments of trust and amity, touched, no doubt, with the fear of sanctions.

In a basement in Chicago sits a motley crew, mostly women, mostly suffering, mostly alienated from formal religion and almost from life itself. They are condemned by a society that blames the victims in prostitution as in other areas of gross injustice, and they sense the condemnation of the clergy and of God. But they are praying together this evening, earnestly and spontaneously, and there are even clergy and other professionals among them. They take courage from one another and from the ethos created for their "liturgy." They are asking for self-confidence enough to hold their heads up, for mutual support, and for strength to step away from addiction. And in the silence of their supplication, a voice interjects quietly (shockingly, to some of the more judgmental and puritanical): "O God, you don't make no shit. Thank you. Help me to believe in *me,* to make it one day at a time."

A profound and pregnant moment, it is a meeting between ethical concerns and honest worship, an encounter between liturgy and life.

The rains should come soon. Clouds gather beyond the horizon. People are hungry, sharing their remaining food. They are assembled, pooling strength and spiritual energies. Some dance a rain dance.

It is not, as ignorant foreigners think, a superstition intended to tease rain from a distant yet gullible supreme being. It bespeaks hope and joy, gratitude and anticipation; it also builds solidarity and unification, reconciliation and collaboration. It is predicated on the certain goodness and timeliness of the Great One, not on the assumption that people can manipulate the divine. It does indeed help bring the rain, like "I baptize you" brings the sacrament. It is an acknowledgment that there are needy people but also that there is a beneficent *Manitou, Wankan Tanka,* Great Spirit. It is as much an attempt to restore harmonious social relationships and be committed to peace as it is to hurry to give thanks in anticipation to the one whose justice is unquestioned and whose desire for peace and creative symbiosis are evident in nature. It is, surely, liturgy.

> A young Christian visits homeless people in unobtrusive service. She finds a woman sick, alone, in serious need of solace and nursing. She reaches out to tend broken skin on rotting feet and notices that she is kneeling, ministering, healing. She remembers the washing of the feet and the injunction to "do this in memory of me." And she marvels that she has been where compassion encounters pain and at the crossroads of life and liturgy.

Sadly, as we know, this is not the total picture. Sometimes liturgy does not mean life, or it runs on a distant parallel; sometimes the two can drift apart and ethics can become estranged from religion. Such a disintegration in relationships is painful to observe:

> A suburban parish of professionals, where the prayers are for vocations but few parishioners think of offering their own service and ministry to the parish; where the organ is magnificent but few people sing; where the parish accountant is a fine steward of the abundant harvest of dollars but where homeless people sometimes get moved on for trying to keep warm in the church porch; where no African-American or Hispanic people happen to come to worship. . . .

> A seminary chapel where the worship space is architecturally stunning, the singing is note perfect, the choreography superb. But children don't come because their parents feel they will embarrass them by making noise; and few women come because they are outraged at the self-importance and privilege; and no young people come because who wants to go to a privileged and out-of-touch place like a seminary? . . .

> Far away in an exotic land there is a small, thatched building made of simple materials, where many children sit facing the altar and a

**Anthony Gittins, C.S.Sp.**

serious and dedicated young American Christian, the missionary. And not far away the sound of machine guns and the smell of death, the exploding napalm from the plane flown by a serious and dedicated young American Christian, the marine. . . .

A private oratory where a private priest says a private Mass and prayer for unity; but he does not know, never visits, and would not think of inviting the local Episcopal pastor to share prayer or play, food or friendship. . . .

### Toward Resolution

I have heard the question asked recently, in various forms, Can there be worship any longer in a world that cannot avoid the accusatory fingers of the exterminated in the *Shoah?* Or, How can we continue to engage in liturgies as a Christian community when, as a Christian community, we failed so abysmally to protest the annihilation of millions? But there is another side of the question: How can we worship—focus on a supreme and beneficent God— in the face of rampant injustice and when God's justice is *not* seen to be vindicated? Where, indeed *is* God in a world gone mad? David Power notes the predicament of the Churches that "find themselves doomed to silence by the inability even to face, let alone make sense of, current reality," and asks, "Can we in truth celebrate eucharist after the Nazi holocaust, and in a world half populated by refugees, in the same way as we did before the occurrence of such horrors?"[15]

My own contention here is, firstly, that there have been always and everywhere throughout the Christian Era cases of human cruelty on a widespread and indiscriminate scale, involving the unimaginable numbers of people we so facilely designate "millions"; the genocide in the 1940s, while the most well known, shocking, and profoundly embarrassing to contemporaries, is, sadly, not unique. And the sorry tale continues, not only in the headlines but in the small print of Tianamen Square or Transylvania, Burundi or Latin America, Liberia or Iraq. Secondly, I try to show that concern about the possibility of the "absence of God" in human affairs is no new problematic. From the "My God, my God, why

15. "Response: Liturgy, Memory and the Absence of God," *Worship* 57 (1983) 328.

have you forsaken me," to the "Why did *my* child get killed?" to the "If God really existed, *my* spouse would not have been allowed to die," cries have burst forth from people begging for a sign that seems to be withheld. The more homogeneous a culture, the more it will stave off the threat of chaos and meaninglessness by trying to maintain an integrated liturgical expression of its ethical concerns; but the more secularized, pluralistic, individualistic, and conscious of alternative possibilities or explanations, the more likely that culture or subgroup will be to experience its own sense of impending chaos and the meaninglessness of life in the face of tragedy.

And so, to address the question of whether there can be worship after the *Shoah* and similar atrocities: Not only can there, but there must be. And can our Eucharist be celebrated in the same way as formerly? Certainly not, but it *must* be celebrated. For whenever we become conscious of our frightening tendency to terrible evil, and whenever we realize just how broad has become the divide between the meaning attributed to our liturgies and the meaning we extract from and attribute to our lives, we must seek to build bridges and to reconstruct our world of meaning or we fall straight through our crumbling "plausibility structure"[16] and into the void. In celebrating future Eucharist then, it must be not with formalism but with appropriateness; not in strength but in brokenness; not triumphantly but repentantly; not in certainty but in self-questioning. Aware of human faithlessness, yet inspired by God's fidelity, we can loyally celebrate the memory of Jesus in order to restore our broken spirits and bring about what it signifies: unity, peace, love, reciprocity, universality.[17]

Religion serves, among other things, to create and maintain meaning, but it is a public realization and succeeds only when committed to a suffering humanity and when addressing the ethical concerns of the contemporary society. If liturgy fails, religion becomes privatized; if privatized, it mutates to something almost unrecognizable. Therefore, after *every* outrage, *every* public

16. On plausibility structure as a base upon which society is constructed, *see* Peter Berger, *The Sacred Canopy* (New York: Doubleday, 1969) 45.

17. *See* John Hadley, *Bread of the World* (London, England: Darton, Longman & Todd, 1989) 44.

**Anthony Gittins, C.S.Sp.**

blasphemy, *every* social act of hubris, there *must* be worship—worship that builds on the newly noticed discrepancy between the reality of human existence and an underpinning worldview. Every time it becomes embarrassingly and humiliatingly clear just how far apart ethics and worship have grown, we *must* reflect, regroup, and reconstruct our worldview lest the blasphemy be extended and we fail to see the accusing finger of that discrepancy.

But as human persons we are challenged to *grasp* the paradox, the contradictions, between our worship-in-isolation and our injustice-in-conspiracy. By standing where holocausts and genocides collide with aspirations and protestations of universal love and defense for the weak, we are called to repudiate the one and return to the demands of the other.

*The Dance of Life*

Somewhere there is told the story of the American academic who, in Japan for a learned symposium on religion, found himself confused. To a Shinto priest he expressed his concern. Having visited several shrines and having attended some ceremonies, he was still unable, he said, to grasp the ideology and the theology of Shinto. The priest responded, "I don't think we *have* an ideology or a theology: we dance." Some religious systems may indeed be more visual, more dramaturgical, more embodied than intellectualized or formalized in theology; they make sense only when seen in action. From South America to East Asia and for thousands of years people have danced their religion.[18] And within Christianity, too, there has been a robust tradition that speaks of "the dance." In the lyrics of a popular liturgical song, Jesus applies one of the great "I AM" descriptions to himself: "I am the Lord of the Dance."[19] If our worship were a dance in which we were to "ex-press" what we "em-body," then not only would our liturgy be actually incarnated, contextualized, and inculturated in as many ways as there are embodied people and different cultures; but the visual, the dramaturgical, the enacted dimensions of our religion would be in-

18. *See* Joseph Campbell, *Historical Atlas of World Mythology* (New York: Harper & Row, 1988) vol. 1, pt. 1.

19. The lyrics to this song, whose melody is based on a Shaker hymn-dance entitled "Simple Gifts," were written by Sydney Carter.

**The Dance of Life**

separable from an authentic involvement with the ethical concerns of societies.

## For Further Reflection

1. What evidence can you gather that suggests that some cultures, groups, or parishes thrive *because* they integrate their liturgical expression (in the broad sense of "liturgical") with their current ethical concerns? And what evidence can you adduce to suggest that a failure to integrate liturgy and ethics will become manifest when cultures, groups, or parishes are in decline?

2. Do you agree that liturgy can and must continue, even or especially in a world marked by atrocities? Or do you think that in such a world, religion is clearly proved to be impotent and therefore irrelevant?

3. Some religions are "religions of the Book," and have scriptures and other codified theological forms. Other religions are "religions of the Dance," and have no such codifications. Do you think it is easier for one or the other of these types to achieve a creative and satisfactory relationship between liturgical action and ethical concern? In which religious type may change be facilitated?

4. Discuss some examples from you own experience that would illustrate what has been discussed above in the section "Liturgy Engaged with Life." Does a consideration of these examples modify your understanding of "religion," "liturgy," or "ethics"?

**Anthony Gittins, C.S.Sp.**

# For Further Reading

Avila, Raphael. *Worship and Politics.* Maryknoll, N.Y.: Orbis Books, 1981.

Balasuriya, Tissa. *The Eucharist and Human Liberation.* Maryknoll, N.Y.: Orbis Books, 1979.

Baldovin, John. "The Liturgical Year: Calendar for a Just Community," *Liturgy and Spirituality in Context.* Ed. Eleanor Bernstein. Collegeville: The Liturgical Press, 1990.

Bergant, Dianne. "Liturgy and Scripture: Creating a New World," *Liturgy and Social Justice.* Ed. Edward M. Grosz. Collegeville: The Liturgical Press, 1989.

Bernier, Paul. *Bread Broken and Shared: Broadening Our Vision of the Eucharist.* Notre Dame, Ind.: Ave Maria Press, 1981.

Bowman, Thea. "Justice, Power and Praise," *Liturgy and Social Justice.* Ed. Edward M. Grosz. Collegeville: The Liturgical Press, 1989.

Brueggemann, Walter, Sharon Parks, and Thomas H. Groome. *To Act Justly, Love Tenderly, Walk Humbly: An Agenda for Ministers.* New York: Paulist, 1986.

Clerq, B. de. "Political Commitment and Liturgical Celebration," *Political Commitment and Christian Community,* 110–116. *Concilium* 84. Ed. Alois Muller and Norbert Greinacher. New York: Herder and Herder, 1973.

Collins, Mary. "Naming God in Public Prayer." *Worship* 59 (1985) 291–304.

Cone, James H. "Sanctification, Liberation and Black Worship." *Theology Today* 25 (1978) 139–152.

Crockett, William. *Eucharist: Symbol of Transformation.* New York: Pueblo, 1989.

Cummings, O. "The Eucharist and Social Justice." *Clergy Review* 71 (1986) 207–212.

Dallen, James. "The Social Activist-Liturgist Confrontation." *Today's Parish* 9 (1977) 44–55.

Duffy, Regis. "Symbols of Abundance, Symbols of Need," *Liturgy and Social Justice.* Ed. Mark Searle. Collegeville: The Liturgical Press, 1980.

Dussel, Enrique. "The Bread of the Eucharistic Celebration as a Sign of Justice in the Community," *Can We Always Celebrate the Eucharist?* 56–65. *Concilium* 152. Ed. Mary Collins and David Power. New York: Seabury, 1982.

Egan, John. "Liturgy and Justice: An Unfinished Agenda." *Origins* 13, no. 15 (September 22, 1983) 399–411.

Empereur, James, and Kiesling, Christopher. *The Liturgy That Does Justice: A New Approach to Liturgical Praxis.* Collegeville: The Liturgical Press, A Michael Glazier Book, 1991.

Fink, Peter. "Liturgy and Spirituality: A Timely Intersection," *Liturgy and Spirituality in Context.* Ed. Eleanor Bernstein. Collegeville: The Liturgical Press, 1990.

Gelineau, Joseph. "Celebrating the Paschal Liberation," *Politics and Liturgy,* 107–119. *Concilium* 92. Ed. Herman Schmidt and David Power. New York: Herder and Herder, 1974.

Grassi, Joseph A. *Broken Bread and Broken Bodies: The Lord's Supper and World Hunger.* Maryknoll, N.Y.: Orbis Books, 1985.

Guerrieri, John A. "Catholic Liturgical Sources of Social Commitment," *Liturgical Foundations of Social Policy in the Catholic and Jewish Traditions.* Ed. Daniel Polish and Eugene Fisher. Notre Dame, Ind.: University of Notre Dame Press, 1983.

Happel, Stephen. "The Bent World: Sacrament as Orthopraxis." *The Catholic Theological Society of America Proceedings* 35 (1980) 88–101.

Haring, Bernard. *The Eucharist and Our Everyday Life.* New York: Seabury, 1979.

Hehir, J. Bryan. "The Liturgy and Social Justice: Past Relationships and Future Possibilities," *Liturgy and Social Justice.* Ed. Edward M. Grosz. Collegeville: The Liturgical Press, 1989.

Hellwig, Monika K. *The Eucharist and the Hunger of the World.* New York: Paulist, 1976.

Henderson, J. Frank, Kathleen Quinn, and Stephen Larson. *Liturgy, Justice and the Reign of God: Integrating Vision and Practice.* New York: Paulist, 1989.

Himes, Kenneth. "Eucharist and Justice: Assessing the Legacy of Virgil Michel." *Worship* 62 (1988) 201–224.

Hoffman, Lawrence. *The Art of Public Prayer: Not for Clergy Only.* Washington: The Pastoral Press, 1988.

Hollenbach, David. "A Prophetic Church and the Catholic Sacramental Imagination," *The Faith That Does Justice.* John Haughey. New York: Paulist, 1977.

Hovda, Robert. "The Ethical Demands of the Eucharist." *Living Worship* 11 (August–September 1978).

_____. "Liturgy: Effective Political Action?" *Worship* 63 (1989) 361–365.

_____. "Liturgy Forming Us in the Christian Life," *Liturgy and Spirituality in Context.* Ed. Eleanor Bernstein. Collegeville: The Liturgical Press, 1990.

# For Further Reading

_____. "The Mass and Its Social Consequences," *Liturgy 90* (April, 1991) 9–12.

_____. "The Saving Evangelism of Our Symbol Language." *Worship* 58 (1984) 531–536.

_____. "Where Have You Been? 'Peace Liturgies' Are the Only Ones We Have!" *Worship* 57 (1983) 438–443.

Huck, Gabe. "The Role of Liturgical Celebration in Fostering Spiritual Growth." *Living Worship* 14 (June–July 1978).

Huels, John. *Disputed Questions in the Liturgy Today.* Chicago: Liturgy Training Publications, 1988.

Hughes, Kathleen. *How Firm a Foundation: Voices of the Early Liturgical Movement.* Chicago: Liturgy Training Publications, 1990.

_____. "Singing of God in an Alien Tongue." *G.I.A. Quarterly* 1:2 (1990) 41–43.

International Commission on English in the Liturgy. "Sexism in Liturgical Language," *Doctrine and Life* 32 (1982) 318–322.

Jegen, Carol Frances. "The Eucharist and Peacemaking: Sign of Contradiction?" *Worship* 59 (1985) 202–210.

Jegen, Mary Evelyn. "Theology and Spirituality of Non-Violence." *Worship* 60 (1986) 119–133.

Keisling, Christopher. "Liturgy and Consumerism." *Worship* 52 (1978) 359–368.

_____. "Liturgy and Social Justice." *Worship* 51 (1977) 351–361.

Kilmartin, Edward. "The Sacrifice of Thanksgiving and Social Justice," *Liturgy and Social Justice.* Ed. Mark Searle. Collegeville: The Liturgical Press, 1980.

Krisak, Anthony. "Liturgy and Justice: Parish Reflections," *Liturgy 90* (April, 1991) 6–8.

Lane, Dermot A. "The Eucharist and Social Justice," *Eucharist for a New World.* Ed. Sean Swayne. Carlow, Ireland: Irish Institute of Pastoral Liturgy, 1981.

Laverdiere, Eugene. "Eucharist as Proclamation, Liberation and Communion" *Eucharist for a New World.* Ed. Sean Swayne. Carlow Ireland: Irish Institute of Pastoral Liturgy, 1981.

Leonard, Maria. "After Sunday: The Work Week, the Marketplace," *Liturgy and Spirituality in Context.* Ed. Eleanor Bernstein. Collegeville: The Liturgical Press, 1990.

Llopis, Joan. "The Message of Liberation in the Liturgy," *Politics and Liturgy,* 65–73. *Concilium* 92. Ed. Herman Schmidt and David Power. New York: Herder and Herder, 1974.

Mahoney, Roger. "The Eucharist and Social Justice." *Worship* 57 (1983) 52–61.

**For Further Reading**

Mannion, M. Francis. "Liturgy and the Present Crisis of Culture." *Worship* 62 (1988) 98–122.

McKenna, John. "Liturgy: Toward Liberation or Oppression?" *Worship* 56 (1982) 291–308.

McManus, Frederick. *Liturgical Participation: An Ongoing Assessment.* American Essays in Liturgy 10. Ed. Edward Foley. Washington: The Pastoral Press, 1988.

Meyer, Hans B. "The Social Significance of the Liturgy," *Politics and Liturgy,* 34–50. *Concilium* 92. Ed. Herman Schmidt and David Power. New York: Herder and Herder, 1974.

Mitchell, Nathan. "Bread of Crisis, Bread of Justice." *Living Worship* 15 (March 1979) n. p.

Moltmann, Jurgen. "The Liberating Feast" *Politics and Liturgy,* 74–84. *Concilium* 92. Ed. Herman Schmidt and David Power. New York: Herder and Herder, 1974.

Navone, John. "Evil and Its Symbols," *Politics and Liturgy,* 51–64. *Concilium* 92. Ed. Herman Schmidt and David Power. New York: Herder and Herder, 1974.

Osiek, Carolyn. *Beyond Anger: On Being a Feminist in the Church.* New York: Paulist, 1986.

Ostdiek, Gilbert. *Catechesis for Liturgy: A Program for Parish Involvement.* Washington: The Pastoral Press, 1986.

Power, David. "The Song of the Lord in an Alien Land," *Politics and Liturgy,* 85–106. *Concilium* 92. Ed. Herman Schmidt and David Power. New York: Herder and Herder, 1974.

Procter-Smith, Marjorie. *In Her Own Rite: Constructing Feminist Liturgical Tradition.* Nashville: Abingdon, 1990.

Ramshaw, Gail. *"De Divinibus Nominibus:* The Gender of God." *Worship* 56 (1982) 117–131.

Routely, Eric. "The Gender of God: A Contribution to the Conversation." *Worship* 56 (1982) 117–131.

Schmemann, Alexander. *For the Life of the Word.* Crestwood, N.Y.: St. Vladimir's Seminary Press, 1977.

Schmidt, Hans. "Line of Political Action in Contemporary Liturgy," *Politics and Liturgy,* 13–33. *Concilium* 92. Ed. Herman Schmidt and David Power. New York: Herder and Herder, 1974.

Schneiders, Sandra. *Women and the Word.* New York: Paulist, 1986.

Schüssler-Fiorenza, Elisabeth. *Bread Not Stone: The Challenge of Feminist Biblical Interpretation.* Boston: Beacon Press, 1984.

––––––––. "Tablesharing and the Celebration of the Eucharist," *Can We Always Celebrate the Eucharist?* 3–12. *Concilium* 152. Ed. Mary Collins and David Power. New York: Seabury, 1982.

# For Further Reading